Dedicated to the sports volunteers in Ireland who have selflessly nurtured and created both our inspirational superstars and the wonderful characters who have made us love sport so much.

Play It Again, DES

MY AUTOBIOGRAPHY

Play It Again,
DES

Sport Media Ⓢ

Written with Mary Hannigan.

First published in Great Britain and Ireland in 2018 by
Sport Media, a Reach PLC business,
5 St Paul's Square, Liverpool, L3 9SJ.

www.tmsportmedia.com
@SportMediaTM

Sport Media is a part of Reach plc.
One Canada Square, Canary Wharf, London, E15 5AP.

1

Hardback ISBN: 9781911613190
eBook ISBN: 9781911613251

Photographic acknowledgements:
Des Cahill personal collection, Inpho, Sportsfile.

Design and typesetting by Sport Media.

Printed and bound by CPI Group (UK) Ltd,
Croydon, CR0 4YY.

Contents

Acknowledgements   7

1   Lucky Man   11
2   First Lessons   21
3   Bobby Charlton Won't Get You A Job   31
4   Making The News   40
5   Sweet Carlow And Caroline   49
6   Welcome To Kerry   61
7   The Kerry Babies   72
8   Home From Home   81
9   The Outsider   88
10   And In Sport…   98
11   Wheels Of Fortune   107
12   Olé, Olé Olé Olé!   118
13   Innocent Seoul   129
14   Golden Girl   138
15   Rolling With The Punches   148
16   Who Does He Think He Is?   157
17   Disneyland To Saipan   166
18   Brendan   176

Contents

19	Son Of Gaybo	180
20	The Sunday Game	190
21	Suspicious Minds	201
22	Three Of A Kind	212
23	Changing Times	221
24	A Tale Of Two Great Men	233
25	The Games People Play	239
26	Proud Role	248
27	Cuala Man	254
28	Gaelic Life	265
29	Sport For All	275
30	Paul And Amy	286
31	Dancing Dessie	295
32	Good To Talk	310
33	Just A Matter Of Opinion	319
34	Looking Up	328

Acknowledgements

When I was first asked to do this book my response was: 'Who on earth would want to read about my life?' I just didn't think my story was all that interesting and so I had no great enthusiasm for the idea. Besides, I'm way more comfortable talking to other people about their lives than I am reflecting on my own, so there was that too.

But then my family and friends pointed out to me that no matter how uninteresting I thought I might be, I had the privilege to witness so many thrilling sporting occasions over the years and to get to know many of the people at the heart of them. Those stories, they reckoned, were worth sharing.

And they also tried to persuade me that after 40 years working in the Irish media, first as a newspaper reporter and, since 1984, as a broadcaster with RTÉ, I was bound to have had the occasional experience that might be of some interest too.

So, I agreed to take the plunge.

And despite my early reluctance, I very much enjoyed the project, not least because it reminded me of just how fortunate I have been through my career – and it allowed me to take several trips down memory lane to relive the most special of sporting days. It also allowed me to relive 'The Dessie Swim' and, as anyone fortunate enough to have witnessed it would know, it can never be relived enough.

It couldn't have happened without the wonderful work of Mary Hannigan of *The Irish Times*.

There were parts of the book I found emotional and difficult, there were times I questioned the value of a story, or how to tell it, and Mary sorted it all out with her calm, cool, judgement and wonderful writing skill. Most importantly of all, she has a similar sense of humour.

Publisher Paul Dove of Sport Media has been a wonderful mentor as he seamlessly guided us through the process while Roy Gilfoyle, Rick Cooke and Chris Collins provided expert contributions with the production and design. Thanks also to Simon Hess, who has shown unwavering support and belief in the project, ably supported by Declan Heeney and the Gill Hess team.

My heartfelt thanks, then, go to those who convinced me that the book was worth doing, especially my beautiful and patient wife Caroline, plus my adoring children Paul and Amy!

Family is the most important thing, so, needless to say, lifelong thanks to my mother Nora, Una, Brian, Declan and Pat, the legion of witty nephews and nieces, and, of course, the small army of Currans in Donegal, who have been very loyal in-laws.

Most of my happiness, fun and good fortune in journalism came from having wonderful mentors and colleagues in the *Irish Press*, the *Carlow Nationalist*, *The Kerryman* and RTÉ.

I don't have a large number of really close friends – in truth I only have a handful. But you only need six fellas to carry your coffin! You know who you are – thanks so much for your friendship, and for carrying me this far.

Finally, a sincere thank you to those of you who have listened to and watched my programmes over the years. I'm sure it hasn't always been easy!

Des Cahill, 2018

1

Lucky Man

*'The Coroner said, in expressing sympathy
with Mr Cahill, that no blame was attached
to anybody, this was a very moving and
frightening tragedy, and he had not only his
sympathy, but that of the general public'*

I have been lucky in my life. I grew up in a family with loving,
supportive parents, brothers and sisters. I had the happiest
of childhoods. I married a woman way out of my league and
we had two great children together.

My working life has given me the thrill and privilege of
being witness to some of Ireland's greatest sporting moments,
at Olympic Games, World Cups, the Tour de France and, of
course, so many special days in Gaelic Games.

It has given me the richest of experiences, allowed me to meet
the most extraordinary of people and taken me to parts of the
world I probably would never have seen. I ended up with the
best job in Ireland.

I couldn't even have dreamt it all.

I'd like to think I have never taken that good fortune for

granted, but I'm not sure I appreciated it quite as much as I should have.

Luck, I think, is a huge factor in everyone's life. Most people get some of the good variety along the way, most get the odd knock-back too. For the majority of us, it evens out.

But some are savaged by misfortune. Savaged.

I was reminded of that when my sister Eileen passed away on January 18, 2018, after a long, tough battle with cancer. It was then that I reflected on her life and ended up feeling that I had got all of her luck. Every drop of it.

Pointless as it was, it was hard not to have some sense of guilt when I thought about the life she had compared to mine. You can't help but wonder about these things, the unfairness of it all. Eileen was as good and selfless a person as you would ever meet, yet her early life in particular was blighted by sadness and loss.

But I didn't hear her complain once in all her days, not once. Whatever life threw at her she went about making the best of it.

But my God, it was a tough life.

• • • • • • •

Eileen was a remarkable woman. She touched the lives of so many people in a hugely positive way.

She joined the nuns after leaving Coláiste Mhuire in Ennis where she was a boarder along with our sister Una. Four of her aunts were nuns, so there was that tradition in the family. I think she would have loved to have had a family of her own, but it wasn't to be. But again, she never complained.

Eileen taught in Spanish Point in Clare, in Ennis, in Birr and then she went to Kenya for a period. She had, remarkably, battled cancer on and off for 28 years, finally losing that battle after she came home from Kenya.

For a spell she had moved in with Una, living in an independent apartment within the house, and I know she loved the craic provided by my nephews, Michael, Colm and Sean.

Eileen had a massive impact on a huge number of families. She would often go to see people when they were ill and would transform how they faced death. Word spread about her. People in RTÉ would say "can we visit your sister?" It was a kind of a religious thing. I was a bit uncomfortable about it, to be honest.

But I understood why people would want to meet her and talk with her, she was a special woman who had such a positive effect on the lives of those around her. Including mine.

· · · · · · ·

It wasn't until I was around 12 that I discovered Eileen was actually my step-sister. Until then I hadn't even thought about it. I just assumed we had the same mother and father, there was never any reason to believe otherwise. And there was never any sense that we were two separate family units joined together. We were just family. Eileen, Una and Brian were my siblings, just as Brendan, Declan and Pat were.

But I had wondered about some things, things that didn't seem to make sense to me as a child.

Like, why was Uncle Jimmy called 'Uncle' when he wasn't a brother of either Mam or Dad?

Why was I never allowed to go to Clare with Dad, Eileen, Una and Brian when they visited there?

And who were Joan and Michael? Their schoolbags were in

the attic. I think Dad had put them there. When I found them I opened them up and saw the names on the copies inside. Joan and Michael.

I sensed something. I'm not sure what. But I just had a feeling about it.

I asked Dad to explain, but he kind of dismissed my questions. I left it there. I knew not to go on. So, there were no answers.

But I always wondered.

It was when Eileen was home from the Convent of Mercy in Ennis, where she was a young nun, that I finally got the answers. I asked her to explain about all the things that had puzzled me.

And I think she was glad I asked. It was as if she had decided it was time I knew my family's story.

We were in her bedroom when she told me that story. What had happened on June 14, 1957.

• • • • • • •

My father, Patrick, known as 'Pappy' to his family, had been married before to a woman who, coincidentally, had the same name as his second wife and my own mother, except spelt with a 'h': Norah.

They lived in Caherbullane, Corofin in Co Clare. They had five children, Eileen, Michael, Joan, Una and Brian. Norah had been a school teacher in Dublin before returning to her native Clare. Dad was the principal at the school in Willbrook near Corofin.

That day Eileen was sitting an exam called the Primary Cert, a national exam that effectively graded pupils before they went into secondary school. Norah had decided to take the other four children to the lake for an outing. Eileen told me what she knew of that day, but I could see from her face that it was very painful for her, so I didn't ask any detailed questions.

It was in later years I went in to the National Library and looked up reports in the local papers, Eileen subsequently giving us copies of some reports too. I found one on the inquest where my father detailed what happened. It left me stunned.

Dad was only home about five minutes from school when Una rushed in alone.

He learnt that Joan had gone in to the lake and disappeared under the water. Michael went in to try to save her and he went under too, and then Norah followed him in and she also went under.

He got in his car and drove to the lake.

There was no sign of Norah, Michael or Joan. He took off his clothes to dive in, but Una pleaded with him not to, she was afraid he would disappear too.

Dad at first assumed Brian had also drowned, he couldn't find him, but he was later found wandering near the lake.

The report read as follows...

> Two of the bodies were recovered shortly after 8pm – seven hours after Mrs Cahill and her children had set off on their day's outing. The third body was taken from the lake after a further two hours.
>
> Guard V. Fanning said he discovered the bodies of Mrs Cahill and her son Michael in about eight feet of water and 12 yards from the shore. They were in bathing costumes. For about seven yards from the bank there was a stony bottom but the water was only two feet deep.

Then there was a ledge and a drop to eight feet of water. The lake covered an area of about two acres and had apparently a number of deep holes.

Guard W. J. Conroy said he discovered the body of Joan floating in the water some 20 yards from the shore.

The Coroner said, in expressing sympathy with Mr Cahill, that no blame was attached to anybody, this was a very moving and frightening tragedy, and he had not only his sympathy, but that of the general public.

Dad had lost his 39-year-old wife Norah, his son Michael, aged 10, and daughter Joan, aged seven, all drowned in Turkana Lake about a mile from their home at Caherbullane.

I felt empty after reading it and discovering the truth.

But I now had the answers to everything that had confused me. The schoolbags in the attic. Joan and Michael were children my father had lost.

Uncle Jimmy was a brother of Norah, my Dad's first wife.

And now I understood why Dad didn't take me to Clare when he went there with Eileen, Una and Brian.

They were visiting the graves.

• • • • • • •

It was when I was 18, working in the *Irish Press* as a student journalist, I was unexpectedly presented with a searing mental image of him after the tragedy.

I had been sent to cover the Dáil, shortly before the summer recess. Michael Barber from the *Press*, Mairtin MacCormac from the *Independent* and Michael Foley from *The Irish Times* were working there on my first day.

When the day was done I joined the three lads for a pint down in the bar. I was feeling glad to be accepted within the group and we settled down to chat.

"So, where are you from?"

"Monkstown in Dublin," I told them, adding that my family was originally from Co Clare.

"Any relation to the Cahill family that suffered the drownings in Corofin?"

I said that I was, but I didn't explain the relationship.

Both Michael and Mairtin then began reminiscing about it. Remarkably, it transpired that both men had gone to the family home that night. They had the horrible task of seeking photos of the deceased. Without realising I didn't know a lot of detail, one of them described how awful it was and said he remembered the father drinking straight from a bottle of whiskey.

My father.

It was an alien image to me. The pain he must have been in.

Hearing that was traumatic, but I didn't say anything to them.

It was later that night I had my conversation with Eileen about it all.

In more recent times I went to the funeral of Sr Mary Senan O'Reilly who had been the last surviving sibling of Norah. I met a cousin there, Pat O'Reilly, who had actually been an altar boy at the funeral of Norah, Joan and Michael. He remembered the other altar boy fainting from the sheer tension and emotion of it all, the scale of it. And he recalled my father visiting his home and crying for an hour.

I'm an empathetic person, I've always been that way, I feel other people's pain. I think it might be because of what my family went through, trying to imagine their pain, the scale of the trauma, without actually suffering it. Because I didn't suffer it. I'd have Clare people, older people especially, saying 'I'm so sorry' when they realise the connection, but it's the strangest of feelings – I never knew Norah, Joan and Michael, yet their loss had such an enormous impact on my family, on the people I loved.

But I've seen old photos of Joan and Michael, some school photos, and the vulnerability is what hits you, it's stark. So young, so small, so innocent.

● ● ● ● ● ● ●

Dad didn't talk about it at all in the earlier years. In later life he would just mention "the accident", but he wouldn't go much beyond that. I would have gone to my mother or Eileen about it more.

Brian was so young, just two, a baby really. He hasn't had a problem talking about it, but he doesn't do so at length.

When I began reflecting on the tragedy for this book, I thought about how difficult it must have been for Una and Eileen that what happened was never really talked about.

I had always been in awe of my father for how he battled on and made a good life for all of us after suffering such unimaginable grief.

At times you sensed the weight of the tragedy on him. There had to be spells of melancholy, but with family and work, he didn't have a lot of time to be melancholic, he had to get on with life. And despite it all, he was a jovial man. He was funny. He was witty. I think I inherited the same sense of humour from him.

He never lectured us about being one family – we were one family. The words 'stepbrother' or 'stepsister' were never mentioned. There was none of that. The only times we ever heard the words were in fairy tales. We were brothers and sisters. He treated us exactly the same, there was no difference. He wanted one tight family bond, and that is what we had.

And looking back, I had enormous respect for him for bringing us up as one family unit. He was a school principal, so he probably had a broader understanding of raising children than most. But there was courage in his determination to keep the family together, and then raise those two 'units' as one.

I also admired him for bringing Eileen, Una and Brian to visit the graves of their mother and siblings, so that they would remain part of their lives and never be forgotten.

Those visits must have been incredibly painful, but he obviously felt they were important to do. I don't think he wanted to burden the rest of us with it, so myself and the younger lads were left at home.

Maybe that was the only way he knew how to acknowledge what had happened, to visit the graves.

Like so many men of that generation – and plenty even now – it would have been such a struggle to talk about something so painful.

• • • • • • •

My father died in 2002. He had cancer for six or eight weeks. I had been working at the World Cup that summer, but after getting off the plane that morning from Japan, he passed away within half an hour of me arriving. He waited for me.

And while we all had a happy family life in Dublin, when I think of what he, Eileen and Una, in particular, suffered, it just adds to my sense of how lucky a man I've been that I never endured pain of that magnitude, that my life has been filled with so much more joy than heartache.

2

First Lessons

*'If it wasn't easy having me as a son at times,
it wasn't plain sailing having your father as
the principal of your school either'*

It was around two years after the tragedy that Dad married my mother Nora. She was a cousin of his first wife and had been nursing in Liverpool before returning home to Clare. They made the decision to move to Dublin to start a new life.

It was early 1960 and by then they had a new baby, myself having been born in Ennis hospital where my mother had worked as a nurse.

When they moved to Dublin my father began teaching in Belgrove School in Clontarf where our first home was, on Mount Prospect Avenue, while my mother was helping Eileen, Una and Brian to adapt, and also looking after me.

Mam has always been an incredibly strong and loving woman and when I look back on the circumstances she found herself in, I'm sure she needed every ounce of that strength. It must have been a tough marriage to put together, although they got great support from both their families.

But inheriting a family by marrying a man with three children can't have been easy for her, and it must have been made all the more difficult by the tragedy they had been through and the loss they had suffered.

In the early years Eileen and Una were with us, but they then went away to school as boarders in Coláiste Muire in Ennis where the principal was an aunt of theirs. So they weren't around to help, as the older girls in families often do.

And in no time Mam had five young boys to look after, myself and my three younger brothers Brendan, Declan and Pat all arriving in around five years. That's some handful. And two of the boys, Brendan and Declan, had their problems.

Brendan was born with severe brain damage that left him with a profound intellectual disability, one that made a normal life impossible. Declan came along a year later and he had huge problems with both feet, spending months in hospital. He had to wear calipers, metal supports, on both legs through his childhood.

I remember waiting for the bus in Clontarf when I was about four years of age, standing by my mother's side. She had a child in each arm trying to board the bus, and was pregnant.

In recent years, I asked her what was going through her head when she was pregnant with Pat, given there had been such huge, but very different, medical complications with Brendan and Declan. She said it was a nightmare, every day she worried that something would go wrong again. You can't even imagine the stress of that.

Thankfully, Pat was born a healthy, smiley baby. And that was our family complete.

• • • • • • •

I was six when we moved from Clontarf to Monkstown in south county Dublin after Dad was made principal of Foxrock National School. Most of my childhood memories would be from there, although there are a couple of vivid ones from our Clontarf days. Like the time the house went on fire.

My mother's sister, Mary, had come home from America and she brought Mam in to town. It would have been a rare day out for her. By the end of it she was probably afraid to leave the house again.

No-one was hurt, but there was a fire that started in the kitchen when a pan spat flames on the wall. I remember being put sitting in the cab of the fire brigade while they dealt with it, which for a young fella was the height of excitement.

There was rarely a dull moment. Having five young boys in the house ensured that. There were regular trips across the road to Dr O'Driscoll (Bill – Brian O'Driscoll's grandfather), like when Pat drank some Parazone.

Years later, when Brian O'Driscoll became an Irish rugby international, my mother recalled the younger lads escaped from their playpen because somebody took three bars from the side of the wooden pen. When she saw (Brian's dad) young Frank O'Driscoll playing cricket, she had her suspicions about what happened! Mam needed eyes in the back of her head.

In fairness to Dad, he did try and help out when Mam went back working as a nurse, often making us dinner. But there are no words for his cooking. No words. It'd be cabbage in a pot of water, or something. Jesus, it was brutal. And he'd be, 'isn't that a lovely dinner now?'

• • • • • • •

I'd say I drove my Dad mad, but I know he liked me a lot as well. I had a good relationship with him, although his boiled cabbage tested it. I was in trouble with him a lot.

If it wasn't easy having me as a son at times, it wasn't plain sailing having your father as the principal of your school either, as he was all through my national school days.

He moved on from Foxrock National School to become principal at Oliver Plunkett School in Dunedin, Monkstown, which was a very different, much tougher school.

There was a world of difference between the two. Foxrock was still a leafy village, one of Dublin's poshest suburbs. The school in Monkstown, although only three or four miles away, was in a far less privileged area, with high rise flats a few hundred yards away. Quite, quite different from the high rise apartments that you see now in Foxrock.

Monkstown was a brand new school when Dad – and I – moved there in 1966. Although the area was full of really decent, hard-working people, it had its problems too. The school was regularly vandalised, young lads would break in, block the sinks, run the taps, and so on. And a few of the guys in the school were often in trouble with the Gardai. Unfortunately for me, they were also regularly in trouble with my father.

Back then when a teacher had a problem with a pupil, he would send them 'to the wall' outside the principal's office. My father would come out, ask them what happened, and depending on the seriousness of it he might use a cane on their hand. This, needless to say, made things difficult for myself, Declan and Pat. My way of trying to handle the inevitable resentment towards me from the lads who were always in trouble, was to use a mixture of humour and diplomacy. It was my defence mechanism.

And I had to use that humour and diplomacy outside of school hours too. Some of my classmates used to enjoy throwing stones at the 'posh' lads going to the nearby Christian Brothers school, CBC Monkstown. That was fine, except virtually every other boy in the estate where I lived went to CBC.

So, I was considered a posh boy at school, and a hooligan where I lived. There was probably an element of truth to both.

Dad was strict, but he had to be. When you're a school principal and you're telling other parents their child is misbehaving, you can't really let your own do the same.

It was tough for him, but tough for me too. "There's fucking Cahill's son!" was the refrain that followed me around through those years. It was worse when I got to 16, 17, when you're going in to a pub or a disco and you're hearing the same thing. I was never actually beaten up, but I was threatened all the time.

I remember going with Dad to The Graduate pub on Rochestown Avenue in Killiney to watch the 1971 FA Cup final between Liverpool and Arsenal. When we arrived, there were loads of ex-pupils of his there, it was like the sheriff walking in and the piano player stops. The whole place fell silent and turned and looked at us. I was thinking, 'Jesus, two hours of this'. Wherever we sat, a big space formed around us.

So, that's how it was back then, but then you get older, in to your 30s or 40s, and you have fellas coming over, "how's your Da?" They realised then that he was very good for them, that he was just trying to put them on the right path. And he would have gone out of his way a lot. He'd often go to family homes, trying to help mothers or fathers who had it tough. So they appreciated him in later years. I still get people coming up to me now talking fondly about him.

• • • • • • •

It came as a complete surprise when Dad asked me how I'd feel about doing my secondary education through Irish, rather than going to CBC Monkstown, where most of the lads on the road went, or to another school nearby.

But he had a friend who had been a teacher at Coláiste Mhuire on Parnell Square, right in the middle of Dublin city, and he felt it might be the right school for me. He liked the idea of me learning through Irish, of me being able to speak the language.

Coláiste Mhuire was one of the oldest Irish language schools in the country. It was set up in 1931 by the Christian Brothers, initially located on Harcourt Street before moving to Georgian buildings on Parnell Square two years later.

While it was a small school initially, it expanded over the years, taking in numbers 23 to 28 on the Square. Number 25 had been the headquarters of The Gaelic League, the movement founded in 1893 to revive the Irish language and culture, where it was believed plans for the 1916 Rising were set in train. So it was steeped in history.

It had an excellent reputation academically and over the years many of its past pupils went on to enjoy great success in a number of fields, men like former Fine Gael leader Alan Dukes, RTÉ's Seán Óg Ó Ceallacháin and Brian Farrell, and two of the legendary Dublin team of the 1970s, Brian Mullins and Robbie Kelleher.

But the prospect of going there and doing all the subjects through Irish was daunting for me because I had so little of the language at that stage. Nervously, I decided to give it a go.

And it was a real culture shock at the start. Most of the other first year students had been educated through Irish in primary school, or came from families where it was the spoken language. But I was lost, I hadn't a clue what was being said, so I found it very difficult in those early days. But it's amazing how quickly you can pick it up – by November I was getting on fine, by January or February I was grand, and within five or six months I was totally at home and doing well.

I loved my time in Coláiste Mhuire. Most schools would have a good mix of students, but it had a greater one than most, with boys from every walk of life.

And there was something hugely exciting about going to school in the city centre, walking up and down O'Connell Street, the city's main thoroughfare, to get there. The school has since moved to Cabra after the building was deemed unsafe in the early 2000s, but back then you were right in the heart of the city, overlooking the Garden of Remembrance.

And they were highly charged times, of course, with 'The Troubles' in the north.

I can remember a boy in my class, a bright, very likeable and witty fella with a shock of red hair, being taken to and collected from school by detectives in an unmarked car. He was the son of Judge Frank Griffin, the first Presiding Head of the Special Criminal Court which had been set up in 1972 to try terrorism and serious crime cases, but without juries because of the fear that they would be intimidated.

There was outrage in some quarters, especially among Republicans, about the new court, largely because of the absence of juries, so being the son of the head judge, Frank was sometimes driven to school by the Gardai, who escorted his father for protection.

There was some irony to it, though, because he was going to a school where many of the lads would have come from strong Nationalist families, most of whom probably had their own objections to the Special Criminal Court.

1972 proved to be the deadliest year of The Troubles, with almost 500 people killed, half of them civilians. Two years later the Dublin bombings took place when three car bombs exploded in the city centre, planted by Loyalist paramilitaries, causing the deaths of 27 people. On the same day there was a bomb in Monaghan that took the lives of seven people.

One of the Dublin bombs was just around the corner from our school in Parnell Street. I was in town on the day, but we'd all gone home by the time they went off, between around 5pm and 5.30. They were horrific. There were kids among the dead, too. They were insane times. But this kind of thing was going on all the time up in the north. We were so close to it, yet it all seemed so far away. Until it came to Dublin.

• • • • • • •

Maybe it was down to the atmosphere of the times but back then in Monkstown, as I saw it, the language and flag meant nothing to most people, including myself before I started in Coláiste Mhuire.

You certainly never saw anyone walking around in an Irish jersey in those days, they were just different times to now. But then I was in a whole new world, surrounded by people who were proud of their language and proud of their flag, and my experience there led me to sharing that pride in both.

I came to understand the passion for the Irish language and the battle to preserve it. If we let it die, what would that say about us? Would we even know who we were?

So, I grew to love Irish and, to this day, am proud to speak it. But in those days, it was decidedly uncool. When we played other schools in Gaelic football they would mock us by shouting gibberish to each other, imitating our calls 'as Gaeilge'.

It's hard to imagine that now. These days parents are queuing up to get their kids in to Gaelscoileanna where the education is done through Irish, with the likes of Coláiste Eoin and Coláiste Íosagáin becoming extraordinarily successful schools.

And Gaelic football has become cool too, which inevitably happened once I took over *The Sunday Game*. I don't think I could ever have imagined that back when I first took it up on going to Coláiste Mhuire. That made me a real oddity on my road, where most of the lads played rugby in either the local CBC or Blackrock College.

Brian Keogh, my best friend growing up, and his brother Mark played on the CBC Monkstown team that won the Leinster Schools Senior Cup in 1976 – the only time the school ever won the trophy. God, I was jealous. The final was played in front of 20,000 people at Lansdowne Road when they beat Castleknock by the pretty remarkable score of 3-0. Brian, although a year younger than all of the other players, was the star at out-half.

In the wake of the victory, the lads became sex gods around Dún Laoghaire, while I was totally ignored by the girls. I was the weird guy following behind them who played the very uncool GAA.

The great irony is that many of the best GAA players in Dublin in recent years have come from both CBC and some of those girls' private schools. CBC Monkstown has produced Michael Fitzsimons who has been one of Dublin's star defenders at senior level, with five All-Irelands, while Conor Mullally and Darragh Spillane, nephew of Kerry great Mick, have won All-Ireland under-21 medals, Conor winning a Minor All-Ireland too.

Changed times indeed.

And just as I had experienced when I went to Oliver Plunkett School, I was kind of caught in the middle. If there was a snobbery from the rugby boys about me going to an Irish language school where we played Gaelic football, I got the reverse from the lads in Coláiste Mhuire because I lived in Monkstown. In fact, Willie Hughes, who sat beside me, christened me the 'snob'. Willie was a rogue then, and he still is.

Most of the school's football team were northsiders so they all regarded me as the posh boy. When I was around 16 we were playing Clonkeen in Deansgrange in south Dublin so while we were out that way they all insisted that they wanted to see my house, to see how big it was. Amazingly, the teacher driving the car agreed to their request.

So, naturally, I directed us past my family's semi-detached and down to the heart of Monkstown village where I pointed to a huge mansion.

"Do you want to come in?" I asked.

"No, we haven't time," said the teacher, so we drove off, the lads left open-mouthed.

I laughed all the way back to school.

3

Bobby Charlton Won't Get You A Job

'With so little broadcast sports news back then, newspapers were essential for the sports fun. I devoured every word about every sport I could find. I was a proper little anorak'

"They've no telly!"

The news spread around the road fast.

I was already an oddity because I was a Gaelic football-playing Coláiste Mhuire lad, and then to top it all Dad decided to get rid of the television at home as an experiment for the academic year.

Jesus, I remember the shame.

Kids wouldn't cope now with how weird having no telly would make them look. They'd run away.

But it's funny looking back at that time, I think it might have kindled a love of radio because in the absence of a television that's all there really was to entertain yourself. So, while doing my homework I'd be listening to the radio in the kitchen, probably

31

a lot more focussed on it than my homework. Sport would have been on BBC Radio 2, in my teenage years, it was on longwave so you could get good quality reception. I loved it. The live matches on a Wednesday night, all that. RTÉ Radio had one sports bulletin in the morning and one at tea-time back then, that's all. Fortunately for me they've expanded their coverage somewhat over the years.

By then sport had become a huge part of my life, but I can see now where my interest in how it was covered in the media developed.

Back when I was in Oliver Plunkett School, Dad would sometimes show a movie in the school hall, usually a comedy, often one of the Norman Wisdom films. The lads used to love them. I did too, but what really captured my imagination were the Pathe News reels that would precede the movies, the clips from FA Cup finals or the World Cup, the big occasions. They just grabbed me. The magnificent deep tones of the guy doing the voiceover, the sense of drama, the cutaway shots of cheering fans. I was mesmerised.

From the age of about nine I'd begun to follow sport avidly. There were several influences. Glasgow Celtic and Manchester United had won the European Cup Final in successive seasons in 1967 and '68. It was easy for a young sports fan to be captivated by the stories of both clubs. Celtic because of their Irish roots, and the incredible statistic that all but one of their 1967 team was born within 30 miles of Celtic Park, Bobby Lennox from Ayrshire the only 'foreigner'.

Then there was the magic of United winning Europe's top competition just 10 years after the club was devastated by the Munich Air Disaster. That Matt Busby, Bobby Charlton and Bill Foulkes could recover from their injuries and subsequently win the trophy was just an extraordinary story. And I'd fallen for West Ham.

I'd seen them win the 1964 FA Cup on Pathe News, then the European Cup Winners Cup at Wembley the year after, and of course three of the team were central to England winning the World Cup in 1966, Bobby Moore, Martin Peters and Geoff Hurst. Hurst scored a hat-trick and Peters scored the other goal when England beat Germany, but Moore was the glamour boy, cool and handsome. A brilliant, composed defender with shiny blond hair. I remember being amazed to see him pouring bottles of milk into the FA Cup in 1964. The weird things you recall.

So, I was hooked on the drama of sport. And while I had been a voracious reader from the age of about six – every Enid Blyton adventure, comics, all that – I was now hooked on sports stories. I could hardly move for my collection of *Shoot* magazines. And starting from then, I'm now the possessor of an enormous book collection which takes up a whole room, lots of them autobiographies. With no internet back in those ancient times, these autobiographies were the best way of researching someone you were going to interview.

With so little broadcast sports news back then, newspapers were essential for the sports fan. I devoured every word about every sport I could find. I was a proper little anorak.

We'd have the newspaper delivered each day. The *Irish Independent* was dropped in the letterbox around 8am. My father, reasonably enough, wanted a quick glance at it before he left for work. A cat and mouse game developed between us. Dad would listen for the delivery, but I used to try to slip the newspaper out of the letterbox as quietly as possible and go in to the front room. I would carefully lay the paper on the floor and go straight to the sports pages.

Dad would come looking for me, scoop up the paper and in a frustrated voice say, "Bobby Charlton won't get you a job!"

• • • • • • •

I wouldn't say I got my love of sport from Dad, but he encouraged it and was really supportive of it. While I had respect for him as a great teacher, though, I had none for his style of football management.

Soccer was the sport played by everybody in the school – many of them played to a very high standard with one of Dublin's top schoolboy clubs, St Joseph's in Sallynoggin, and a couple of them went on to be team-mates of Paul McGrath at Pearse Rovers. But there was no soccer competition for primary schools in the '60's, so we entered the GAA league – even though nobody played for a GAA club.

There was one year when Dad ended up as our manager because there was no other suitable teacher available. He hadn't a clue.

Because so many of the lads were good soccer players, the team was competitive, but my father insisted on letting every sub play part of the game. So even if we took a narrow lead in the closing minutes, against the odds, he would indiscriminately take off five or six players and replace them with subs who were enthusiastic, but not very good.

This 'it's not the winning, it's the taking part' policy resulted in us narrowly losing a play-off game in Fairview Park on the north side of the city – many miles from Monkstown. One of the players who was substituted, Bobby, was furious. So he refused to get back in to Dad's car after the game where around seven of us were crammed in. Bobby stormed off, but he hadn't an idea about the geography of the area. He set off walking towards Clontarf. The wrong direction.

People on the street stared as my father drove alongside him, pleading with the long haired little 11-year-old, still in his football gear, to get in.

"Get in the car, Bobby!"

"No sir, I won't. I can't believe you put them subs on," came the indignant reply.

The other seven players in the car all muttered their agreement and quietly gave my father the disdainful look players give managers who they reckon should be sacked.

Bobby strode on, in to the unknown. And my father couldn't just drag the child in to the car which was already packed with miserable-looking kids. God only knows what people were thinking as they watched.

So we had to go for about two miles along by the Clontarf promenade before Bobby's boots became too uncomfortable, and he reluctantly squeezed into the back of the car.

I don't think he ever forgave Dad. For Bobby it was the winning, not the taking part.

• • • • • • •

I loved playing Gaelic football, but nobody else on my road, Windsor Park, was interested in the sport until a young couple, Frank and Pauline Dargan, moved in around the corner in Windsor Drive. Frank would chat to us all when we were out playing football on the road and he told us that he was born beside Croke Park and was a big Dublin GAA fan. So, at last, I had a kindred spirit in my neighbourhood.

Frank was in his mid 30s, three times my age, but we got on famously. On Sundays we'd head off to Dublin's league games around the country. Everyone else in Windsor looked upon us kindly and affectionately, but considered us a right pair of gombeens.

Frank was a very warm man, hugely popular with the neighbours, he had a kind word for everyone. He didn't drink, but my God, when we went to some of those Dublin matches in the mid '70s, he got very excited – there were times when he would lose the plot.

With the Dubs on a successful run in that decade, everyone wanted to see them lose. I could understand that, but Frank thought there was a conspiracy amongst the 'culchies' to drag Dublin down, at any cost. (He wasn't the first Dub to think that).

I remember a game in Roscommon where one of Frank's favourite players, Bobby Doyle, was in a fight with the local legend, Dermot Earley. As a result of the incident, Dermot was sent off. The home crowd was absolutely furious with Bobby because Dermot, apart from being one of the best footballers I ever saw, was also deemed to be one of the fairest.

So the locals were hurling abuse at Bobby and the 'Dirty Dubs'. Frank wouldn't have a bad word said about Bobby, so at one stage I thought we would be taking on about 5,000 furious Rossies as he told them all where to go. I had to act as a teenage peacemaker, nudging Frank away from the home supporters who were keen to kill him. I started asking a bunch of random questions just to take his mind off engaging with 'the culchies'. We were probably lucky to get out unscathed.

But they were happy days. We had the best of fun together, and when I was 18 and started college I even played for a season on the same soccer team as Frank. He was the oldest player in the league, but boy was he still competitive. We actually got to a cup final in Tolka Park, but lost 3-2, before I then dashed off from the dressing room to play an under-21 Championship game against Ballymun up the road in Parnell Park.

This was how life had become, legging it on the final whistle in one game and criss-crossing Dublin to play in another code. And I loved every minute of it.

Meanwhile, the other lads in Windsor were progressing well with the rugby. Blackrock College RFC backed on to Windsor and myself and best friend Brian Keogh would watch all of their home games. They had a host of Irish internationals and Lions. What a treat it was to go and watch the likes of Ray McLoughlin, Fergus Slattery, Willie Duggan and Ned Byrne playing their club rugby every fortnight.

Ironically, Brian was to end up playing alongside them as he made the Rock first team a year after leaving school as an Irish schoolboy international.

By then, my local GAA club Cuala was becoming a huge part of my life, and has remained so ever since.

It was in its infancy at the start of the 1970s, based originally in Sallynoggin and then up the road in Dalkey when the juvenile club Cuala Casements merged with Dalkey Mitchells. It was a marriage of convenience. Cuala Casements had a host of talented young players, and Dalkey Mitchells had an adult pitch.

It would have been a lot easier for me to play for Cuala, but I waited until after my Leaving Cert to join them because Coláiste Mhuire past pupils had formed their own club, Clann Coláiste Mhuire. So I stuck with them until I left the school, and we had some good times, winning the Leinster Colleges B final which, for such a small school, was a big thing. I played midfield. And the final was in Croke Park too. Although whenever I'm tempted to brag about playing in the great stadium, I might have Henry Shefflin on one side of me, and Tomás Ó Sé on the other. Fellas who played in Croke Park more often than I've had hot dinners. So, my feat doesn't stack up so well. (But did I mention I got three points from midfield?).

The only downside of playing with Clann was that it took me two buses and about an hour and a half just to get to our home games at Islandbridge. And the away games took us all over north Dublin.

There was one long-term advantage to my loyalty to the club. Tom Quinn, along with Denis O'Neill and Sean Lynch, was one of the stalwarts of Clann, a fantastic volunteer, the three of them driving 20 or more of us to venues all over Dublin. Tom was to pop up in my life again a few years later when I went for my interview with RTÉ.

By now I was also going to a lot of soccer games, starting with TEK United who played up the top of the road. They were an exceptional non-league team, at 18 Pat Devlin would have played for them. And I loved the experience of going to League of Ireland games – the atmosphere, the humour and wit of the terraces.

And then my brother Brian brought me to my first international in December 1968. It was such a generous thing for him to do, he was working as a lounge boy at the time and he wasn't a sports fanatic, but he still took 15-year-old me to the game.

It was a midweek World Cup qualifier between the Republic of Ireland and Denmark at Dalymount Park.

It's hard to describe how excited I was going to the game, especially when it was under lights. I loved the noise around the ground, the smell of the chip vans, the sense of anticipation as the fans made their way in.

And then, with the fog that night, we could barely see a thing from the main terrace opposite the stand.

Alan Kelly, Tommy Carroll, John Dempsey, Tony Dunne, Charlie Hurley, Eamon Dunphy, John Giles, Eamonn Rogers, Johnny Fullam, Alfie Hale and Frank O'Neill. They were all out there. Apparently. Giles equalised from a penalty after the Danes had taken the lead. Apparently.

The game was abandoned after 51 minutes, the first time an international match in Ireland was not completed…and I was there.

But by now I had become immersed in sport, whether playing it or watching it or reading about it or listening to it on the radio. It had become an all-consuming passion.

And thanks, in part, to Pathe News before those Norman Wisdom films and the radio in the kitchen and the newspaper dropping through the door, I knew from an early age the path I wanted to take. Maybe not intentionally, but it was a path Dad had put me on.

4

Making The News

*'There was no problem with the cows, but the
deer were proving harder to shift. So I wrote
the undeniably immortal line, 'there won't
be a single cow, holy or otherwise, in the
Phoenix Park when the Pope comes to visit"*

I t's one of my favourite memories, the images and sounds are
still powerfully strong in my head.

A winter's evening in Mulligan's pub on Poolbeg Street
with a gang from the *Irish Press*, which was just next door.

It's raining outside, people are rushing by, heading for the train.
There's the steam, the heat, the smoke, the laughter, and you're
there listening to them all telling stories.

I loved it, they were who I aspired to be, I wanted to be part of
that world. I wanted to be a journalist.

Back then the only journalism course in Ireland was in
Rathmines College, unlike nowadays when there are so many
other routes in to the profession.

There were only 20 places available, so it was a real battle to get in. I had been good academically in school, I got all As in what would now be called the Junior Cert. But then, much to the annoyance of my father, I did nothing really. Too many distractions.

I remember one Sunday night coming home from a pub… and I was only in fifth year. Dad had an ad from the papers for an Air Corps apprenticeship. You'd learn a skill, a trade, like a mechanic or an electrician.

"You're applying for that tomorrow," he said.

But I was brutal with my hands.

"I'll go for the Cadets," I said.

"You're not going for the Cadets, you're going for this."

He was just fed up with me. But by then I knew what I wanted, in fact I think as early as 12 or 13 I knew I wanted to do journalism.

In fairness to Dad, when I did something really bad he didn't make a fuss, but he did react to the little things.

The night of the Leaving Cert results I was out with a gang of friends and neighbours – Caroline Burke, Liz Hughes, Mary Daly and Brian Keogh included.

I'll spare you the sordid details, but after being introduced to pints of 'snakebite' – a mixture of cider and beer – they literally carried me home. They put me in a bin, and took a photo, and then Brian brought me into the house and put me lying on a sofa. There was a coat hanging in the hall, so he put it over me and tiptoed out of the house.

The next morning my dad went looking for his brand new camel-coloured cashmere coat. When he couldn't find it in the hall, he stuck his head into the sitting room, to see his new coat covered in vomit.

It was never worn again. But he never mentioned it.

I nearly got caught in my Leaving Cert, though. You needed a B in English to get in to Rathmines. I was good at English, especially essays, but I didn't put in the work and then had to gamble on what prose and the poetry would turn up on the paper. I got lucky.

In the end I got five honours, which was enough. I had also applied to Thomond College to train as a PE teacher and I got offered a place there too, but it was Rathmines for me.

• • • • • • •

Journalism back then would have been seen as a more glamorous job than it is these days. The industry was booming, but unless you went down the traditional route, starting out as a copy boy at a newspaper, there were limited enough opportunities to get in to it. The NUJ controlled the intake of 20 in Rathmines, so if you got in you had a real chance of making a career out of it.

And most of the people in my year did, like Vincent Hogan, chief sports writer with the *Irish Independent*, Eoghan Corry, who went on to become sports editor of the *Sunday Tribune*, and two people from out my way who I travelled to Rathmines with by bus every day, Barbara Fitzgerald, now a news editor in RTÉ, and Jackie Coogan, daughter of Tim Pat, the legendary editor of the *Irish Press* for almost 20 years.

Vincent has been a long time friend. Although I remember one particular day when he must have doubted that friendship. He rented a house in Cabra with his sister Flo and we went back there on my birthday in December. Flo cooked us a meal and we ended up drinking whiskey. A lot of whiskey. The problem was, we had our Christmas politics exam in Rathmines next morning. I remember us sitting upstairs on the bus. We were both dying. And when we went to get off we bumped in to our politics lecturer, Ellen Hazelkorn.

"Oh my God Des, are you not well?" she said when she saw the state of me.

"No, I'm very sick Miss," I replied.

"Oh you couldn't do the exam feeling like that, you go home." So I did.

As I walked away I was saying to myself, 'don't look back at Vincent, don't look back at Vincent'.

But I did, and it was a mixture of rage, envy and pain.

I think he got about 10 per cent in the exam.

• • • • • • •

I loved my two years in Rathmines, and because there were only 20 of us we were close as a class, we became good friends and had some great times.

There was a guy called Brian Merriman in our class, a nice fella, and girls loved him, I'd sit at the back resenting all the admiration they were showering on him, hanging on his every word.

He was going for class rep in the Students Union so out of pure devilment I decided to stand against him – for no good political reason. And there were genuine issues to campaign on, many of them much the same as we have now, like student accommodation, the cost of it and the limited supply. Brian, who later worked with Fine Gael, fought a very good campaign on these issues and deserved to win.

But Monty Python's *The Life of Brian* had been banned in

Ireland because it was deemed to be blasphemous, so that became my election issue – opposition to censorship, freedom of information, all that, my platform. And my promise was that if I won we'd all go on a trip to London to see *The Life of Brian*. That pledge meant the outcome was fairly inevitable. A silly prank had backfired on me. Big time. I romped home. I was the new class rep.

I had no choice but to keep my campaign promise, there would have been a riot if I hadn't, so two classes from Rathmines, ourselves and the year behind us, set off for London by boat and train, staying in a hostel when we got there.

The trip was great fun, we got to see *The Life of Brian* and I arranged for us to go to a football game (West Ham, of course). I also organised visits to *The Sun* and *The Observer*, in an effort to make the trip seem at least loosely connected to our course.

It was a strange experience. There had been an IRA bomb in London in the previous few weeks and there had been fatalities. I couldn't exaggerate the anti-Irish feeling spat out by *The Sun* guy who had to meet us. We were brought in the back door of the print room and just left there. It was grim. Looking back on it you could understand the resentment towards us, but everyone was pissed off.

But then we had the trip to *The Observer* where Conor Cruise O'Brien, later to become a government minister, was editor. There was some contrast with the way we'd been treated at *The Sun*, we were brought in to the boardroom, the News, Features and Sport editors came in to meet us, they had laid on coffee and biscuits for us.

I remember the lads grabbing the biscuits and stuffing them in their pockets, I gave them a 'Jesus, I'm so disappointed in you' look.

The course in Rathmines was a really interesting one, I loved the politics especially which was divided in to nationalism, socialism and liberalism. I found it fascinating, especially looking at American elections. But it lacked a practical element. It wasn't much help when you ended up covering council meetings, as I did, so it left you having to do a lot of learning on the job.

The one course that was helpful in a practical way was Mairead Doyle's shorthand and typing. Not to be too immodest about it, I was one of the best in the class. So, naturally enough (he says), I was her favourite.

On a Monday morning we'd have two hours with Mairead, who is an aunt of the comedian Neil Delamere. She was a kind, warm, older lady. She used to go around the country with a Padre Pio exhibition every weekend, campaigning for him to be made a saint.

My role on a Monday morning, so everyone else could get their work done for the later classes, was to ask Mairead how the weekend had gone. I'd find out on the Friday where she was going and then I'd be asking her all about it, like "how did Tullamore go?", while everyone else was scribbling away. And she'd be "stop it Des, I know what you're at".

But Padre Pio was canonised by Pope John Paul II in 2002, so Tullamore and the rest of the trips obviously went well.

The key part of the two years in Rathmines was the work placement during the summer. If you were any good you'd make an impact wherever you got in.

My placement was with the *Irish Press*. I wanted to do sport but I ended up doing news too, which made for great training that stood me in good stead later.

You were thrown in at the deep end and had to learn the ropes fast, but I would have been very enthusiastic and I took to it well.

And it was a real thrill to be working in the same paper as the legend that was Con Houlihan. I used to cut out his columns, especially the ones on the back page of the *Evening Press*. He was a master, one of a kind. He was good to me too, fond of me. When I later joined *The Kerryman* he was both amused and bemused by this young Dub moving to his home-place.

I ended up doing a bit of everything in the *Press*, from match reports to advertising features to going along to press receptions with Terry O'Sullivan, father of Nuala O'Faolain, author of the famous *Dubliner's Diary* in the *Evening Press* and 'Mr High Society'.

They'd be on between five and seven and there was free drink everywhere. I, of course, found it all very entertaining, I loved the novelty of going to these things and meeting these people, it was a party atmosphere, it was the buzz. When Terry turned up it was like God had arrived. He had huge status.

But the drinking culture was evident, journalism back then renowned for it, and you had to be careful not to be sucked in to it. Around then, when I was 18, 19, I was on the first-team for Cuala, but I would have missed training a lot, I just found it more fun to go drinking with the lads.

I remember Michael O'Toole, who was a news editor with the *Press*, taking me in to Kennedy's pub under the bridge at Tara Street station, and giving me a bollocking about it, telling me to cop myself on. It was a valuable talking-to. Although I suppose it was ironic where it took place.

Back at work, I had my first front page story during the Pope's visit in 1979. I didn't actually get a by-line, it was too short a piece, but still, you never forget your first front page. The story? Well, the Office of Public Works had to move the deer and the cows out of the Phoenix Park ahead of the Pope saying Mass there. There was no problem with the cows, but the deer were proving harder to shift.

So I wrote the undeniably immortal line, 'there won't be a single cow, holy or otherwise, in the Phoenix Park when the Pope comes to visit.'

To this day I can't believe I didn't get the Pulitzer.

• • • • • • •

I began getting regular work with the *Irish Press*, getting the odd full day's shift – for which you were paid £33. It was huge money, kids are barely getting that today.

There was no local radio then, and there was no *Irish Daily Star*, *Irish Daily Mirror*, *Irish Daily Mail*. There was the *Indo*, the *Press* and the *Times*, the *Examiner* was still a quasi national paper, and there was RTÉ. That was it at a national level. There were some magazines, but they were the only outlets. But it meant if you got a job you got paid properly.

The *Press* were hiring 12 or 14 journalists at the time, juniors and seniors, and I was pretty much guaranteed a job in sport because I was already there and I was getting on well, they trusted me.

But Michael O'Toole said to me that you can move from news to sport, but it's very hard to move from sport to news if that's what I wanted one day. He and another of the news editors, Paul Muldowney, both advised me to go and work for a provincial newspaper where I could cover both, and where I would get the best training.

And it was in May 1980 that a letter arrived that would set me off on that very path.

Dear Mr Cahill,

It has been suggested to me that you might be available to take up a position as a junior reporter. If you are interested please contact me at....

Yours sincerely,
Liam D Bergin
Managing Director & Editor,
The Nationalist and Leinster Times, Carlow.

It was a huge decision, one that would require leaving the course in Rathmines before finishing it, and turning down the chance of a position with the *Press*.

I agonised about it for a while, but I trusted Michael and Paul, they knew the business as well as anyone, so I took their advice and accepted Liam's offer of a job as a junior reporter.

Vincent, meanwhile, got one of the positions in the *Press* and was soon covering big sporting events while I was doing small local stories.

'Jesus, was I mad heading off to Carlow, did I make the wrong decision?' I asked myself.

It turned out to be the perfect move.

5

Sweet Carlow
And Caroline

*'He asked to see a photograph of her. So
Jimmy comes back with a photo after lunch
and your man says, 'oh yeah!' I looked at the
photo and said, 'hold it, I'll ask her out"*

My first day with the *Carlow Nationalist* was a memorable one, if not entirely for the right reasons. The plan was to stay in digs in the town but I decided to drive down from Dublin early in the morning instead.

I had to have a car for the job, I would be working across three counties, the newspaper having different editions for Carlow, Laois and Kildare. So, with the help of my dad, I bought a car the previous Friday – a very old Renault 4 that cost £400. I think we paid around £350 too much.

I got a puncture on the Saturday.

I got a puncture on the Sunday.

I just remember thinking to myself how lucky I was that it didn't happen on the way to Carlow on the Monday morning.

And then I got a puncture on the way to Carlow on the Monday morning.

I had set off hoping – praying – that I wouldn't have a problem, and then I could get the spare tyre repaired in Carlow. But a couple of miles outside Castledermot in Co Kildare…my worst nightmare. So, while wearing my brand new suit, I had to thumb a lift to the nearest garage carrying my punctured spare tyre.

It transpired that the tubes were way too big for the cheap tyres, causing them to puncture. A fella from the garage gave me a lift back to the car with the repaired tyre, so I then drove on to Carlow, and – almost two hours late – turned up to start my new job.

If I thought things could only get better, I was wrong.

• • • • • • •

I called to the front desk, and was sent to the office of the editor, Liam D Bergin, where we were joined by company secretary, Tom Geoghegan.

I was given a warm welcome, and then Tom walked me to the small newsroom where I would begin work. I introduced myself to the two reporters who were there, Charlie Keegan and Jim Humphries, both of whom were to prove hugely helpful to me.

But it all became a bit awkward when I realised that they didn't know a new reporter was starting, and it got worse a few minutes later when the News Editor, Seamus O'Rourke, came out of his office. He looked quizzically at me, and I explained I was Des, the new reporter. He looked even more puzzled. He hadn't been told either by Liam that I was starting that day.

It was all, to say the least, awkward.

Seamus wasn't sure what work to give me, but as we chatted, a man came in to complain about the terrible state of a caravan given to him by Carlow County Council. Seamus was delighted to have something for me to do, so he suggested I go with the man to have a look at the condition of the caravan which was parked by the local GAA pitch, Dr Cullen Park.

I was shocked by what I saw. There were literally hundreds of maggots behind the cooker and under the seating. I couldn't believe it, so I rang the office and they arranged for the local photographer, Karl McDonagh, to come and get photos of the conditions the family were living in. I returned to the office and immediately rang Carlow County Council to ask why such a dreadful caravan could possibly be given to this family. They said they would investigate and get back to me in a couple of days. But as I sat at the news desk, being watched by my new colleagues, I felt I had to show them that I wasn't going to be a soft touch.

So, I told the Council official that we were going to print that evening with the story and that we would need a statement from them before then.

I was eventually put through to the Carlow County Manager, Mr Michael Boyce, and went through the story again, telling him that this was his opportunity for a right to reply. He quietly asked me when I began with the newspaper, and when I told him it was my first day, he welcomed me warmly. But I wasn't going to be thrown off by his pleasantries. I remained stern, I wanted answers.

Mr Boyce assured me that the Council was most unlikely to give a caravan like I described to anybody. But it would take him 24 hours to investigate if, and how, this happened.

I warned him once more that I would need a statement by

6pm, otherwise we would go to print with the story that evening. I wasn't backing down.

"Well, I won't be able to get back to you by then," he replied. "I'll get in touch with you tomorrow – and in the meantime, welcome again to Carlow, and I hope you have a happy time here."

We held off on making it the front page story, carrying the article, with a photo, on an inside page instead. Luckily.

Mr Boyce rang me early the next morning. "I see you went ahead with the story," he said.

"Yes we did," I replied, defiantly. I sensed he had a smile on his face as he explained what had happened.

The gist of it was that this man had previously been given a caravan, but then left the area. When he returned his caravan was gone, so he asked for another one. But he was told the only one available was not fit for habitation, so he would have to wait. But he said he would take it any way. And then he came to us to complain about the state of it.

Turns out he had sold the first caravan, and then used this cub reporter's youthful enthusiasm – and innocence – to get himself another one. From having felt like The *Carlow Nationalist's* Woodward and Bernstein, I ended up with my head in my hands. It had been some first day.

• • • • • • •

I spent 18 months with the *Carlow Nationalist* – or *The Nationalist and Leinster Times*, to give it its proper title – and loved every minute of it, both the life I had there and the training it gave me covering local sport and news.

I was 20 when I moved to Carlow and it was my first time living on my own. I couldn't get over the freedom I had, having no parents in the house, being able to come and go as I pleased. Being that free was a real novelty.

I took advantage of it too, there was plenty of partying. Charlie Keegan's wife Margaret called me 'the magpie' for stealing her husband away. We'd go out the odd time and he'd finish up by trying to sing a song from all 32 counties. It was never quick.

I had my 21st when I was in Carlow. It was a disaster. It was at the rugby club and a lot of the Cuala lads came down from Dublin, some of them only arriving near eleven. And then the rugby club closed the bar at midnight because we hadn't applied for an extension to the licence. Let's just say, the lads weren't impressed.

Tom Geoghegan, meanwhile, introduced me to Éire Óg, the GAA club based in Carlow town. Tom, who was really good to me during my time at the paper, was a giant of a man, six foot four or five, and played midfield for Éire Óg.

So I went along training with the club, although I wasn't able to be very committed because I had to cover matches at the weekend. But through them I almost ended up playing for Carlow once. Seriously.

We got to a Leinster Club final against Walterstown from Co Meath and the club got permission from the Carlow County Board to represent the county in a National League game to give them a warm-up before the final. I was a sub, but I never got on – which is probably just as well because I was sitting in the dug-out with my notebook covering the match for the *Nationalist*.

I always regret not having the opportunity to write 'and then I came on for Carlow and scored a stunning winner in the last minute.'

Thankfully, things improved for me at the paper after that calamitous first day.

The following week I had the lead story on the front page of the newspaper about an industrial dispute at the local sugar factory which would have huge implications for the local economy.

Unemployment was a major story through my 18 months in Carlow. I can remember reporting on the figure rising 120 per cent in one year in Carlow town alone, between February 1980 and 1981. There were constant worries about the future of the sugar factory and Erin Foods, the main employers in the county.

I would have done stories too on concerns about the rise of the use of hard drugs, such as cocaine and heroin, with talk of the town's college being targeted by pushers from Dublin. They were tough times, all over the country, with unemployment a desperate blight everywhere, and drugs a major problem in the towns and cities. And occasionally you'd have to cover horrendous crime stories too. There was a particularly devastating murder/suicide story where an elderly man shot a relation who was living next door, and then he shot himself in the head.

When I went out to the house the Gardai brought me around the back and didn't tell me the suicide victim was lying there. They did it for the laugh. I just remember the stubble on his face, and then nothing above it, blown away. I'll never forget it. They thought my reaction was hilarious. It was grim.

• • • • • • •

There was huge variety to the work, which I really enjoyed, from politics to sport, from crime to economic issues, any local stories at all that cropped up.

And I tried to contribute in as many ways as I could, at one point suggesting we start a youth page in the paper, which Liam was enthusiastic about. It turned out that there had been a similar section in the paper a few years before under the guidance of none other than Olivia O'Leary, who went on to become one of our very best current affairs presenters.

What I really enjoyed too was covering elections, few as memorable as the 1981 General Election which featured an extraordinary battle for the last of the five seats in the Carlow-Kilkenny constituency between two men who had been senior Fianna Fáil Government Ministers, Tom Nolan, from Carlow, and Jim Gibbons, from Kilkenny.

To this day I'll never forget the tension in the count centre. Both men had large families and they were all leaning over the desks checking every single vote being counted.

Eventually, at 4.35am, after a marathon 19-hour count, it was announced that Nolan had held his seat by 23 votes.

After the Returning Officer, Tom Crotty, announced the result, and as the cheers and boos subsided, Gibbons raised his hand. In a quiet controlled voice, he sought a total recount. That was dramatic enough, but nothing compared to what was to come.

The Returning Officer and his senior counsel, Declan Budd, found that about 30 voting papers had not been stamped, as is required. The *Nationalist* had learnt that stamping machines in at least one polling centre had broken and unstamped ballots may have been given out prior to the arrival of a new machine at the centre.

By now the saga was leading the national news, dragging on for four days. The tension built to a climax when the Returning Officer came to the microphone in the count centre and said he had an important announcement.

The crowd hushed. Crotty said that when he checked over his figures he feared there was something wrong. A box of votes, which had not been counted, had been found.

This was extraordinary. The Gibbons and Nolan camps waited in stony silence to find out where the box was from. Everybody knew if it was a Carlow box, Nolan would benefit, while a Kilkenny box would boost Gibbons' hopes.

When it was announced that the box was from Rathanna, Co Carlow a huge cheer went up from the Nolan contingent. Shouts of "Up Rathanna!" filled the air as his supporters jubilantly lifted Nolan shoulder high.

Out of the 176 Rathanna votes, Gibbons got just nine while Nolan picked up 89 – game over.

Gibbons accepted defeat, but questioned the legality of counting votes from an unsealed box that had been left unguarded for four days.

It was an incredible few days of drama with endless rumours and counter-rumours.

I have covered every General Election since then, even while working for RTÉ Sport, and I've loved it. There's been plenty more drama through the years, but it would be hard to top that 1981 fight for the last seat in Carlow-Kilkenny.

• • • • • • •

I can't say I ever got close to Liam Bergin, but he was a kind and helpful man and I had the height of respect for him. He was a legendary name in Irish journalism, and editor of the *Nationalist* for a remarkable 50 years.

He was a lovely, well-read gentleman with white hair, glasses, and a pointy goatee beard. He looked just like Kentucky Fried Chicken's Colonel Sanders.

He travelled extensively and his great passion was international affairs. And while the editorials in provincial newspapers tended to focus exclusively on local issues, his often dealt with world affairs, which made the paper unique in Irish provincial journalism.

Liam retired while I was working for the *Nationalist* and was succeeded by his good friend, and a former Head of News in RTÉ, Des Fisher. Des's son Michael was a stalwart in the RTÉ Belfast newsroom for many years, and his daughter Carolyn was to be a colleague of mine in later years.

I have one stand-out memory from Liam's going away celebration. After several tributes were paid to him, he wrapped up his few words with a poem that I have never forgotten, and always promised myself I would recite on the day I retire.

The Indispensable Man,
by Saxon White Kessinger.

Some time when you're feeling important,
Some time when your ego's in bloom,
Some time when you take it for granted,
You're the best qualified in the room.
Some time when you think that your going,
would leave an unfillable hole;
Just follow this simple instruction
And see how it humbles your soul.

Take a bucket and fill it with water;
Put your hands in it up to your wrists;

Pull them out – and the hole that remains;
Is the measure of how much you'll be missed.
You may splash as you please when you enter;
You may stir up the water galore;
But stop – and you'll find in a second,
That it looks just the same as before.

The moral of this is quite simple;
Do just the best that you can,
and be proud of yourself – but remember;
There is no indispensable man.

• • • • • • •

Caroline Curran, though, has proved to be an indispensable woman since I first met her during my time in Carlow.

Her sister Ruby was married to one of the news reporters at the paper, Jim Humphries, a Scouser. From Ballyshannon, Co Donegal, she's from a family of 14 and her mother was the eldest of 17, so they're related to half the people in the town. Or more, probably.

Caroline was down visiting Ruby one time and Jimmy asked me if I'd take her out because she was hanging around the house bored. I didn't fancy the idea of a blind date, though, so I said no.

So Jimmy asked this Dublin fella who was there on a training scheme if he would take Caroline out. He asked to see a photograph of her, the cheeky bugger, before he'd agree. So Jimmy comes back with a photo after lunch and your man says, "oh yeah!" I looked at the photo and said, "hold it, I'll ask her out".

She was a really good looking woman. Still is. Way, way out of my league. She was too good looking for me. I was a realist, I knew my level. But she must have been seriously bored because she agreed to go out with me.

We just hit it off. Apart from being beautiful she has a great sense of humour, which was a big part of the attraction. We clicked. Although Caroline soon learnt that going out with me can be a pain in the neck. She prefers smaller groups, I like big ones. And because I'm informal on the radio and cheeky to people, they're naturally cheeky back. Wherever you'd go there'd be lads coming over with a few drinks in them. There's no harm in it, none of it is nasty, but they will literally sit down with you. You might be there having a quiet meal with Caroline and they'd be pulling their chairs in. She didn't know what she was letting herself in for.

But, yes, she was definitely out of my league. Some fellas would swagger around the place if they had a good looking girl with them, whereas I'd just be nodding at everyone going 'I know, I know, I'm out of my depth'.

So, amazingly, she agreed to go out with me and although it was a hell of a trek from Donegal, she'd travel down when she could.

Our most memorable moment in Carlow was probably the time we got arrested in an outdoor swimming pool on the way home from a Carlow Chamber of Commerce dinner. These things happen. The Gardai arrived and then realised I was the reporter from the *Nationalist*. The story didn't make front page news.

If the journey from Donegal was a long one for Caroline, the distance between us was about to get longer. The length of Ireland, in fact.

A job was advertised for *The Kerryman* and on a whim, really, I decided to go for it. It was partly because *The Kerryman*, part of the Independent Group, paid better than *The Carlow Nationalist*, but it was also one of the best provincial papers in the country. So I went for an interview, was offered the job, and decided to take it.

I don't know what possessed me, in a way. I liked Carlow. I cried the night I left it, at my going-away do. But after two months in Killarney I was going 'Jesus, what was I doing crying leaving Carlow?'

6

Welcome To Kerry

"Aren't you Des Cahill from The Kerryman?"
"I've an auld court case coming up next
week, if you could keep it out of the paper..."

"Jesus, hard luck number 14!"

I was mystified. By now I was covered in so much muck it was a wonder the umpire could even see my number.

The first high ball comes in and I misjudge it so badly it hits my chest and bounces back out 30 yards to the half-back line.

I slip. I fall. The full-back gets it.

"Ooooh, you're lucky there Johnny!"

Johnny, the full-back, looks back at the umpire.

I look back at the umpire.

"What?!"

There was no luck about it. Johnny was destroying me.

By now Dr Crokes must have regretted getting me out of the pub to play for them against Firies out at Farranfore. The conditions were abysmal, the wind howling and the rain torrential. And I was not in the best of shape.

It was a Saturday and there had been a tourism conference on in the Great Southern hotel earlier that morning. I'd met a young journalist from Manchester there and he was a bit lost, he knew no-one. He asked me would I have a pint with him in one of the town's pubs so I told him I'd bring him to The Laurels but I wouldn't drink because I had a junior match that evening.

But the rain was bucketing down, and getting heavier by the minute, so I asked some of the lads in the pub if they thought the match would be called off.

"Ah Jesus, it won't be on in that," they said.

So I had a few pints with your man.

Around 5.30 I hear: "Is Dessie Cahill in here?"

The match was on.

Jesus.

The smell of beer off me put me in the serious bad books with the lads when I arrived. I wasn't in peak condition.

There were about four people from our club at the game, but considering the conditions I was surprised there were that many. I'm walking across the pitch and it was splish, splash, splosh, from my feet. And my stomach.

I was playing full-forward and this giant of a fella was marking me. The umpire was standing there with his brolly in the driving rain. Every time I lost the ball, which was often that evening, he'd shout "Jesus, hard luck number 14!"

Then we got a couple of frees, I kicked them over and he was cheering wildly.

At half-time he shouts at the full-back, "Jesus, you're in trouble there with that man!" He was hammering him.

Then he followed the two of us down to the other goal for the second half, which was unusual.

He kept cheering me on and telling the full-back how blessed he was every time he got the better of me.

At the end of the match I went up to him and said, "do I know you?"

"Aren't you Des Cahill from *The Kerryman*," he replied.

"I am."

"I've an auld court case coming up next week, if you could keep it out of the paper…"

Welcome to Kerry.

• • • • • • •

It seemed like it took forever to drive from Carlow to Tralee for my interview. I knew it would be a long enough trip, but it felt like I was travelling to another world.

And in many ways I was. Kerry was a new world for me and I had a lot – everything – to learn about the place and its people. Not least the lengths they would go to to keep their names out of the court reports in the paper.

The decision to join *The Carlow Nationalist*, rather than stay in Dublin, had turned out to be the perfect one, I learned so much in my 18 months there having been thrown in at the deep end.

But both myself and Caroline look back on our three and a half years in Kerry with a special affection, we absolutely loved the place and the life we had there. We were youngsters having a ball.

She joined me in Killarney within the year and I was lucky that she did, it made everything so much easier. Initially I was lost, despite the kindness of so many locals in those early days, but her arriving just helped make it an adventure. We were both a little homesick at first, Caroline now at the opposite end of the country from her family, and that was something that probably brought us even closer together. We helped each other find our fect in this town far from home and grew to love it so much we really would have happily stayed there forever, Caroline made great friends in Killarney, they're still friends to this day, our only regret that we rarely have the time to visit. But it will always be a special place for us.

Our bond with the town, and our fondness for the place, was made all the stronger by the fact that it was there that we married in 1983. We wanted the wedding to be in the cathedral in Killarney but the Bishop, Kevin McNamara, wouldn't give us permission because we were living together. We were a bit taken aback, but we didn't get too upset about it. Those were the rules.

Our next choice was the church at Fossa which has a window behind the altar looking out on the lakes and mountains; it's simply stunning. But that was booked out.

Finally, we got a free date at Muckross Church, also out by the lakes, a beautiful setting, Bill Murphy, a friend of Eileen who later became the Bishop of Kerry, marrying us. But not before we had to do our pre-marriage course with a Dr Norrie Buckley who was sent to speak to us. Again, those were the rules, we accepted them, even if we found the whole process a little strange.

But our wedding day was perfect, ending with a reception in the Gleneagle Hotel. One of Caroline's brothers had driven a coach-load of her family down from Donegal…and I thought my journey from Carlow was epic.

So, somehow, around four years after meeting her, the woman who was way out of my league had married me. Not for the first or last time, I felt a lucky man.

• • • • • • •

I was worried at first that there might be some resentment towards this young Dub coming in and working for the local newspaper. 'Who does this fella think he is, he knows nothing about us?' I remember Mick O'Dwyer, the legendary Kerry manager, being particularly wary of me initially. He couldn't fathom a Dub being given a job with *The Kerryman*.

People would look at you out of the corner of their eye and they'd be sizing you up, and they wouldn't make any bones about it either. They'd throw loads at you, I loved their humour, but if you were cheeky enough, able for it and you could bat some back then you'd be accepted. It was a bit like school all over again. I had to be funny and cheeky to survive there too.

So, you had to win people over.

Donal Hickey, the local correspondent for *The Cork Examiner*, was unbelievably helpful to me from the day I arrived in Kerry and would advise me on reading the mood of people, who to approach or not to approach, who'd be comfortable or uncomfortable with this loud young Dub talking to them.

Unfortunately Donal, who was from Gneevgullia, a small village in East Kerry, also decided that I needed to toughen up the soft hands I had acquired from my cosseted lifestyle. So he took me out to the bog in Gneevgullia one day where we collected the peat, put it in to bags and then threw it up to two local farm hands who were in a trailer on the back of a tractor.

It was all too much for me, by mid afternoon I was knackered. By late evening my last attempt at throwing a bag up to the lads ended with it falling short of its target, turning upside down with the peat tumbling all over me.

"Christ," said one of them, "you newsagents are useless."

A newsagent with soft hands. The city boy had failed the test in the bog.

The paper was based in Tralee but I would be living in Killarney from where I would cover south Kerry news. For the first week, though, I was put up in Benners Hotel in Tralee so I was able to go to the office, get to know everyone and see how they operated.

The hierarchy in Carlow had been stronger, Jim and Charlie were the main news and sports guys, I was the number three in both, but when I went to *The Kerryman* it was very different. The paper had three editions, for Kerry north, Kerry south and Tralee, and while most of the content would be the same they'd each have a different front page and three or four different news or features pages inside, as well as different local notes. That meant, then, that I would be solely in charge of south Kerry news, so with that came a certain freedom.

There was, though, a sadness around my arrival at the paper because I was succeeding Ian O'Leary in the job, a reporter who had tragically passed away in his 40s. Ian's father had been a reporter with the paper too, so it was a dynasty. The editor, Seamus McConville, whose support and friendship I came to value so much during my time there, brought me to meet Ian's family, his widow Mary and their young kids. I stayed in contact with them while I was there, it was a desperately difficult time for them.

Everywhere I went it was 'oh, you're Ian O'Leary's replacement', it was strange for me, but it was obvious how highly regarded he had been. But it didn't inhibit me, I really felt I could do this job having taken a lot of confidence from how things had gone in Carlow where I'd been an outsider too.

After my week in Tralee I stayed in the Failte Hotel in Killarney for a fortnight, to give me time to find somewhere to live, and to find my bearings.

The hotel was owned by Dermot O'Callaghan, a Fianna Fáil

councillor. He and his family were very kind to me and helped me find my way in Killarney. One of Dermot's sons, Niall 'Botty' O'Callaghan, became a key man in the backroom team for the Kerry football team. Well, he told me he was key!

It was Dermot who recommended a visit to Tatler Jack, a famous GAA pub in the town, which led to me joining and playing for local GAA club Dr Crokes. And as I had learnt in Carlow, playing sport for a local club is a great way of getting to know and becoming part of the community, of getting accepted by them.

There are two GAA clubs in Killarney, Legion and Dr Crokes, the rivalry between them going back to the Civil War – you're either from a Crokes or Legion family, back then never the twain would meet. I'd never experienced anything like it, there's nothing similar in Dublin. To this day I'd have Legion people asking me why I joined Crokes. But I hadn't a clue at the time, Dermot was a Crokes man so he sent me to their pub – if I'd been sent across the road to Murphy's Bar, I'd have ended up playing for Legion.

Tatler Jack, a dark pub festooned with intercounty jerseys, was owned by Eddie O'Sullivan who had been a publican in New York before he and his wife Bridie brought their young family to Killarney, one of them, Patrick, going on to become chairman of the Kerry GAA County Board in later years.

Eddie was steeped in Gaelic football and was a senior Kerry selector under both Mick O'Dwyer and Paidi Ó Sé. He became a good friend during my time in Killarney, we'd often go to see St Brendan's in Munster colleges matches together, and when I told him I played Gaelic football he organised for me to go and play a game with their second team.

It was a similar situation to Éire Óg in Carlow, because I would be covering matches at the weekend for the paper and was just generally busy with work, I wasn't able to give a full commitment. But we had great success with the second team, I got to play in a Kerry Junior final. About seven of that team, who were all around 18 or 19, me being in my 20s, played in the All-Ireland senior club final two years later. Seanie O'Shea captained them in Croke Park. His brother Pat was manager when Kerry won the All-Ireland senior title in 2008. Connie Murphy went on to win an All-Star, Mike Buckley, Ger O'Shea, John Clifford…they all came through our team as kids on their way to bigger things. So, a decent side, and a lovely bunch of fellas.

It was one of my less memorable outings for Crokes, though, that day the umpire was inexplicably shouting "Jesus, hard luck number 14!", that gave me a real insight to the community in which I now lived.

• • • • • • •

Like in Carlow, I was covering a bit of everything for *The Kerryman*, general local news, sport, the council, and so on. But working as a court reporter in Killarney probably gave me the best understanding of local life and I soon came to appreciate the shame attached to being involved in a court case.

It was probably greater then because the local paper carried so much power, and people would do anything to keep their name, or that of a family member, out of it. You'd even be offered money not to file a report on a case. They were quiet people, they just didn't want their business in print for everyone to read.

The biggest thing was not to have your name in the paper for drink driving. You would be approached by people pleading with you not to publish their name, never aggressively, just in a genuinely pained kind of way. And Caroline would also have people coming to her crying, begging her to ask me not to cover a particular case, it carried such a stigma. But there was nothing you could do. I would have made it far more difficult for myself if I got involved in all that.

The hardest part was when some court stories I filed wouldn't get carried because there wasn't space, a huge local story might have come up or several pages might have been taken up by a big Championship match, especially for an All-Ireland semi-final or final. Then you would have people asking why some other fella's name wasn't in the paper but his was. "You're out to get me", and all of that. There would be real resentment towards you, they wouldn't speak to you any more. But that's a small community, that's what happens. It was especially tough on the editor, Seamus, because he was the one who had to make the call on how we used the space, what went in and what was left out.

A lot of the court cases were the usual humdrum stuff, straight-forward motoring offences, whatever, but there were the tragic ones too, sometimes where human error might have cost a life, sometimes the life of a loved one. They were heart-breaking cases, the pain on the faces of the families hard to bear, and there were times you felt you were being horribly intrusive by just being there with your notebook.

And there were the zanier days, like when a jarvey was up on a charge of being drunk while driving his horse and cart. I'd never even heard of a jarvey before going to Killarney. People were tittering in the court. I truly was in a different world.

Election time used to cause plenty of grief too. Kerry South was a constituency on its own and because I was the reporter there I had a big role in covering its politics and election campaigns. It was one of my favourite parts of the job. But *The Kerryman* was a weekly paper which meant that there would only be two or three editions during a standard election campaign, and every candidate was, of course, desperate to make the front page with a positive story. The news editor would ultimately decide.

Needless to say, those decisions caused plenty of resentment too. I still remember Fine Gael TD Michael Begley calling to my door after midnight, raging. He'd just got a copy of *The Kerryman* from the printers where it was being readied to go first thing in the morning. Michael Moynihan of Labour, a TD with a huge personal vote rather than a party one, was on the front page and Begley, understandably enough, thought that this would give him a big push. He was incensed.

The next week Labour and Fianna Fáil would be equally annoyed with you, you couldn't win.

As it turned out, Begley topped the poll, so it didn't do him too much harm. But elections were rarely short of tension or frayed tempers. I even ended up in court as a witness to a heated encounter during the February 1982 campaign.

Jerry Kennelly, who went on to become a very successful entrepreneur and whose family owned the Kerry's Eye newspaper in Tralee, was working as a freelance photographer during the election and had been assigned by three Dublin newspapers to cover polling day in Killarney.

He saw a group of men lifting an elderly man in a dressing gown from a voting booth and he began taking photos. The men asked him to stop, but he continued. It finished up with one of the men, Daniel O'Leary (brother of Fianna Fáil TD and junior minister, John O'Leary) hitting Kennelly in the face with the elderly man's walking frame, and come November of that year it ended up in court.

O'Leary was found guilty of common assault and fined £15. It was an awkward one for me because I knew both men well, but I just described what I saw.

> *Kerryman journalist Des Cahill said he was in the vicinity of the polling station on the occasion. He heard parties shouting at each other. Canvassers from Fine Gael were shouting at Fianna Fáil, saying that they were carrying in patients from the hospital. Kennelly was taking photographs and Fianna Fáil people were telling him to go away, but Kennelly kept saying that he was just doing his job. Witness said that the argument continued for five or 10 minutes. He saw O'Leary hit Kennelly on the face with a semi-circular walking aid.*
>
> *(From my report in The Kerryman)*

I had become used to writing about matches in which I'd played, but this was the first – and mercifully only – time I had to write about a court case in which I was a witness.

When Michael O'Toole and Paul Muldowney advised me to go and work for a provincial newspaper, I had no idea what experiences lay ahead.

7

The Kerry Babies

'It resulted in a horrible, suffocating atmosphere of suspicion, and a lot of bad blood. I was shocked by it all, life in Dublin was so different'

I left Kerry in 1984 to join RTÉ, but the following summer I went back down for the Munster football final which, as was usually the case, was between Cork and Kerry. It was in Páirc Uí Chaoimh that year, but I went to the game from Killarney with the lads, for old time's sake.

It was a beautiful scorcher of a day, Kerry won by six points, so the form was good. On our way back to Killarney we stopped in a small hotel in Ballyvourney, just on the Cork side of the border, for a few pints.

When we arrived at the hotel I spotted the slight figure of a woman sitting on the window sill outside. I recognised her immediately.

Inside, in the bar, there were people standing up on seats trying to get a look at her through the windows. The image will never leave me, it just made me wonder about what her life had been like after she had become one of the most recognisable faces in Ireland, how people reacted when they saw her. Staring, pointing, whispering.

She was Joanne Hayes, the woman at the centre of 'The Kerry Babies' story, an extraordinary and tragic series of events that began the year before, just a couple of months before I left *The Kerryman* for RTÉ.

• • • • • • •

It was a Sunday morning in April 1984 when Donal Hickey, the local correspondent for *The Cork Examiner* rang me. I was due to play a match for the Crokes that day, but Donal told me that a baby had been found dead in Caherciveen and that Sergeant Paddy Reidy, who I knew as an administrator in the GAA, would be bringing the remains up to Killarney for the Assistant State Pathologist to examine.

I recall sitting in the sunshine with Paddy, while he waited for the State Pathologist to visit, and I sent up a couple of paragraphs about the story to the Dublin papers, which is what local correspondents would do, Donal and myself being the first to report on the story.

Distressing as it was, I never for a moment imagined just how big the story would become, or how enormous the consequences would be. My first report in *The Kerryman* simply gave the earliest available details on the saddest of discoveries:

> *The young baby found dead on a Caherciveen beach at the weekend may have been murdered, according to Kerryman sources. The newly born male infant had a broken neck and*

*chest wounds ... the grim discovery was made at White
Strand on Saturday night at 8.30pm by Mr Jack Griffin
of Kimego, Caherciveen, who was walking along the beach
at the time. The child was lying on the rocks with a plastic
fertiliser bag beside it. There was a hole in the bag and
Gardai believe the child had fallen out of it ... the little
infant was buried on Monday afternoon. He was in a tiny
white coffin and the funeral was attended by local clergy as
well as young schoolchildren ... Gardai launched a public
appeal for information. They say anyone who comes forward
will be treated in the strictest of confidence.*

The post mortem on the baby boy, who was later to be named
John and buried in the town's Holy Cross Cemetery, showed
that his neck was broken and that he had 28 knife wounds. It
was horrific.

The Gardai then put out an appeal seeking information about
the mother of the baby, and I found the nature of that appeal
disturbing. Effectively, they wanted to know about any woman
who had been pregnant but, subsequently, there was no sign of
her baby. The Gardai didn't state it publicly, but if there were
suspicions about a neighbour, people were asked to come forward
and report them.

It's hard to explain to people who haven't lived there, and life
has changed so much since then, but parts of Kerry were so rural
and remote, electricity had only come in to the Black Valley 20
years before. I had come to understand through reporting on
court cases that these were a people for whom privacy was so
important, they didn't want their personal or family business
aired for everyone to know. So the social fall-out from this appeal
was enormous, it resulted in a horrible, suffocating atmosphere

of suspicion, and a lot of bad blood. I was only a young man in my mid-20s and I was shocked by it all, life in Dublin was so different.

The Gardai would be told about a girl next door who, neighbours believed, had been pregnant. In some cases they were right, in some they were wrong. Maybe the girl had just put on weight. Or maybe she had gone to England to have an abortion.

If that wasn't traumatic enough, the Gardai were now being dragged in to her life and asking such personal questions about what must have been a difficult and lonely experience, one she would have wanted to be kept private. And travelling to England for abortions happened way more than was ever acknowledged back then; we looked the other way. Those journeys must have been desperately hard.

Even getting the information they needed in those days would have been a challenge. And there would, no doubt, have been plenty of girls and women who needed to make that journey, but were unable to do so because they lacked the wherewithal, either financial or just even knowing how to go about it.

I thought of those girls and women again in the wake of the 2018 referendum being passed in Ireland, when the constitutional ban on abortion was repealed. I thought about what it meant for women in Ireland, especially having listened to people like Roisin Ingle talk about their own experiences of having to travel for abortions.

When the referendum passed I couldn't but think of the Kerry Babies case again and how Ireland has changed for the better since then.

• • • • • • •

Joanne came to the attention of the investigation after she had gone to the hospital in Tralee that April saying that she had had a miscarriage, but a scan showed that she had carried her baby to full term. The Gardai spoke to the medical staff there and concluded that Joanne was a suspect.

What followed was the most bizarre and dreadful sequence of events that, to this day, is still hard to take in.

Joanne, 24, lived with her mother, two brothers and her sister at her aunt Bridie's farm at Abbeydorney, a few miles north of Tralee, and they were all questioned by the Gardai who by now were being helped by detectives from the Murder Squad in Dublin.

Joanne had become pregnant by a local married man, Jeremiah Locke, with whom she already had a daughter, and she told the Gardai that she had buried the baby on the farm after it had been stillborn. Her aunt, Bridie Fuller, who was a midwife, had delivered it.

The Gardai didn't believe her, suspecting that the Caherciveen baby was hers. After their interrogation, Joanne and her family signed confessions, admitting that she had killed her baby and then the family helped dispose of the remains in the sea, many miles from their home. Joanne was charged with murder and four of her family were charged with concealment of birth.

That appeared to be the case resolved. But then the body of another baby was found hidden on the farm, just as Joanne said it would be. She had been telling the truth. That October, the Director of Public Prosecutions dropped the charges.

When I look back on the case I feel ashamed to have been part of the reporting. With a few honourable exceptions at the time, most of us were unquestioning of the Gardai, just as we were of all our major institutions in those years, the Church included.

I knew some of the people involved in the investigation so I was getting snippets of news as it progressed. The discovery on the farm of the remains of Joanne's baby appeared to rule her out of any involvement in the Caherciveen case, but then a Garda called to my door and told me that she'd had twins, the one found on the farm and the one in Caherciveen. I just remember saying, "you're joking?"

And that's how we reported it, Joanne had had twins. We just accepted this as fact. We didn't question the Gardai.

The country had been horrified by the nature of the death of the baby, the Gardai had provided an explanation for how it happened, and it was as if everyone was relieved by that. We could move on and put the horror behind us. No questions asked. Case solved.

Except it wasn't. The forensic evidence showed that while the baby on the farm belonged to Joanne and Jeremiah Locke, the one on the beach had a different blood type to both of them, so it could not have been theirs.

But the Gardai had an answer for that, too: they put forward the theory that the babies were twins by different fathers. 'Superfecundation', a word I, and probably most of Ireland, had never heard of.

And this was casting an even greater slur on Joanne, as it would have been viewed at the time, she'd had sex with two different men within a short space of time and became pregnant with twins, each man fathering one of the babies. And that's how the papers carried it.

These days if you heard mention of an unfamiliar medical phenomenon, you'd go straight on the internet to research it and get some understanding of it, or you would consult with experts. But, again, we were unquestioning, when the Gardai told us superfecundation explained how Joanne had had twins by two different fathers. That's how we reported it.

· · · · · · ·

It was the following January that the Kerry Babies Tribunal opened in Tralee, its purpose to examine how criminal charges had ever been brought against Joanne and her family. By then I was working for RTÉ, but I followed the tribunal closely and was both shocked by the treatment of Joanne and the nature of the questions put to her over five harrowing days, and the allegations made against the Gardai and their behaviour towards the Hayes family.

Joanne claimed she had been slapped during the interrogation and threatened with losing the daughter she already had with Jeremiah Locke, that she would be placed in an orphanage. She was treated appallingly and asked the most personal of questions, to the point where she was left in tears. And I remember the endless jokes told at the time about it all, about Joanne's relationship with Locke. There was a cruelty too to some of the media coverage, it was a dreadful way for people to be treated. And Locke had a wife and family too, they were suffering through it all as well. They were all such easy targets.

But Joanne received plenty of support too, her neighbours and various women's groups in particular, horrified by her treatment, protested outside the tribunal.

Eventually the superfecundation theory in the case was dismissed by experts, but the verdict of Justice Kevin Lynch, who chaired the tribunal, was shocking.

Despite there being no evidence to back him up he declared

that Joanne had choked her baby to death in her bedroom after it had been born alive. And rather than the Gardai being held to account for Joanne and her family signing confessions for something they could not have done, receiving just a mild rebuke for their behaviour, the judge insisted the family alone were responsible for those confessions.

It was an extraordinary conclusion.

• • • • • • •

Almost 34 years later, in January 2018, Joanne finally received an apology from the Gardai after they secured a DNA profile that confirmed she could not have been the mother of the Caherciveen baby. Speaking at the Garda Station in Caherciveen, Supt Flor Murphy of Killarney said:

"It is a matter of significant regret for An Garda Síochána that it has taken such a long time for it to be confirmed that Ms Hayes is not the mother of Baby John. On behalf of An Garda Síochána, I would like to sincerely apologise to Ms Hayes for that, as well as the awful stress and pain she has been put through as a result of the original investigation into this matter, which fell well short of the required standards."

The Taoiseach, Leo Varadkar reiterated the apology, while the acting Garda Commissioner Donal O'Cualáin wrote and spoke to Joanne by telephone to also apologise for the Garda handling of the investigation. Three and a half decades later.

• • • • • • •

Three months before the baby was found on that Caherciveen beach, 15-year-old Ann Lovett died after giving birth beside a Grotto dedicated to the Virgin Mary in Granard, Co Longford. Fifteen.

It was heart-breaking, her isolation, loneliness, desperation and fear simply unimaginable.

It is often said that Ireland began to change that year, because of Ann Lovett and because of what Joanne Hayes endured. And I believe that too. It was the start of us beginning to question our society and its powerful institutions, including the Gardai and the Catholic Church once we began to learn of the abuse of children that had gone on in the religious orders. And the appalling treatment of 'unmarried' mothers.

When the members of the Hayes family signed confessions, few of us, including me, went after that story at the time, we just accepted it. I went along with it. It was only when the tribunal came around and we heard the allegations about what the Gardai had done to the family that I understood why they signed those confessions. They were terrified.

And it was then I thought, 'Jesus Christ, those people were so vulnerable but they had nobody supporting them'. So, I do feel shame and guilt looking back. Feelings that were stirred again that summer's day in Ballyvourney when I saw that slight figure of a woman sitting on the window sill outside. All I hope is that her life since has been a good and happy one.

It's the very least that Joanne Hayes deserves.

8

Home From Home

*'The place is full of people who move there
with the intention of staying for just a year or
two, and end up never leaving. Caroline and
myself were hugely tempted to do the same'*

The courts and council meetings were the staple work for
the paper, that's where you'd often get the biggest stories.
Reporting on the urban council in Killarney was rarely
dull – they'd fight like hell, mainly for my benefit, to get in the
paper.

They'd be looking over their shoulders at me to see if I was
writing. They'd bicker from start to finish, and then when they
were done we'd all go across to the Ross Hotel for a few pints
afterwards. No more bickering. You could only throw your eyes
to the heavens and laugh.

And I can only laugh looking back at the rather unconven-
tional means I used to get my copy in after a day in court or the
council. *The Kerryman* didn't have any copy-takers so if you were
squeezed for time that made it tricky getting it from Killarney to
Tralee. The solution? Send it by train.

At the end of each court day I would go home, only a few hundred yards up the road, and start typing. If I needed a little more time to get finished I would ring Christy Horgan, a Labour councillor who worked at the station. He would regularly hold up the Dublin to Tralee train, which stopped in Killarney, while waiting for me to get done. I actually think that made me good with dealing with deadline pressure – there aren't many reporters who have a train waiting for them while they're trying to finish their story.

I'd put the sheets in an envelope and hand it to the train driver and he'd bring it to Tralee where the legendary Teddy O'Dowd, a famous footballer with the John Mitchels club whose son Timmy later won three senior All-Irelands with Kerry, drove the van for *The Kerryman*. He would collect the envelope and deliver the copy to get it set that evening.

Once the train departed the station, my day was done.

I can only apologise to those passengers all those years ago who could never understand why they were being held up in Killarney.

• • • • • • •

While local news took up a huge part of my work during my years in Kerry, Gaelic football was, of course, central to my time there too. Between 1975 and 1985 Kerry and Dublin met in the All-Ireland final on six occasions, Kerry winning five of them. That era was, then, the peak of the rivalry between the counties and I was lucky to be there for four years of it. And it wasn't a bad time to be a Dub living in Killarney. There was plenty of slagging and no end of fun.

The football was fantastic with some of the game's greatest ever names playing in that time. I can remember seeing one of them, Jack O'Shea, playing for South Kerry against Castleisland in a Championship match. The sun was splitting the rocks, it was a Saturday evening in Cahirciveen, Jacko was playing centre half-back marking Cork's Christy Kearney – and Jacko scored five points from playing in defence while marking an inter-county player. He was a magnificent player. They were exciting times. At Kerry training sessions in August and September, coming up to an All-Ireland final, there'd be a couple of thousand people there. There'd be huge interest in 'who's going well', as they always asked, although the team rarely changed.

I discovered a remarkable depth of knowledge of the game, you'd have little old ladies talking about Kerry the previous Sunday in the greatest of detail, 'we're too weak at corner-back', everyone knew the team inside out. I went from being a Dubs fan who would always have shouted for whoever Kerry were playing to having the greatest of respect for them. They were a fantastic team with incredible skill, strength and flair.

I was gutted for them as I watched from the press box in Croke Park when Séamus Darby got that late goal for Offaly in 1982 to deny them the five-in-a-row. Back in Kerry all the five-in-a-row t-shirts were ready for sale, there had been complete confidence in the team achieving the feat. The loss, then, was devastating.

But they still came back to win a three-in-a-row between 1984 and '86 which showed their strength of character. That Offaly loss would have floored most counties for years to come.

I got to know Mick O'Dwyer well during those years and after his initial scepticism about the wisdom of *The Kerryman* hiring a Dub, we got on really well. Whenever we've met since he'd note the fluctuating nature of my weight.

"You're a bit stronger than the last time…" And if I'd lost a few pounds… "you're not as strong as you were the last time."

'Strength' was a delicate way of putting it, he was the Fitbit of his time, closely (and alarmingly accurately) monitoring my battle with the bulge.

It's as well I didn't play for him. Around March he'd get the players back together again for training, in preparation for the Championship, but some of the stars on the team would put a good bit of weight on over the winter, so they became known as the 'fatties' within the group. Without naming names they would have included Eoin 'Bomber' Liston, Paudie O'Shea, Jimmy Dennihan and the late, great Tim Kennelly and John Egan.

Micko would get them in to shape. Savage training it would be, wrapped in plastic bags, doing lap after lap, until he felt they'd shed enough weight. Then the rest of the panel would come in and the serious Championship preparations would begin.

The lifestyle of most of today's inter-county players has changed completely since then. Back in those days, though, the Kerry players would be having their pints, and there'd be no reporting of them to management by someone who spotted them in a pub. They were winning, so there was no reason to doubt them, and they stopped drinking when they needed to.

They, too, were wary of me initially – 'who's this fella from Dublin?' – but through my involvement with Crokes they got to know and, I think, trust me. The Crokes second team had a lot of mid-week games and I would play in them, so I'd be all around the county and became a familiar enough face for them.

Even if they broke Dublin hearts on many an occasion, it was a real privilege to have watched them at close quarters and got to know them. They were an extraordinary bunch, wonderful characters, and among the most gifted players we've ever seen.

If Micko and his players were among the most memorable people I came to know in Kerry, Jackie Healy-Rae was another. He had been Fianna Fáil's director of elections in Kerry South but left the party before the 1997 general election when he failed to receive a nomination to run. And then he won a seat as an independent, his son Michael succeeding him in 2011, Danny, incredibly, making it two seats for the family in 2016.

I got on very well with Jackie and had great time for him. And contrary to the sometimes sneering attitude towards him, especially from people in Dublin who regarded him as a 'gombeen', I grew to learn what an astute and smart man he was – as Michael and Danny are too. Witty and kind as well.

Those who mock the Healy-Raes just don't understand them at all. People don't vote for them because they're 'characters', they vote for them because they get so much done for their community. And with people in so many parts of rural Ireland feeling neglected or abandoned by 'Dublin', people like the Healy-Raes are saviours, they're the ones people turn to when they need help, whatever it might be. I think Michael in particular is the most effective voice for rural Ireland in the Dáil.

And I'd add Maurice O'Donoghue to the list of people who made a huge impression on me while I lived in Kerry. He was an extraordinary pioneering man who, before his death in 2001, contributed enormously to turning Killarney in to the most successful tourism centre in the country.

I've always said that if my time with RTE ended tomorrow, the one job I'd love to take on would be promoting tourism in Donegal. I grew to love the county once I came to know it through Caroline, for both its spectacular beauty and its people. But like many other counties, it really could take lessons from how Killarney has promoted itself over the years, its tourism potential still untapped. Although it is, of course, severely hampered by having no train links.

And it was Killarney's train link to Dublin that Maurice, very brilliantly, put to good use from 1980 when he launched the Showtime Express, an off-season weekend train and accommodation package that brought so many visitors in to the town in the quieter spells of the year.

The idea was just to get the visitors in at cost, or close to it, and once they were there they would spend money on food, drink, music, horse racing, whatever was going on.

Maurice owned both the Gleneagle and Scott's hotels. He might have Joe Dolan on one night in the Gleneagle, Brendan Grace the next, and jazz sessions in Scott's. He had a waterbus on the lake, he had just about every tourism angle covered, there was something for everyone. And if you wanted to work, there was a job for you in Killarney, in the hotels, B&Bs, restaurants, bars, so many tourism outlets, and there were conferences on all the time in the hotels. And he put a lot back, especially through sport which he loved. He was a big GAA supporter and sponsored the county team, as well as a basketball team and the annual car rally in Kerry.

He really was a visionary. He brought tourism to a whole new level, and it fascinated me. His legacy is an extraordinary one. Now, if only I could do that for Donegal.

• • • • • • •

It's often said that Galway is the best place to live in Ireland, and I can see why, but I'd put Killarney right up there with it.

The place is full of people who move there with the intention of staying for just a year or two, and end up never leaving. Caroline and myself were hugely tempted to do the same, we really couldn't have been any happier, we just loved the place. By then I'd even considered trying to buy *The Killarney Advertiser.*

It was owned by Danny Casey, a great character, and he mentioned at one stage that he might sell it. He must have thought it was ludicrous that a young fella like me would talk to him about buying it, but I was interested, the thought struck me that you could have a good business and really develop it.

Danny had a very successful formula, the paper was free but advertising paid for it, but I doubt he took me seriously when we spoke. Apart from anything I just wouldn't have had the money to buy it. Anyway, God knows what kind of accent I would have ended up with if I'd stayed there for 25 years.

In the end it was partly down to ambition, partly money, that we made the decision to move on. I would be returning to my home place too, close to family, and Cuala, so that eased the wrench of leaving Kerry. We weren't long married and provincial papers didn't pay well, so I decided that the next journalism job that came up in Dublin, I'd go for it.

And, as it turned out, that was a position as a news reporter with RTÉ in 1984.

I have two oil paintings of Killarney at home, they must have been selling them cheap – one was a gift from the council after I reported on a meeting for the last time, the other from Dr Crokes. They mean a lot to me.

We packed the paintings and everything else we owned and headed for Dublin, teary-eyed, for a new chapter in our lives.

The one we had just closed had brought us nothing but happiness. Even just heading out the road, I was already missing the place.

9

The Outsider

*'I remember Fergal being particularly
generous after my first report for television,
which actually was the Ideal Homes
Exhibition. "And everyone had a good time!"
Cringey...'*

Caroline wouldn't be a particularly religious person, but
she sat in the car with her rosary beads praying for me
when I went in to do my interview in RTÉ. Hard as we
knew it would be for both of us to leave Kerry, we also knew that
this was a great opportunity career-wise and once I'd decided to
go for it, I really wanted the job.

Her prayers were answered, partly, I think, because of the
divine intervention of Tom Quinn.

"Dessie Cahill?!"

"Tom!"

"What are you doing here?"

"I'm going for an interview."

"Oh my God!"

Just when you think the world can't get any smaller. I was on my way up to the third floor in the RTÉ administration building, I got out of the lift and there was Tom walking by. He stopped and did a double-take.

It had been a long time since we'd seen each other, at least 10 years, so when he got over the shock he walked me to the interview room. And he told the five people behind the desk to, under no circumstances, consider giving me the job.

They looked a bit bemused. "Why?" they asked.

Because, he told them, I had failed to turn up for Clann Coláiste Mhuire for an under-15 league semi-final, opting instead to go away for the weekend to the birthday of a Wicklow girl I had met at the Gaeltacht. (This was true).

He smiled as he left the room, which was fortunate.

Otherwise my time in RTÉ might have ended before it started.

· · · · · · ·

After 40 years with RTÉ, Tom Quinn retired in 2009 having risen to the position of Group Secretary. He was a Coláiste Mhuire old-boy who, along with Sean Lynch and Denis O'Neill, gave up so much of his time to transport 20 or more players around Dublin for Gaelic football matches, six or seven of us crammed in to his Mini.

Tom was entitled to be livid with me for failing to return from Wicklow in time for such an important game. Even a decade or so later.

But his intervention ahead of my interview proved to be a big help, the panel amused to learn that he had been a football manager, a side of his life they knew nothing about. And they couldn't but laugh at this reprobate, who'd let Tom down all those years before, turning up looking for a job in his place of work. It broke the ice and made the interview a lot more relaxed than it might have been.

And even though I have since reflected on my reporting on the Kerry Babies story with no great pride, the fact that I had worked on it from its earliest stages stood me in good stead. It was such a huge story at the time, so they had lots of questions about it.

What helped too was that I had worked for two highly respected provincial papers and picked up invaluable experience at both, covering every kind of story imaginable. I'd had my doubts when Michael O'Toole and Paul Muldowney at *The Irish Press* advised me to go down that route, when I thought the obvious choice was to stay with the *Press* in Dublin, but it turned out to be up there with the best advice I ever received.

I also had to do an aptitude test – Jesus, when I think of it – and a voice test, the latter the one that worried me the most. To this day I really don't have a good broadcasting voice, it's undeniably squeaky, so I feared I would perish on that rock.

We were brought in a mini-bus from Donnybrook to a training studio in Ballsbridge to do the voice test. There was a woman on board who was also going for one of the jobs, I remember her saying to me, "you mightn't have a voice for broadcasting". It wasn't exactly the kindest of remarks at that particular time, but she was right. In the end, though, my weakness was forgiven and I got one of the positions. She didn't at that time, but got one later on. She actually turned out to be a nice person, but on that occasion at least, perhaps a little too forthright.

So, I was one of four reporters given positions in news, also hired were Michael Ronayne, who later had a spell as Fianna Fáil press director, Fergal Keane, who went on to the BBC, and Maggie O'Kane, who went on to *The Guardian*. Both had outstanding careers, including spells as war reporters. In later years, Fergal used to say to me that some of the junior hurling matches I covered were more barbaric than any of the wars he had reported on.

He was probably right.

·······

It wasn't a conscious decision at all to move from print journalism to broadcasting, in fact it had never entered my head. I'd only ever considered going to one of the national newspapers to cover sport, and back then there were only three, *The Irish Press*, *Irish Times* and the *Indo*.

But I'd had a chat with Michael Fortune, who was the Group Sports Editor of *The Irish Press*, and he told me I was pissing people off by applying for jobs and then backing out. Which I had done, getting cold feet when it looked like I'd get the job, opting instead to stay where I was.

"Don't be annoying people, make up your mind," he said. "If you want to stay in Kerry, stay there!"

And Caroline and myself *were* tempted to stay because we had been so happy, so it was probably the most difficult decision we ever had to make.

But in the end we felt that it was the right thing to do. So I said I would go for the next job that came up in Dublin, whatever it was – and I'd stick with it. No backing out.

And that was the RTÉ job.

Thirty-four years later and I'm still there.

·······

When we left Kerry we just weren't in a position to buy our own home in Dublin, so we moved in with my parents. They were very good to take us in, but it was difficult enough for us – and probably for them too – after we'd been used to all that freedom in Killarney.

And it was hard for Caroline. In some ways I felt like I had to start all over again being back in Dublin, but at least I had Cuala and all my friends there. Caroline had lived in Dublin for a year before, but that wasn't long enough to establish any great roots in the place, so it really was like starting from scratch for her. We'd had much the same circle of friends in Kerry, but she wouldn't have known the ones from Cuala as well.

And living with my parents was quite an experience.

We'd go to bed. Mam would knock on the door, but walk in at the same time.

"Are you alright there lovies?"

It reached the stage where I'd lie frozen in case she appeared.

We were there for nine months until we got a house…no, six. It just felt like nine.

• • • • • • •

In those early days I was one of three news reporters on the TV desk, along with Charlie Bird and Joe O'Brien, who I had replaced at *The Carlow Nationalist* a few years before.

Charlie and Joe were best friends, still are. I was the junior of the three, so didn't exactly get the plum jobs. Charlie was a divil – he would look at the next day's markings and would write his name beside the most attractive. Always. And Joe would just look at me and shrug his shoulders. He'd end up getting the second best story, and I got, well, the Ideal Homes Exhibition, that kind of thing.

I remember Fergal being particularly generous after my first report for television, which actually WAS the Ideal Homes Exhibition. "And everyone had a good time!" Cringey. So, it didn't merit any generosity at all, but he was exceptionally kind about it, he was that type of fella, someone who had a word of encouragement in those early days.

Just about everyone in there had come from the newspaper industry, television was still relatively new – RTÉ1 had only been launched 23 years before. There were no local radio stations, at least not legal ones, the pirates going for music rather than news.

I was mainly doing television at first but you got moved around different desks. I did 2FM News for a while, and when *Morning Ireland* started up on radio that November I began working on that.

And there was a poignancy to the first big story I did for *Morning Ireland*, just a week after it took to the air. Only a couple of months before I'd had a few beers in Killarney with a bunch of journalists who were down for a tourism visit to South Kerry, and here I was reporting on their deaths in the Beaujolais plane crash.

Nine men in all died after the plane, which had been en route to France to bring home the first Beaujolais Nouveau wine in what was an annual tradition, crashed during bad weather in to a hill near Eastbourne on the south coast of England.

Among the dead were the pilot, a number of businessmen and some of the biggest names in Irish journalism at the time, Kevin Marron, the *Sunday World* editor and columnist, Niall Hanley, editor of the *Evening Herald*, *Herald* columnist John Feeney, and Tony Heneghan, a columnist with the *Irish Independent*.

The news was utterly shocking when it came in. I had to do a piece profiling each of the people who had died, and it was well received. It was, though, painful to do.

It was the start of a long relationship with *Morning Ireland*. If I ever need reminding that I'm not as young as I think I am: I'm the only one still working on the programme who was there from when it began.

• • • • • • •

Starting out in RTÉ was daunting, as it would be for anyone going into a new, large workplace. And like in any big organisation, some people will take to you, some won't. Some will rate you, some won't. I think that happens everywhere. From early on, for example, I knew Shane Kenny, who presented the lunchtime news, didn't rate me at all. He'd give me fairly menial jobs to do. But I never took any of that personally, he had his two or three favourites, his gang, people whose style he just preferred or who he believed had more ability or potential.

And I definitely wasn't one of the cool kids coming in at that time either. There was a certain condescending attitude from some of the younger crew, my peers, towards provincial papers, so when they asked you where you had worked and you said *The Kerryman*, you sensed their disdain. The more experienced journalists, or ones who had come from the same background, wouldn't have reacted that way, they knew the value of working for a good provincial paper. But the younger ones just didn't.

I wouldn't push myself forward in the newsroom as they did. They'd be going to the main news people saying "there was a really interesting story in *The Guardian*…", and I'd be sitting there thinking 'ah Jesus'. It's not that I have anything against *The Guardian*, it's a great paper, but you just felt they were doing this because they thought it was what they had to do to get ahead. I just wasn't a player that way. I can't do it, it's bullshit to me.

I remembered Michael O'Toole telling me that if I went to the provinces to work, it would knock the edges off me. And it did just that, especially in Kerry. You wouldn't have any notions about yourself there like you might have done if you had stayed working in the media in Dublin, hanging around south Dublin with your south Dublin friends with their south Dublin mindset. You'd never leave that world – from school to college to work to your social life, it's all you'd ever know.

And it was uncomfortable deciding to leave it behind for those few years, it would have been much easier to stay. I was hanging around with a good gang of fellas and girls, I was enjoying life. It was, I think, a brave decision. I had wondered at the time if I was mad, but the experience has stood me in good stead ever since.

When I look back on my early days I see a common thread through it all, I was an outsider in many ways from when I was a kid right through to joining RTÉ. I was just about the only lad on my road who went to Oliver Plunkett School, most of the others going to CBC Monkstown; I was the young fella whose Da was the headmaster; I was the 'posh boy' in Coláiste Mhuire; I was the weirdo who loved GAA when all the others were in to rugby; I was the Dub in Carlow and the Dub in Kerry. You learn to adapt, you have to, and I think I always managed to do that.

So if, in some ways, I felt like an outsider in RTÉ in the beginning, it didn't worry me at all. I'd adapted before, I'd adapt again.

• • • • • • •

I got a break from my Ideal Homes Exhibition-type reports when Charlie and Joe were tied up with other stories. Word came in to the newsroom one day that Dominic McGlinchey would be handed over by the RUC to the Gardai at the border that day.

McGlinchey, the head of the Irish National Liberation Army, had been extradited to Northern Ireland in March 1984 after being captured by the Gardai following a shoot-out in Cork and was to stand trial for the murder of a postmistress in the north when he had been a member of the IRA. He was tried and convicted the following December, but the conviction was later overturned on a legal technicality. The authorities in Northern Ireland had, then, to hand him back to the south.

Myself and cameraman Brian Miley headed for the border in his RTÉ van. The crowds of Republican supporters – and the tension – were growing when we got there, we were being jeered, the cameramen jostled, the atmosphere was ugly. After a long wait a convoy of jeeps appeared over the hill on the motorway from the north. And at the same time, the convoy from the south came in to view. It was all done with precision.

There was shouting and roaring, women screaming, police trying to push them back, it was chaotic. Brian got up on a wall with his camera to avoid the mayhem and get the best view, capturing the moment the handover took place, as well as all the shoving and fighting.

I had spotted a big advertising poster for Visa card, which said 'Visators Welcome', so we got shots of it amid the mayhem.

We were really happy with the report, we felt we'd done a good job. I called Barney Kavanagh, the news editor, "that sounds great, son," he said, "get back as quick as you can."

Those were pre-satellite days so we couldn't send it back. We had to jump in the van and drive back to Dublin.

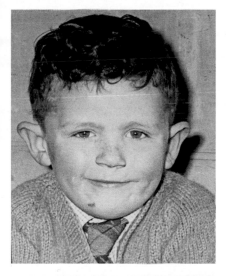

My dad telling the joke about the wide mouthed frog…and me (left). That's right, I was born good looking…

My sister, Eileen – a gem

(Above) Me, middle right, with some of my school mates from Coláiste Mhuirc – Willie Hughes, Aidan Devanney, John Slevin, Eamon Rice, John Kavanagh and Mick Leonard

Caroline (front centre) introducing Paul to some of the Cahill family. (Back row) Declan, Brian, Mam, Dad, Geraldine, Una; Eileen, Shane, Barry David, Colm, Michael, Sean, Pat, myself

A Cuala team from around 1984. (Back row) Ciaran Irwin (always needed his coat), Derek Spain, Nobby Comerford, Denis Browne, Mick Murray, Sean O'Toole, Fintan Quill, Mick Quinn, Noel Timlin, Damien Byrne. (Front) Johnny Sheanon, Eamon Brennan, Davy Hudson, PJ Holden with Tommy, Johnny Carroll, Kelly, and the Goal Machine

(Above) Taking notes at a Killarney Urban Council meeting, while Cllr Murt O'Shea speaks. Murt and his wife, Bridie, became good friends to us and their sons Seanie and Pat are Dr Crokes stalwarts. (Above right) Getting notions about myself at the Rose of Tralee ...

(Above) Ian Dempsey. Love the man. We had very little in common, but so much fun together on the 2FM Breakfast Show. (Left) the switch from newspapers to broadcasting was a smooth one

(Above) With Producer Ian Corr and Jimmy Magee at the Seoul Olympics in 1988

(Above) Some of the RTÉ team for the 1992 Olympics – with Bill O'Herlihy, Jimmy Magee, Roy Willoughby, Myles Dungan and Tom Rooney

At the Giro d'Italia, 1987. The first victory in the extraordinary triple success for Stephen Roche (on the right) with his loyal team mate, Eddy Schepers

As a West Ham fan, you can see my delight to chat with Geoff Hurst, the only man to score a hat-trick in a World Cup final. Former Finance Minister, Brian Lenihan Snr, also looks impressed

With Ian Corr, Jim Beglin and Gabriel Egan – the team that reported on Irish sport's greatest odyssey – Italia 90

Finalists in Irish Sport's bushiest eyebrows competition – World Cup hero Packie Bonner (bronze) and former World Snooker champion, Ken Doherty (silver). Two gentlemen

Guaranteed fun with these fellas – Niall Quinn and Kerry legend, Bomber Liston. I'm standing on Nicky English's back to reach up to them

Schoolboy error by friend and colleague, Tony O'Donoghue. He fell asleep on the flight home from the World Cup in 2002. Steve Staunton and I tried to enhance his facial appearance. We failed

Jack Charlton called to the house to see Caroline after Paul was born

I always enjoyed Mick McCarthy's dry sense of humour. I often wonder how close he would have got to the World Cup in 2002 if Roy Keane had played

A historic place! When the crowds left the stadium in Stuttgart, Noel King and I wandered over to get a photo of the exact spot where Ray Houghton put the ball in the English net in 1988

Nigata, Japan, where Matt Holland scored a great equaliser to earn Ireland a 1-1 draw with Cameroon in the 2002 World Cup. I took this photo (right) of Ian Harte's penalty v Spain as Tony O'Donoghue and I were put sitting literally against the hoarding behind the goal at the World Cup game in Korea

Imagine Eddie Jordan got to create his own team and have a 1-2 success in Formula One. He's good company too!

Not long after his famous Gold Cup victory on Dawn Run in 1986, Jonjo O'Neill successfully overcame a long battle with cancer

Joe Hayes of Tipperary leads the sing-song, with the feeble help of his team mate, Nicky English, Ann and Angela Downey (Kilkenny), Colman Corrigan and John Fenton (Cork) Ogie Moran, Bomber Liston, Ger Power & Mikey Sheehy (Kerry)

You can see the excitement on the faces of some of the press corps in Rome's Olympic Stadium ahead of the 1990 World Cup quarter-final against Italy

(Above) A few proper Kerry legends here: Mick O'Connell, Moss Keane and Jack O'Shea. In the background is the wonderful poet and raconteur, Brendan Kennelly

(Right) With Kevin McStay and Pat Spillane on radio coverage of the All-Ireland football semi-final replay in Limerick, where Kerry controversially beat Mayo

With two fantastic stalwarts of RTÉ's GAA coverage – Michael Lyster, the rock solid anchor of The Sunday Game for so many years, and the national treasure himself, Micheal O'Muircheartaigh

It was like my journey to Carlow that Monday morning all over again: we got a puncture.

By the time we arrived in RTÉ we were met by a deflated silence. It was around twenty to seven, we'd missed the *Six O'Clock News*, they'd ended up having to use pictures from ITV or the BBC.

From the sense of excitement we had about these extraordinary pictures, this being the biggest news story I'd ever covered, to complete and utter dejection. It made the *Nine O'Clock News* alright, which was some consolation, but it had turned in to a day of the highest of highs to a subterranean low.

● ● ● ● ● ● ●

I neglected to mention to the lads in Cuala what happened on the way back from the border, the slagging would never have stopped. They always found it hard to credit that anyone would deem me worthy to cover a big story or send me anywhere to do it, so I wasn't going to give them added ammunition.

It was a few months before the McGlinchey story when I did a television news report on the hijacking of a plane en route from Cairo to San Diego, the hijackers diverting it to Beirut, Algiers and back again to Beirut.

The next day I was in Cuala and the lads were amazed to see me.

"Jaysus," said one, "you got back from Beirut quick."

I could have admitted that I'd covered the story from Montrose. But I liked the idea of them thinking I'd jetted to the Lebanon for the assignment. It was hard to impress them in Cuala.

10

And In Sport...

'I was reading the sports news on his show and he was doing his level best to distract me. First he stood up on his chair, then he stood on the table, then he dropped his trousers'

Considering the amount of coverage sport gets these days, it's hard to imagine now that it was often no more than an afterthought in the news 20 years ago or so.

"And in sport…" the newsreader would say at the end of RTÉ's Sunday bulletin, followed by the briefest of mentions of the day's major sporting events. There was no separate sports section in the news then, it just wasn't considered important enough.

To me, this was crazy. It just seemed like there was a complete lack of awareness of the interest people had in sport and the need to respond to that by covering it as news – we didn't even have a sports correspondent, never mind a team of them.

I kept pushing and pushing for one to be appointed, but the attitude was, 'why would we need one?'

We had our flagship *Sunday Sport* programme on radio, and

Sports Stadium filled much of Saturday afternoons on television, but the gaps were sizeable elsewhere. Val Joyce's *Airs and Races* on a Saturday was a popular programme, but aside from covering horse racing, mingled with music, all you'd really get were a few soccer results.

So I kind of took it in to my owns hands and started covering the bigger events, doing previews of All-Ireland finals or Triple Crown matches, whatever. And on my Sundays off I would cover a League of Ireland or GAA match for radio. I got paid a few extra bob for it, but I was mainly doing it because I just enjoyed being at and covering the games.

Unbeknown to me at the time, I was about to get an opportunity to make a bigger contribution to our coverage of sport. Caroline Murphy had decided that she wanted to switch from radio sport to news and that opened the way for me to make the opposite move.

Caroline was a great journalist who blazed a trail in RTÉ by becoming the first female sports journalist in there. Later she worked in television as a producer. I always thought if she wanted to she could easily have become the first female head of TV sport, but she chose not to go down that path.

She had spoken to the bosses about moving to news and once she cleared it with them she came to me and asked if I would be interested in the swap. Going from news to sport back then was an uncommon enough move, but I loved the idea and really wanted to try it out, to see how it would go.

So, in 1985, the year after I joined RTÉ, I moved to radio sport.

And they haven't got rid of me since.

And around a year after that, News appointed Vere Wynne-Jones as a sports reporter.

So, at last, we were getting more than "and in sport…" at the end of a bulletin.

• • • • • • •

It was a very different era back then. When I arrived in radio sport there was a tough love policy. If you made a mistake they weren't slow to let you know about it, especially the producer Ian Corr.

He was a tough guy, he wouldn't hold his feelings back if he wasn't happy with how you had done something. He was hard on me, *very* hard on me, he would say it straight, with a liberal sprinkling of 'f' words. But that was all good for me. You learnt quickly that way, you had to.

I think that kind of approach would be good for a lot of people now, to be honest, you certainly wouldn't have any notions that you were a star – if you did, it would soon be knocked out of you.

Everyone is kinder and more polite now to the new people coming in and while that makes life in the workplace more pleasant, I'm not sure it actually helps make them better reporters or broadcasters. I just find now with some of the younger crew that their interviews are as much about their own opinions as the person they're speaking to and we don't have people any more to ask: "What are you doing?"

If I had done that I would have got it in my ear from Ian Corr, "I don't give a shit what your opinion is, ask the person opposite you for theirs – no-one wants to hear your view". He knocked it out of you, which is what you needed.

Maurice Quinn, who was the head of radio sport then, was a

very different character, a real gentleman and an exceptionally bright man. He had been Irish correspondent for the *Observer* and he used to set *The Irish Times* sports crossword. A bridge player, too. He was a lovely man and a huge help to me. He'd show you how to improve your writing skills, he'd advise you on every aspect of the job, he'd go out of his way to help you along. Similarly Dermot Kelly, another producer, I learnt a lot from them all.

In those early days sports presenting would have been quite formal, you wouldn't have had much fun with it, but although I've always taken my sport seriously and love it with a passion, and there are plenty of times when issues arise that have to be handled with seriousness, I've always believed that the essence of sport is fun.

I've been criticised for that a lot over the years, my informal style or approach to sport wouldn't be to everyone's liking, especially those who take it very seriously, but I think most people enjoy having a laugh with sport, especially when there's so much grief out there. And there would be plenty of days when I'm working on *Morning Ireland* and the news is so dismal, it just puts it all in perspective for me.

• • • • • • •

It was when I started working with Ian Dempsey on his 2FM Breakfast Show that I was really free to have fun with it all, it was the first slot that allowed me to do that. And it was probably the first time that sport became conversational fun on the airwaves. That type of programme is so much more common now.

I had already been doing sport on the breakfast show before Ian took over, but it was then that the slot really took off. Initially it was just meant to be me coming on the show with a two-minute sports bulletin, but often it would turn in to 10 or more because we'd just be chatting. And it became very interactive, people would send letters in – God be with the days – or jokes that you wouldn't dream of telling now.

Ian was brilliant, he had that Gay Byrne knack of knowing when something was working and being generous enough to sit back and let it run. Like Gay, he didn't pretend to be an expert in sport, when a lot of people do, when he saw it was going well he was quite happy for me to drive it. And he would always credit me when it went well. He was not only generous but he was confident in himself too, he was secure enough not to need to be claiming credit for himself.

Sometimes I was out and about and reporting from around the country for the show. Like the time I was in Limerick but when I went to the studio there it was locked, I couldn't get in. So, I had to do the first bulletin in to Ian's show from a phone box on the street, making the mistake of reporting my whereabouts because cars started coming around and beeping the horn at me. It was a 'Dessie's in trouble again' moment, which the show loved, although Ian Corr hated all that stuff and certainly didn't want me bringing it to Radio 1.

But it was a hugely successful show, produced by John Clarke who would later become head of 2FM, and really increased my profile in RTÉ. It allowed me to be myself, show my personality, as opposed to just reading sports news. There was a great mix on the programme, everything from Zig and Zag to Simon Young doing his "Ger owa dat garden!" comedy slot. Simon was hilarious, but went on to have a very tough time of it personally, later talking about his struggles with alcoholism and depression.

I thought of how I remembered him from Ian's show, this larger than life jovial character who was full of fun, and it struck me how we just don't have any idea what goes on in people's lives, how we don't see past the front they present to the outside world.

• • • • • • •

The whole ABU thing – Anyone But United – grew out of that slot on Ian's show. If Manchester United had lost, our audience would actually increase because of the laugh we'd have with it, I'd be playing 'Zip-a-dee-doo-dah, zip-a-dee-ay, my, oh, my, what a wonderful day', and everyone used to crack up at that. It was childish, completely juvenile, but it was great fun. All we were doing was reflecting the slagging of United fans. Ireland was (and still is) jammed with them – and that slagging was going on in the schools and workplaces around the country.

The irony was that even though I'd been a West Ham fan since I was a kid, I'd always had a soft spot for United mainly because of their history and the brilliance of Best, Charlton and Law. How could you not love them? They were the Messi and Ronaldo of their day.

Mind you, not everyone saw the funny side of the ABU business. Most people got it, it was just a laugh, but I had a few people threaten me, usually ones with plenty of drink in them. And it could be tricky when I'd go over to Old Trafford with some of the lads for games, you'd have fellas coming up to you, "you fucking bastard, we'll get you", "we're going to tell the English lads you're here", all that. I'd be like, "get a life", but inside going 'oh shit'. And the lads with me would be like, "for fuck sake Des, what have you done?"

And then there was that 'FUCK OFF DES CAHILL' banner hanging from a pub in Tallaght after United had won the league in 1993.

I didn't drop in for a pint.

It would probably have amused them to know my son Paul was a United fan in his very young days, before switching allegiances to Sunderland.

A switch that has brought the poor fella only pain.

• • • • • • •

So, I loved those days on 2FM, apart from the traumatic moment that is still etched in my memory: the sight of Jim O'Neill's bare and hairy bottom.

I was reading the sports news on his show and he was doing his level best to distract me. First he stood up on his chair, then he stood on the table, then he dropped his trousers. At that stage I was only a quarter way through the bulletin, so I left three quarters of it out and suddenly handed back to him. He had to jump off the table, with his trousers still around his knees, on to his chair, the wheels sending it spinning away. All the listeners could hear were loud crashing sounds from the studio, and the rest of us howling with laughter.

It was, I think, Des 1, Jim 0.

Meanwhile, I kept working with Ian until 1998 when he left RTÉ to take over the breakfast show on Today FM which had started up the year before.

I could have gone with Ian, the offer was there, but it really would have made no sense for me. RTÉ had all the sport then so I would have been doing nothing but sports news, instead of actually covering events. If I'd gone with Ian there would have been no World Cups or Olympics for me. So no regrets.

RTÉ offered me an improved contract to ensure I stayed, which was a measure of how successful working with Ian had been. So, I had benefited from it, both financially and career-wise.

There will always be a bond between myself and Ian because of our time working together, we were good for each other. I've the greatest of respect for him, he's had a fantastic career and continues to enjoy great success with his Today FM breakfast show, now, remarkably, 20 years old.

We didn't hang around socially, but three or four times a year we'd go out for a few pints. We decided one morning to head for Houricans pub on Leeson Street for a pint after the breakfast show ended. This, I promise, wasn't typical, we just decided to do it that day for the hell of it. When we arrived in the pub, at around 10.30 or 11am the chairs were still up on the table.

Unfortunately for us, an RTÉ employee happened to be passing on the top deck of a bus as we settled down with our pints and saw us through the window. The word went back to Montrose.

I think there might have been some concern about our lifestyle.

• • • • • • •

By then I'd landed the presenting role on RTÉ radio's flagship sports programme, *Sunday Sport*. Jimmy Magee had been the presenter before me, but in 1987 he told RTÉ that he was sick of being tied in to it, he wanted to be free in '88 to go to the European Championships – and at that stage it looked unlikely Ireland was going to be in them. And he wanted to attend the Tour de France, which Stephen Roche had won in '87.

I think there was an element of RTÉ wanting to show Jimmy that they could get by without him, that's just how I interpreted it. So they put me in to present *Sunday Sport* in '87. And then they left me there.

Jimmy never begrudged me, but the irony was that come '88 we had qualified for the Euros and as the *Sunday Sport* presenter I went to Germany, the Tour de France and the Olympics, which was all that he had asked to do. But Jimmy and I were always kind of close and that was never an issue with him.

Besides, it freed him up on Sundays to be out at matches, and he loved walking in to press boxes, like it was the royal arrival. He'd shake hands with everyone in the room. And that meant a lot to him, just to be free to be out and about again.

And, later, he got to do his GAA commentaries for UTV, which he was always desperate to do but couldn't with RTÉ because those positions were taken. He had a kind of child-like enthusiasm for it all, he'd say to me, "why won't they let me do that?" And I'd say because you want to do the All-Ireland final this week, the World Cycling Championships the week after, and something else the week after that. You can't be everywhere!

But Jimmy didn't see the problem, he thought he could be.

His wanderlust had, in the end, opened up a wonderful opportunity for me. *Sunday Sport* had no rival at the time. Munster finals and all the major GAA games, bar the finals, weren't on television, so we were getting remarkable audiences around the 800,000 mark.

And just even being a part of all that, on RTÉ Radio 1 on those sunny Sundays, was a privilege. The soundtrack of my youth was Micheal O'Hehir, a Championship match and the sound of the beach. Joining the team that hosted those sounds was a very lovely thing.

11

Wheels Of Fortune

*'I ended up interviewing Stephen (Roche)
in what was effectively a broom cupboard
in his team hotel...'*

I t was the Friday before the end of the 1987 Tour de France when I got a call at our Tour de France commentary position from PJ Mara, the Government Press Secretary and Taoiseach Charlie Haughey's right-hand man. I didn't know PJ, but he wouldn't have been someone who'd struggle to get hold of a phone number. Any phone number.

"Is Roche definitely going to win?" he asked.

"Well, I can't say he's definitely going to win, but he's looking good. It's all down to the time trial in Dijon. Why?"

"The Boss might be coming out."

The Boss being Charlie.

"So is he or isn't he going to win?"

If PJ wanted certainties, sport wasn't the place to be looking for them.

Again I said it was impossible to be sure.

The phone rang again on the Saturday.

"How's it looking, will he win?"

"I think so."

And come the end of the final stage on the Sunday, there was Charlie on the podium on the Champs-Élysées alongside a victorious Stephen Roche.

If The Boss had ended up standing beside Pedro Delgado, PJ would most probably have hunted me down.

• • • • • • •

It was earlier that year that I was following the drama of the Giro d'Italia from back home in Dublin, the race developing in to one for the ages because of the bitter battle between two Carrera team-mates, Italian Roberto Visentini and Stephen Roche, the 27-year-old from Dundrum.

Based on their form going in to the Giro, Stephen really should have been team leader with Visentini riding for him, but Carrera gave the honour to the local hero, the defending champion, their plan being that the roles would be reversed for the Tour de France.

But Stephen did the unthinkable; he defied team orders. Instead of riding for Visentini he rode for himself, convinced he could win the race while doubting the Italian's ability to do so. That made Stephen public enemy number one to the Italians. Breaking your team rules was the ultimate treachery, especially when the team leader was the home favourite. He was booed and spat on by the crowds, kicked and thumped, the atmosphere was poisonous.

"We should go out to cover this," I said to Maurice Quinn, my boss in RTÉ at the time. I thought that it just wasn't getting enough attention back home. He gave me the go-ahead so I contacted Frank Quinn, who was Sean Kelly's manager and who did some work for Stephen as well. He was about to travel out to Italy so I went along with him.

It turned out to be an extraordinary race. Visentini took the pink jersey on day one by winning the prologue in San Remo, but Stephen took over the lead after stage three. He kept it for 10 more days before Visentini reclaimed it for 48 hours, before Stephen got it back again after stage 15 and held it until the 22nd and final stage. An epic battle. It was dizzying.

The drama through it all was unending, the ill will towards Stephen from all of his Carrera team-mates bar Eddy Schepers venomous. There were a couple of evenings I recall when Stephen invited me to join him, Eddy and his mechanic Patrick Valcke for dinner. We were seated at one end of a long table, the rest of the Carrera team at the other, with about five empty chairs between us. They were shouting at Stephen to get me out of there, he was shouting back that I was staying. Even at their team dinners Stephen, Eddy and Patrick were isolated and ostracised.

On reflection, sitting with Stephen at the team meal was one of the most extraordinary places I ever found myself in my career. To witness the internal tension at first hand was gripping.

He was distressed by it all, but the hostility towards him only strengthened his resolve, his attitude ending up being 'if they want to do me, I'll do them'. Even he, when he reflected on it, couldn't believe where that mental strength had come from.

But the tension and pressure of it all was enormous, and at times it took its toll. Frank said that Lydia, Stephen's wife at the time, wanted to come to Italy in the middle of it all, but Stephen reacted with fury when he saw her at the end of a stage. He lost his head. The atmosphere was so ugly he just didn't want her there, exposed to it.

It got even nastier on what was the most dramatic day of the Giro, the 15th stage on the mountainous trek to Sappada.

Stephen broke away, against team orders, the team manager driving up to him to order him to drop back. "No, let Visentini come up and join me," Stephen recalled saying to him, convinced Visentini hadn't the strength. He was right. Johan van der Velde ended up winning the stage, but Stephen had done enough to reclaim the pink jersey, and he never lost it again.

Visentini, like his supporters, was seething, but by winning the Giro, Stephen had spectacularly proved his point – he was Carrera's main man.

• • • • • • •

It was the start of what proved to be a truly remarkable year for Stephen when he completed the Triple Crown in cycling, the Giro d'Italia, the Tour de France and the World Championships.

With both he and Sean Kelly in their prime, it really was a golden age for Irish cycling. The journalist Barry Ryan had a great line in his book 'The Ascent' about that era, he said Ireland producing Roche and Kelly around the same time was like Tupelo, Mississippi, producing 'a second Elvis Presley shortly after the first'.

They were very different characters, a city boy and a country boy. Stephen had the twinkle in his eye, there was a bit of the rascal about him. Sean was quiet, suspicious of people, you had to earn his trust. He could come across as dour, but he had a wonderful dry sense of humour. Stephen had flair, and he had one incredible year. Sean was dogged, there or thereabouts all the time. Fearsome too – in sprints he would hold his line, if somebody went out over a wall, then they'd go over the wall. So be it. He was tough as nails.

And both of them were incredibly good to me during my time covering their races, especially at the beginning when I was new to it all. I had a bond with Stephen after that Giro d'Italia, probably because I had been a friendly face at the end of each harrowing day when not only had he pushed himself to the limits on his bike, he'd had to endure the crowd's abuse too. Witnessing close up what he went through, both during the race and in those behind-the-scenes moments with his team, was an incredible and revealing experience, one I'll never forget.

During the 1987 Tour de France, when they were surrounded by reporters at the end of each stage, Stephen and Sean would insist on me being allowed in to the middle of the scrum, they wouldn't start any interview until I was let through. The first couple of days the camera crews would push me away, but they soon realised neither man was going to start talking until I was put front and centre. And they would always make sure I got an interview afterwards, that level of access to them both making covering the race for RTÉ a joy, the listeners at home hearing direct from them both after every stage.

And in one of the weirder episodes of my career, I ended up interviewing Stephen in what was effectively a broom cupboard in his team hotel. He had collapsed with exhaustion after an astonishing effort to catch up with his chief rival Pedro Delgado on a climb at La Plagne, needing an oxygen mask at the end to revive him. He looked like a ghost. Never mind the assumption that his race was over, at that point there were just serious concerns for his health. He was unable to move, lying on the ground for close to 10 minutes surrounded by flashing cameras and reporters screaming questions at him, before he was taken away by ambulance.

That he was back on his bike next morning was astounding.

When he had been brought back to the team hotel there was a huge number of journalists and camera crews waiting to interview him. He was being led through, ignoring them all, but when he saw me, he brushed them aside and looked for a private room to talk to me. And all he could find was one under the stairs, pretty much a broom cupboard.

It was pitch dark, and I couldn't find a light switch. "Come on, just do the interview," said Stephen. We were hunched there in the dark, nose to nose, with me struggling to find the record button in the pitch black. Stephen's understandable tension was making me nervous, and I was terrified I was going to inappropriately burst out laughing, because I was imagining what somebody might think if they opened the door.

I've done interviews in some strange locations in my time, but that one will always be hard to top.

• • • • • • •

My most vivid memory from the day Stephen won the Tour de France, apart from seeing The Boss on the podium, was meeting Irish people in Paris who had been steeped in cycling all their lives and seeing how much that day meant to them.

Their joy was unconfined. Their pride too. I remember how I felt when Cuala first won an All-Ireland club title – these things weren't meant to happen to clubs like Cuala. Multiply that hundred-fold – Irish cyclists weren't meant to win the Tour de France.

And it was only actually being there that first year that I realised the scale of the challenge of even finishing the race, never mind winning it. The Alpine stages in particular were extraordinary, some of them would be two or three times the height of Carrauntoohil. There could be three or four climbs in the day, one after another, and then they'd go again the next day. It struck me as almost inhuman.

I've driven up some of those climbs in first or second gear, it's all you can do. And I've been driven down one too. From sports writer Jeff Connor's brilliant book, 'Wide-Eyed and Legless: Inside the Tour de France':

> *With a muttered prayer and Des Cahill as a passenger I set out down the hairpins out of La Plagne. Halfway down on the approach to a sweeping corner I put my foot on the brake and there was no answering pressure. With handbrakes pulled full on and to the accompaniment of screeching metal and helped by a large bank and convenient lay-by, I wrestled the Iveco to a stop.*

Jeff and I probably aged 20 years during those moments, how he wrestled that Iveco to a stop I'll never know. So, even taking on those climbs in a car, ascending or descending, was a challenge. On a bike? Savage. And TV and the sponsors want the most dramatic and scenic routes, all those spectacular helicopter shots, they want the drama, there are so many commercial elements to it all. I just wonder if too much is asked of the cyclists, if their welfare is given any consideration at all.

• • • • • • •

Myself and the other Irish reporters went to Kitty O'Shea's in Paris to celebrate that Sunday night, Stephen dropping in to say hello. He had just left the Carrera team dinner where the atmosphere would have been considerably warmer than it was back in Italy, not least because Visentini didn't ride in the Tour.

It was an incredible time in Stephen's life, and there was more to come in September in Austria when he, Sean, Paul Kimmage and Martin Earley represented Ireland at the World Championships.

This time the team was working for Sean, the aim to have him in contention at the end for a sprint finish, which was his strength. But Sean was being 'marked' all over the place, giving Stephen the chance to break away, Paul and Martin having put in huge work for him right up until the end. It was a brilliant team effort and come the finishing line Stephen had completed that Triple Crown, capping what was a magical year for him.

There is, of course, a poignancy looking back on that day now in light of the subsequent rift between Paul, after he wrote his book *A Rough Ride* in 1990, and Stephen and Sean.

From the outside looking in, it seemed as though their friendship had been a genuinely deep one, the three having been together so much through their careers, Stephen and Paul room-mates for a while. What I always remember about Stephen and Sean is that the first thing they would ask me after a stage was how Martin and Paul had done. There was a bond between them all that I found striking.

By the time Paul quit professional cycling, during the 1989 Tour, he had already started writing a column for *The Sunday Tribune*. It was a great column too, one that was hugely well received, it gave a real insight to the unforgiving life of a professional cyclist, the at times brutal hardship of it all.

It was during that 1989 Tour that Paul asked me over to

his hotel to talk to me about sports journalism, he was full of questions about it all, what was it like covering GAA and soccer games, what was Jack Charlton like to deal with, what were his players like to interview, and so on. I said I'd take him to some games when we got back, which I did, introducing him to the fellas in the press box in Croke Park.

I stayed way later at his hotel than I expected, we chatted for hours, it was around 11.30 when I left. And it was the next day that Paul dropped out of the race. I think his head had moved on to journalism already.

• • • • • • •

It was after the publication of *A Rough Ride*, which exposed the level of doping that was going on in cycling and how the sport's authorities overlooked it, that Paul's friendship with Stephen all but ended. Sean largely remained silent about it all, but Stephen bit back repeatedly in interviews through the years.

It wasn't that there were any allegations in the book against them, but Stephen was angry about a *Late Late Show* appearance when Gay Byrne asked Paul if he was suggesting that just about everyone was doping, did that include Stephen and Sean?

Paul dismissed the question, insisting the book wasn't about them, it was his story, but Stephen was incensed that Paul didn't defend them, claiming that he had left a cloud of suspicion over them.

While Sean had failed two tests in the 1980s, Stephen didn't fail any at all, but in subsequent years there were allegations made against him, all of which he denied, including a report by an Italian judge following a doping investigation in which he claimed that a sample of Stephen's blood from 1993 had contained the performance-enhancing drug EPO. It was alleged that Stephen and his Carrera team-mates had been part of an EPO experiment conducted by Italian sports doctor, Professor Francesco Conconi.

To this day Stephen denies ever doping, but in light of what happened with his sport in subsequent years he admitted that he'd had his 'head in the sand' when it came to the issue, that he had been hopelessly naïve.

Paul, of course, was entirely vindicated, the sport's reputation left in tatters. And he had been incredibly ballsy to keep chasing the Lance Armstrong story as he did, as David Walsh had done too. It took some guts to ask those questions at the press conferences, to be the unpopular guy in the room with all the focus on him, and the sneering answers from Armstrong in reply. There were other journalists who were equally suspicious, but he was the one who went in there and took Armstrong on. And I always had the greatest of respect for him for doing that. He wouldn't give up, no matter what resistance he met, no matter the personal cost.

It's not as if the issue died when Armstrong confessed, plenty of questions have been asked of some of the leading names in cycling since, but it was a remarkable moment to see him admit that his whole sporting story had been a lie.

And the most unforgivable part, of course, was that that story was built around him fighting back from cancer to become one of the greatest sportsmen of all time. He was just a fraud whose ego was out of control.

● ● ● ● ● ● ●

I talk later in the book about how it was probably Ben Johnson's failed test in Seoul 1988 that truly shattered our innocence about drugs in sport. Until then, while of course it was happening, I think most of us were largely oblivious to it, so we believed what we were seeing.

Paul's book came out around two years later and while by then it would have been less of a surprise to learn that it was happening in cycling as well as athletics, the scale of it was shocking, as well as the suggestion that the sport's governing body was largely turning a blind eye to it.

It made me reluctant to cover cycling again because I didn't feel equipped to do it, it seemed like it was now as much about the science of doping as it was about riding a bike. And in time, I think like most people, I ended up wondering what was even the point of watching the Tour de France, cycling's reputation had been destroyed so if you saw a remarkable performance your cynicism just told you to dismiss it.

Back when I was reporting on cycling I had no doubts, few of us did, but everything that has happened since makes you look back and wonder. And not just at cycling, at every sport, it seems like they're all tainted to some degree now.

I went to the 2017 Tour which was, shockingly, the 30th anniversary of his win. I remember him getting a fantastic reception from the crowd, three decades on there was still huge warmth towards him. Many other previous Tour winners are not invited back because of their links with drug taking, but Stephen was still loved by the French public.

The allegations didn't appear to have lessened that affection, but, I suppose, rightly or wrongly, they will always hang in the air for some.

12

Olé, Olé Olé Olé!

*'My most vivid memory from Italia 90 was
standing between the two dug-outs, Jack to
my left, the Romanians to my right, as the
players prepared for a penalty shoot-out
after a dire goalless draw'*

I talk a lot about the luck I've experienced throughout my
career, but when it came to covering soccer for RTÉ that
luck came in spades during a magical six-year spell when the
national team qualified for Euro 88, Italia 90 and USA 94, and I
got to work at each tournament.

Those days were just a rollercoaster of joy, excitement and,
more than anything, fun.

And then I contrast my good fortune with that of Philip
Greene who first commentated on a soccer international for RTÉ
Radio as far back as 1951. And he remained in the role until
his retirement in 1985, missing out on that wave of qualifying
success that was just around the corner for the Irish team.

Having soldiered through all those barren years, in terms of
Ireland missing out on reaching major tournaments, it was the

unluckiest of timing for Philip, and I always felt for him. I was delighted, though, when the FAI brought him to Ireland's game against England at Euro 88, it was a lovely touch.

I remained conscious of my luck all through those years, having spent time in the company of media colleagues like Con Houlihan, Peter Byrne and Noel Dunne, men who, like Philip, had covered the Irish team for years. And whether it was teams never realising their potential, or suffering from dubious refereeing decisions along the way, they must have doubted that they'd ever see the day when they'd get to report on Ireland competing at a European Championships or World Cup.

I had only left *The Kerryman* less than four years before, and here I was, watching Ireland beat England in Stuttgart in '88, play in the quarter-finals of the World Cup in Italia 90, and beat Italy in the Giants Stadium in USA 94.

Is it any wonder I feel lucky?

· · · · · · ·

Not that had I anticipated us qualifying for Euro 88 when I sat down with Jack Charlton and a group of reporters at an Opel-sponsored night in Dublin to watch Bulgaria play Scotland.

There's always hope, of course, but there was no real expectation that Scotland would beat Bulgaria in Sofia, as we needed them to. And then, lo and behold, Gary Mackay scores the winner and we'd qualified for our first major tournament.

I had done a vox pop for radio that afternoon with fans after Ireland's final game of the campaign and 50 per cent of them wanted Jack to go because the assumption was that we wouldn't qualify.

And here we were, a few hours later, one of just eight nations to make it through to Euro 88, Jack going from sinner to saint in one fell swoop. To top it all, our opponents in our first ever game in a major tournament would be, of all teams, England, which only heightened the sense of anticipation as the tournament drew closer.

And when we left for Germany the following summer, I just remember the giddy excitement when we gathered at the airport, it was like a school trip.

• • • • • • •

I don't think it would ever be possible to recapture the atmosphere of Euro 88. It wasn't only that it was our first major tournament and that it produced such special memories, they were just different times.

These days most young Irish people are off on their travels during their gap years, they're inter-railing, they're going to America on their J1s, they're visiting Asia and South America, they're all over the globe. When I think of most of the young fans who travelled to Germany in 1988 I'm always reminded of that line from Christy Moore's 'Joxer Goes to Stuttgart', which captured it all so perfectly:

> '…*some of the lads had never been away from home before. It was the first time Whacker put his foot outside of Inchicore…*'

And Inchicore must have been half empty during Euro 88, I think I met most of its residents in Germany.

I doubt there'll ever be that same sense of innocence or wonder again. Or an atmosphere quite like the one in Stuttgart that day. Or an explosion of joy quite like the one that greeted Ray Houghton's goal against England.

I was sitting beside Gabriel Egan and Noel King in their commentary position, Gabriel did his South American style 'gooooooooooooal', while Noel was yapping beside him like a puppy. I can still hear the commentary now. Goosebumps.

Later, myself and Kinger went down to the pitch to get a photo of where Ray had scored the goal, there's one of me in the corner of the net where the ball went in. Talk about hallowed ground.

Before the game came what looked like would be my single most catastrophic moment in broadcasting, but one that turned in to the best.

I was presenting the *Sunday Sport* programme on RTÉ Radio 1. But as we neared the start time of 2 o'clock, the broadcast lines to Dublin were still not through. I felt ill. There was absolute panic. They still weren't through as we went on air, so Noel Spillane of the *Examiner* came to the rescue and offered us a loan of his telephone, and from 2 o'clock until kick-off at 2.30pm, I presented the programme on a crackly telephone line, passing the phone around to Gabriel, Noel and our other guests. Just before kick-off, the lines came through from Dublin…and we broadcast the game in high quality.

It was definitely one of my favourite programmes of all time. We still had an hour and a half to fill after the game ended, and that was just pure excitement and joy. There was one GAA Championship match that day, Armagh v Donegal. The other provinces switched games to avoid clashing with the soccer, but the Ulster Council didn't.

We went briefly for commentary, but the listeners just wanted to hear more from Stuttgart. So back we came. I didn't have a panel of famous footballers with me (apart from Kinger), but there was so much laughter and hugging going on at our commentary position that we were joined by some big names from the BBC and ITV who came over to say well done.

First a delighted Liam Brady, who was there working with ITV, joined in our party, and then came the BBC's Trevor Brooking and Ron Greenwood, the former England manager. They were generous and magnanimous and added to the fun. It made for great radio.

Trevor was particularly generous for helping us out because he'd played for England against Ireland in our media match that morning and I think when he saw how pumped up the Irish media were to win, we terrified the living daylights out of him. He played up front with Mark Austen, the newsreader who was then ITV Sports Correspondent. I was centre half along with John Givens, but Trevor barely got involved. I said to him before the game that I was a big West Ham fan, and he looked so relieved. I think he was afraid he'd have black eyes and broken limbs when he appeared on TV later in the day. We were quite fired up. And we won 1-0. So that was two 1-0 wins over England in the one day. Good going.

I remember thinking what a shame it was that more people wouldn't hear that radio report because I assumed most would have been watching television, but it turned out that it was a scorcher of a day in Ireland and so many people headed for their back gardens or the beaches, and had their radios with them. Caroline said all around her at home she could hear the radios on in the back gardens over the walls. The memory lifts my heart even now. How lovely it was to have been part of something like that, however small your role.

The school trip continued by train to Hanover where we were playing the Soviet Union, one of the fans commandeering the speaker on board, the chat going from very efficient German information about the journey to "I'd like to welcome youse all on to the train, youse are all looking great".

I'm not sure if we ever played better than we did against the Soviets, the shackles were off, Ronnie Whelan scoring that wonder goal. It was only later I realised it was a shinner, but it was still a wonder goal. Maurice Quinn, my boss, who wouldn't be given to outbursts of emotion, hugged me tightly when the goal went in.

The draw left us starting to believe we were actually unbeatable, so Wim Kieft's bizarre 82nd-minute winner for the Dutch in the final group game, when we just needed to draw to go through to the semi-finals, was a complete heartbreaker. To this day I will never understand how the ball spun as it did as it went past Packie Bonner, it was like a cricket delivery. Packie's face suggested he couldn't understand it either.

There ended Ireland's tournament, but what an unforgettable week it had been, the size of the crowd that greeted the team on its return to Dublin a sign of how much it had meant to the people back home.

• • • • • • •

Myself and the rest of the press had just left Ireland's training session that morning during Italia 90 when we spotted a group of Irish fans, in very high spirits, who'd made their way out from the local town to cheer the players on.

At that point we were a bit puzzled to see a brass band come around the corner. The group of fans were too, but they decided to have some fun so started running between the lines of the band, jumping up and down while waving their flags and singing 'Olé, Olé Olé' Olé, which didn't remotely blend with the tune the band was playing.

It was then that the hearse came around the corner, the band leading the cortege in honour of its deceased former member.

Oh Jesus.

The lads were mortified.

The Olé Olés ground to a halt and they all began furiously blessing themselves as the hearse went by.

If Joxer had gone to Stuttgart, several thousand of them had made their way to Italy for our first World Cup.

• • • • • • •

I think my most vivid memory from Italia 90 was standing between the two dug-outs, Jack to my left, the Romanians to my right, as the players prepared for a penalty shoot-out after a dire scoreless draw.

Having been drawn in a group with England (again!), the Dutch and Egypt, there wasn't a huge amount of confidence about us progressing to the knock-out stage, and a failure to do so would have given me time to get back home to see Caroline before I set off again to cover the Tour de France.

Caroline was pregnant with Amy at that stage, while also looking after a one-and-a-half year old Paul, so it was really tough for her, especially because she didn't have family in Dublin, most of them in Donegal.

I knew then it would be hard for her, but I think it's only

looking back on it I realise now just how tough it must have been.

So here, incredibly, were Ireland going in to a penalty shoot-out where the prize was a place in the quarter-finals of the World Cup. And I'm thinking, 'Jesus, if we get through I'm not going to get home at all before the Tour de France'. Talk of mixed feelings.

And then it was a case of 'Jesus, David O'Leary?' when he stepped up to take the fifth penalty, and I wasn't alone in being mystified by him taking any penalty at all, let alone the fifth. Jack, beside me, looked a little puzzled himself.

And then David scored and disappeared under a scrum of celebrating bodies.

It was beyond belief. We were in the quarter-finals.

Joyous as it was, I couldn't but think of Caroline.

• • • • • • •

It had actually become an issue back in RTÉ that I was having too much fun during Italia 90, that most of my reports were about the fans drinking and partying. But that was such a huge part of the experience for the fans who had travelled there, all I was doing was reflecting it. That's where you got their stories, being in the middle of them all, and considering I had to be up at the crack of dawn every day to do my reports for *Morning Ireland* and Ian Dempsey's *Breakfast Show*, I wasn't exactly in a position to be joining in on the partying.

It was tough going work-wise, but I was young, and able for it. Aside from some TV reporting, I was mainly doing radio work, following up the morning reports with updates for the lunchtime and teatime news.

It seemed like most of Ireland was in Italy that summer, everywhere you went you bumped in to someone you knew. I remember meeting Jimmy Keaveney, Paddy Cullen, Roddy Collins and Mick Leech who, as a Shamrock Rovers player, had been one of my heroes as a kid. They all travelled over together, as did Maurice O'Donoghue, the owner of the Gleneagle Hotel in Killarney who I had got to know during my time in Kerry. He came to Genoa with a few lads, driving all the way from Killarney. And I thought my journey from Carlow to Killarney was a long one.

It was just a wonderful time, and the fans were such a part of making it so brilliant, the fun they had with the locals and other groups of fans earning them a deserved reputation for being far more interested in having a laugh than a fight.

Having battled their way out of their group, the highlight Kevin Sheedy's equaliser against England in the savage rain of Cagliari, and past Romania on penalties, the team found itself in a quarter-final against Italy in Rome. It really was pinch-yourself territory.

And I remember causing considerable laughter in the media centre when I turned up with my big suitcase for the game, which didn't demonstrate a great deal of optimism about our hopes. But Tim O'Connor, then Head of Sport, had agreed that instead of flying straight to France from Italy for the Tour, I could return to Dublin on the Saturday night if we lost to Italy, and then leave for France at seven on the Monday morning, which is what happened after Toto Schillaci ended our World Cup journey.

Apart from Charlie Haughey doing his lap of honour, what I most remember was the depth of Packie Bonner's disappointment after the game, when most of us were just thinking the team had been great to get that far.

When I asked him for a quick interview in the tunnel he looked at me angrily – "we've just lost a fucking World Cup quarter-final!" It was a perfectly understandable response, it's just I had never seen Packie like that – it would kind of be like hearing Daniel O'Donnell curse. Packie said a bad word!

Andy Townsend stepped in and rescued me, doing the interview instead.

• • • • • • •

It was another one of those wonderful experiences that had myself and Vincent Hogan reminiscing about our days doing journalism in Rathmines.

I recall us going out one night in Sicily, near Palermo, for a meal with Jim Beglin, all of us having been warned in advance about the danger of getting ripped off in local bars and restaurants.

With that in mind, when the bill came I gasped and showed Vincent a figure on the receipt, while kicking Jim under the table. Vincent looked at it and turned ashen-faced, it was a colossal number of Lire, a few hundred pounds.

Vincent would be a quiet enough fella, but he was incensed.

He called the waiter over.

"NO PAY! NO PAY," he shouted, crossing his arms like an umpire, going bananas.

"RIP OFF! NO PAY!"

Jim and myself dissolved.

I had been pointing to the date, 220690.

• • • • • • •

My favourite story of Ireland's homecoming was that, famously, Nelson Mandela arrived at Dublin Airport the same day as the team, and we all wondered if the South African delegation thought the thousands upon thousands lining the route from the airport in to town were there for their President.

A cry of 'Ooh aah, Paul McGrath's Da' went up in Whitehall as a waving Mandela was driven by.

It's stories like that which make me love Irish sports fans so much.

•••••••

I got home, then, late on the Saturday night, spent Sunday with Caroline and Paul, and then left first thing Monday morning for the Tour de France where I spent the next three weeks.

It might have been a magical summer of sport for me, but I was probably lucky my family still recognised me by the time it was done.

13

Innocent Seoul

'"But what about the failed test?" he interrupted. That stirred me from my sleepiness. Failed test? What? Jesus...'

I t was 2004 and I was at the Olympic broadcast centre in Athens when I had to go back to my hotel in the middle of the day to get another microphone for my tape recorder. The hotel, where some of the RTÉ and BBC teams were staying, was deserted because everyone was off working at the Olympic venues.

I was waiting for the lift in the lobby, it was coming up from the car park below. It arrived and the door opened. There were three big men inside who filled the small lift. My jaw hit the ground. My eyes darted from one to the other. The three burst out laughing at my reaction.

I squeezed in and told them no-one would ever believe I shared a lift with them. One of them asked me if I had a camera, I said I had but it was in my room. He said to go and get it, they were on their way up to do a roof-top interview with the BBC but they'd wait for me. So I legged it, got my camera, ran back and to this day I smile when I look at the photo: Mark Spitz, Carl Lewis, Steve Redgrave and Des Cahill, 23 gold medals between us.

It was a lift that was crammed with Olympic history.

And me.

• • • • • • •

That's just one of a lengthy list of special memories from my years covering the Olympic Games for RTÉ. When I went to my first, in Seoul in 1988, I was like a child in Santa's Grotto. I had grown up watching the Games on television, they were magical to me, so for them now to be part of my working life was beyond the stuff of dreams.

Since '88 I've worked at every Olympic Games, in Barcelona, Atlanta, Sydney, Athens, Beijing, London and Rio. And while so much has changed through those years, in sport and broadcasting, our innocence well and truly shattered by the blight of doping, the thrill of covering them has never diminished for me.

I've been privileged to have had a ringside seat for some of Ireland's greatest Olympic days, literally when Michael Carruth and Katie Taylor won their gold medals. They are memories that will never leave me.

I won't forget the controversies too quickly either, and we in Ireland have had our fair share of them, from a horse testing positive for banned substances to the president of the Olympic Council of Ireland being arrested in relation to alleged ticket-touting. There was, at times a 'you couldn't make it up' quality to the Irish experience at Olympic Games.

I remember having a meal out with Vincent Hogan one balmy 2004 night in Athens, he was there covering the Games for the

Irish Independent. I thought of our days getting the bus together to Rathmines for our journalism course. And here we were together in Greece covering the Olympic Games. It was another one of those moments in my life when I felt like a very fortunate man.

Even after eight Olympic Games I still get a thrill from visiting the venues in each city, but I truly thought I was in dreamland when I saw the Olympic Park in Seoul. Since then most host cities have spread their sports around, there would be a lot of politics in it, trying to keep every district happy. But in Seoul it was much more centralised, the stunning Olympic Park staging a bunch of sports including cycling, gymnastics, tennis, fencing and weightlifting.

If you had a couple of hours off you could go and watch the gymnastics and three minutes later be at the weightlifting, all within walking distance. And the broadcaster's pass allowed me access to the commentary boxes for all the events. It's changed completely since then, you have to apply for passes for each event, but I really was in heaven. Watching sports you'd never seen live before, like weightlifting and gymnastics, the drama and tension of it all, it was fantastic.

There were to be no Irish medals to celebrate in Seoul, but in a team of 61 – remarkably, just nine of them women – there were names that were to make a major impact in later years, among them Michael Carruth, Wayne McCullough, Billy Walsh and an 18-year-old Michelle Smith. One of her swimming team-mates was Gary O'Toole. In time, their stars would cross in very different ways.

I didn't know Michelle well, but I had done a feature on her when she was 13 or 14 and now here she was at the Olympics, although in her four events she didn't advance beyond the heats. But because we both spoke Irish I interviewed her every few days for Raidió Na Gaeltachta, she would talk not just about swimming but the Games in general, her impressions of Seoul, and so on. I got to know her reasonably well at that stage.

I also got to meet Pat Hickey for the first time, a man with whom I – and most in the Irish media – would have a long and interesting relationship with. More of that later.

At that stage Pat was on the executive committee of the Olympic Council of Ireland, becoming its president the following year, a role in which he would remain for a remarkable 27 years.

In all my time covering the Olympics, our boxing teams have provided the most incredible drama and the most absorbing of stories, Billy Walsh central to much of that during his time as head coach of the Irish team. In Seoul, though, he was in the ring instead of in the corner, captain of a seven-man team and was fancied to progress after being drawn against a South Korean he had beaten a few months before. But a cut over his left eye led to the fight being stopped, the pleas from the Irish corner to let it continue ignored. Billy was devastated.

The night he was beaten we went out on the town, Billy hadn't had a drink in months so he was more than ready to unwind. We had GAA in common, Billy had been captain of the Wexford minor hurling team and could easily have gone on to play for the seniors but decided to focus on boxing. We had a good night. That started a bond between us. Michael Carruth and Wayne McCullough, meanwhile, both won their opening fights, but were then beaten in the second round.

It wasn't to be the end of their Olympic stories, though.

• • • • • • •

Roy Jones' 'defeat' in the light-middleweight final would have been by far the biggest story from Seoul if it hadn't been for events on the track. The American, who went on to have a brilliant professional career and is regarded as one of the greatest fighters of all time, landed 86 punches on Park Si-Hun, to the South Korean's 32, yet somehow lost the fight 3-2. It was laughable.

The three judges who voted against Jones were later suspended and the farce led to the scoring system being changed for the 1992 Olympics in Barcelona. But it wasn't the last time there was a controversial boxing decision at the Olympics. Ask Michael Conlan, for one.

Overshadowing all of that was 'the dirtiest race in history', as it became known. And I had a spectacular view of it all thanks to Irish photographer Billy Stickland.

Billy had an arrangement with a group of photographers from other smaller nations to ensure they would have all the events covered between them. They would pool their work so they wouldn't miss out on anything important, especially to their own countries.

When it came to the men's 100m final they decided, brilliantly, to do a photo essay of the event together so the race would be covered from every angle. There would be someone lying down behind the start, someone else facing the start line, another half way up the track, another photographing it from on high, and so on.

Billy's vantage point was from on high and he asked me if I'd like to join him. Nowadays, with security so tight, I would never be allowed up there, but things were a little more relaxed back then.

It was a spine-tingling experience. The noise in the stadium was deafening, 100,000 people roaring in anticipation of the battle between the fastest men on earth. I had never experienced anything on that scale in my life

And before the gun went there was a hush in the stadium, pure silence, and then it erupted again when the gun fired. And 9.79 seconds later, Ben Johnson was the Olympic champion. Incredibly, the three men immediately behind him, Carl Lewis, Linford Christie and Calvin Smith, all broke 10 seconds too, Smith not even winning a medal.

The experience of being there, watching it from on high, had been breath-taking.

• • • • • • •

It was two days later when the phone in my hotel bedroom rang at around four in the morning. Because of the time difference sleep was a rare enough luxury, you were usually watching the events during the day, Korea time, and reporting on them for radio for part of the night.

You'd rarely go out for a meal, you'd be eating on the go, although one night myself, Jimmy Magee, George Hamilton, Roy Willoughby and a couple of others ventured out, and I'm reluctant to confess that many a juvenile joke was shared among us about all the talk we'd heard in advance about dogs being Koreans' staple diet. If a dog passed us on the street, a cry of "dinner!" went up.

Our excuse is that there was no internet at the time, so we were going in to the unknown. All I knew was that Irish priests went on the missions to Korea, so I was expecting a very backward country. And then I arrived in Seoul and was blown away, it was as modern a city as you could imagine. The crowning glory for us all was that there was even a TV in the sauna at the hotel. "Jeeeeesus," went up the cry.

We were innocent – and easily impressed – then.

But there were no mobile phones, no notifications alerting you to breaking news in the middle of the night, so you slept on blissfully unaware of what was going on in the wee hours. Like Ben Johnson failing a drug test.

When RTÉ rang they told me Pat Kenny's programme was nearly over so they needed to get me on immediately to discuss the news about Johnson.

I thought 'Jesus, two days later and they're still talking about the 100m final?' I reckoned it had been reported to death at that stage, but if that's what they wanted, fine.

Pat says, "so Des, tell us all you know about Ben Johnson."

I was like, "well, it was a great race and…"

I'd say Pat was sighing about my meandering build-up to talking about the breaking news. Which I knew absolutely nothing about.

"But what about the failed test?" he interrupted.

That stirred me from my sleepiness.

Failed test? What? Jesus…

I was just about alert enough not to make myself look stupid. And then Pat copped on that I had been sleeping soundly when the news broke, so he started saying things about what was known to allow me to repeat them. So I could save a little bit of dignity for myself.

But Ben Johnson failing a drug test well and truly woke me. Maybe in more ways than one.

● ● ● ● ● ● ●

It wasn't as if 1988 was the first time a major sporting event had been won by someone fuelled by drugs, but it was probably the first time most of us became aware of it as being a major issue in sport.

I had covered the Tour de France the year before and doping in cycling just wasn't talked about then. The sport's reputation gradually imploded through the years, and come 2013, when Lance Armstrong admitted that he had cheated his way to all that glory, it lay in tatters. And from then on, whoever won the Tour de France was simply disbelieved, people had lost all faith in the sport.

But in 1988, there was still an innocence among most sports fans, and I'd include myself in that. It was the first time, really, that I became aware of how major an issue doping was, and I date it all back to the 'the dirtiest race in history'.

As we later learnt, Ben Johnson was far from the only offender in the race. Lewis had tested positive three times at the 1988 Olympics trials and shouldn't even have been allowed to compete in Seoul. Christie tested positive for a stimulant in Seoul but was cleared after it was accepted that he had unwittingly ingested it through a cup of ginseng tea. In all, five of the athletes who started that 100m in Seoul failed drugs tests.

Calvin Smith, who was upgraded to bronze after Johnson's medal was taken away, remains the only man in the first five who never failed a test, later arguing that he should have been awarded gold.

There had been suspicions about Ben Johnson in advance, particularly from the Americans, with Carl Lewis, ironically, seen as the clean guy. He was the goodie, Johnson was the baddie. Lewis was handsome and eloquent and articulate, he was likened to Muhammad Ali, humorous and charming and all of that. Johnson had a stutter, he was inarticulate, he was from a poor working class background, an immigrant from Jamaica to Canada. There were all those elements to the story.

Sport was irreparably damaged by it all, I think our suspending of belief about great sporting performances dates back to that.

And I think back to my giddy excitement about looking down on that race from on high alongside Billy Stickland. I'm not sure I looked on so innocently ever again.

Jesus, sport was clean until I arrived.

My first Olympics, then, had been an extraordinary experience.

14

Golden Girl

*'It's a strange story to look back on. Michelle
still has those medals, but she's effectively
been struck from Irish sporting history
because of what happened later'*

How lives can change. In Seoul and Barcelona I would
sometimes be the only media person waiting to speak
to Michelle Smith after her heats. She hadn't progressed
from any of them, so there was no big story.

But come the first week in Atlanta in 1996, she was the only
story – one that had more than a few chapters added to it in the
subsequent years.

By then it seemed like the whole of the world media wanted
to question her. Her press conferences were crammed. There
was never any need for one in her previous two Olympic
appearances, but after winning three gold medals and a bronze
everyone wanted to know about this Irish woman with no record
of success in the Olympics who was suddenly top of the world.

A divisive story it was too, one that created so much tension
that summer, not least among the Irish media where former

friends fell out when they found themselves on opposite 'sides' of the Michelle Smith story.

And even a couple of decades later it can create division.

When we were working on the 'Ireland's Greatest Sporting Moment' series in RTÉ in 2017 there was agreement across the team that Michelle would not be considered, despite her achievements in Atlanta still sitting on top of Ireland's Olympic roll of honour. None of the panellists who appeared in the series nominated her for inclusion, there was no disagreement about her omission, the consensus being that because she had been found guilty of tampering with a urine sample in 1998, for which she received a four-year ban, her Atlanta success should be disregarded for the series.

But there would still be people who would argue passionately that because she never failed a test, which she didn't, her medals from Atlanta should not only be recognised, they should be celebrated. Jimmy Magee always held that view and was heavily criticised for including Michelle in his 'Greatest Sporting Memories' DVD and, later, a similarly themed book.

I think that damaged people's view of Jimmy towards the end of his career, I would have argued with him that he should have left her out because of the tampering offence. But Jimmy was insistent: as our most successful Olympian, who had never failed a drug test, she deserved to be included.

And he never swayed from that belief.

• • • • • • •

RTÉ made a strange decision in 1996. They put me living with an Irish-American family in Atlanta for the duration of the

Games, reckoning that because I was the colour guy it would be a good arrangement, that the family could show me around the city and introduce me to other members of the Irish-American community.

And it did work very well from that point of view, the family, who lived in a beautiful suburban house, was lovely and very good to me. The only problem was that because of the time difference I was taking and making calls to RTÉ from the phone in my bedroom in the middle of the night, doing live stuff for Ian Dempsey and other radio shows. It was kind of mad. You'd get a couple of hours sleep and then you had to go live on air and sound all chirpy and bright, and then it would take ages to get back to sleep.

And once Michelle started winning medals, the phone never stopped ringing.

• • • • • • •

Even now looking at the medal table from the '96 Games leaves you doing a second take. Britain won a single gold, Matthew Pinsent/Steve Redgrave in the rowing, Michelle Smith won three. In light of Britain's more recent success, that's staggering. As is the fact that between 1928 and 1996 Ireland had won five gold medals, now there were three more in a week.

And from the moment she won her first gold on day one, things got tense among the media, journalists like Tom Humphries, Paul Kimmage and David Walsh having long had their doubts about her. Not that we had that much time to sit around arguing, we were all busy, but that tension was real.

They would all have been hugely critical of RTÉ's coverage

of Michelle in Atlanta and accused me and other reporters of being nothing more than flag-wavers, that we were just ignoring what they viewed as the real story, that we were glossing over the suspicions.

But while I could understand their frustration, I still believe RTÉ had no choice but to take the line they did. I know it was discussed at the highest level during the Games and it was decided that because she had never failed a test we could not accuse her of anything nor raise doubts about the legitimacy of her performances. RTÉ had to be responsible about it, not least legally.

Her doubters argued that you can't apply 'innocent until proven guilty' to sport because of the failure of the testing to keep up with the doping, and the evidence over the years shows that's hard to dispute. And they would have seen it as our duty to ask the hard questions. But I don't think they ever fully appreciated the difficulty of the situation for RTÉ and that of the Irish media generally at the time. Some of them were having their own problems getting their work on the issue in to print because their employers were taking a similar stance on the story as RTÉ.

And to this day, broadcasters the world over are faced by the same dilemma when there might be plenty of circumstantial doubts about a sportsperson's form – dramatically improved performances, a link with a suspect coach, and so on – but there are no failed tests to support them. And without a failed test, you are on very shaky ground when you start making allegations.

I think it was hardest for Bill O'Herlihy as the presenter of our Atlanta coverage.

His daughter Sally was a competitive swimmer so he was well aware of the talk in the sport. It was difficult too for the swimming analyst and Michelle's former Irish team-mate

Gary O'Toole, who had predicted that she would win medals. Gary was troubled by Michelle's dramatic improvement, and he has spoken about it all since, but it was such a tough position for him to be in he was relieved when the instruction was issued that he not be asked about the suspicions, RTÉ insisting that he be very cautious.

Because of this atmosphere I felt uncomfortable through it all. On the one hand you had this jubilation over an Irish Olympian performing so spectacularly, on the other Tom and the rest were making a compelling case for why we should be asking questions of these performances.

Michelle was peaking at 26, which was late for a swimmer, and had been knocking big chunks off her personal bests. One fact was regularly quoted, that she had been ranked 90th in the world in the 400m individual medley in 1993, and here she was in 1996 winning gold in the event.

And 1993 was the year she began working with her future husband, Erik De Bruin, who she had met at the Barcelona Games. Erik was a Dutch discus thrower who had failed a drug test in 1993, the same year in which he was asked about doping in the Dutch newspaper De Volkskrant.

"Who says doping is unethical," he said. "Who decides what is ethical? Sport is by definition dishonest. Some people are naturally gifted, others have to work very hard. Some people are not going to make it without extra help."

Quotes like that hardly helped Michelle, especially when she was crediting Erik's training regime for her vastly improved performances.

It only led to more questions.

• • • • • • •

Someone who did raise questions about Michelle was Janet Evans, the American swimmer and four-time gold medallist who had carried the torch on the penultimate leg during the Games' opening ceremony, passing it to Muhammad Ali who lit the cauldron. That was an indication of her status in American sport where Olympic swimming is bigger than I think most of us in Ireland realise.

"Are you asking me if she's on drugs?" she said to a reporter at a press conference when she was asked to comment on Michelle's performances. "Any time someone has a dramatic improvement there's that question. I have heard that question posed in the last few weeks about that swimmer. If you're asking if the accusations are out there, I would say yes."

For that, Janet got slaughtered, even by sections of her own media who accused her of being a sore loser after being beaten by Michelle. And back home I think it had the effect of making people rally around Michelle who they saw as being bullied and slandered by this American.

Pat Hickey, president of the Olympic Committee of Ireland, accused the Americans of 'Uncle Samism', while President Bill Clinton said to Michelle "don't mind all of that crap" when they met after she had won her third gold. She wasn't without friends in high places, then.

I was sitting in the same row as Seán Bán Breathnach at the press conference when he challenged Janet...in Irish. Needless to say, that caused some confusion in the room. But Sean would have got a lot of praise back home for taking on the American and standing up for 'our girl'. And there was an element of 'America aren't the cleanest in sport to be lecturing us' to it as well.

Initially my feeling was, 'Jesus, Janet Evans is bitter', but then you step back from it and reflect, and you can understand the anger and frustration of any sportsperson who, in their heart, believes they are being cheated. Whether true or not, that's clearly how she felt.

There was added ill feeling because the American had missed out on a place in the 400 metres freestyle final by one position, a dispute having arisen over Michelle being allowed to compete in the heats when she hadn't set the qualifying time by the cut-off date. But the International Olympic Committee overturned a decision by Fina (the world swimming body) to exclude her, accepting that there had been confusion about the date and that she should be allowed to compete at the distance. The US, supported by the Australians and Germans, were raging about the ruling, the Americans even more so when Janet ended up not qualifying for the final. And Michelle took gold in that too.

Lots of bad blood, then. But my abiding memory of Michelle when she was challenged at a press conference, repeatedly questioned about drugs and asked about Janet's comments, was how composed she was. Completely unruffled. It was an extraordinarily collected performance in light of what was swirling around her.

She talked about how many times she had been tested, four times in May and June alone, people calling to wherever she was staying early in the morning, and how she hadn't failed a single test. "I'm the most tested athlete in Ireland," she said. "All I can say is just look at all my drug tests."

"I think it would be really stupid of me to take drugs," she added. "When you're in the top 20 you're subject to testing at any time. I was sitting at home at 9 o'clock one Sunday morning when the Fina people came to my house looking for a urine sample. You're not going to be that stupid."

But what was most striking about that week was the atmosphere of suspicion and the absence of joy, when it should have been the most euphoric time of her life.

• • • • • • •

It's a strange story to look back on. Michelle still has those medals, but she's effectively been struck from Irish sporting history because of what happened later. If you mentioned her name to most people born after 1996, they'd probably barely be familiar with it because it's been all but erased.

On a purely human level, it was a hard one. I always liked Michelle, I'd got to know her a bit more doing those Raidió Na Gaeltachta chats in Seoul and found her bright and engaging. I had huge respect for her, she was an incredibly articulate woman who I think could have become such a powerful advocate for young women getting involved in sport. If things hadn't worked out as they did.

She got her open-top bus parade through Dublin when she came home, in the pouring rain, and I think the majority of the public were on her side. Her main sponsor, TNT Express Worldwide, rewarded her with £15,000 for each of her gold medals, but she didn't get the number of new sponsorship deals or advertising work that she might have expected. The benefits were short-term, they faded away soon enough. I think people became uncomfortable with her story.

And when the news broke in August 1998 that she had been banned from swimming for four years, that, effectively, was the end of her career.

She had been found guilty of manipulating her urine sample in an out-of-competition test at her Kilkenny home the previous

January, the International Swimming Federation's doping panel finding that her sample contained an alcoholic content that was 'in no way compatible with human consumption'.

It was a bizarre story, 'the whiskey in the jar', the closing chapter on her sporting life coming at the Court of Arbitration for Sports in Lausanne where, two years after Atlanta, her appeal against her ban was dismissed.

She remained defiant.

"I reaffirm what I have always told you that I have never used any banned substances in the course of my career, nor have I ever been charged by FINA of using any banned substance in the course of my career. I am proud of what I have achieved and assure those who have supported me and believe in me, that my victories in Atlanta and Seville are not hollow and have been achieved without the use of any illegal performance enhancing substance. I will forever cherish my moments of victory and hope that those who still believe in me will also cherish their memories of those times."

And while she can always point to the fact that she never once failed a test during her career, and while she insisted at the time that she did not tamper with the sample, there will, inevitably, forever be a question mark over her achievements.

As one of the testers who visited her home on that January day, Kay Guy, put it: "It's a sad day for Irish sport. I'm sorry that the pleasure and joy some people got from Michelle's successes has been overshadowed now.

"But sport has to be protected."

• • • • • • •

I thought back to that early feature I had done on Michelle when she was swimming at Newpark in Blackrock, her dad Brian driving her there for five in the morning and sleeping in the car while she trained. I remember being struck by the extraordinary commitment and sacrifices that the sport demands, both from the swimmer and their parents. And then to see the story unfold over the next decade and a half, there's a poignancy to it all.

I think there must have been a desperate loneliness to being in the situation she found herself in from January 1998, being erased from our sporting history because of the loss of faith after the whiskey in the jar.

Michelle moved on to become a barrister, the rest of us moved on to other stories, but there's unlikely to ever be another quite like her own.

15

Rolling With The Punches

'I can remember Michael talking about signing on for the dole during a later period when he couldn't find work, when most of us might have thought that is something that could never happen to an Olympic champion'

A nineteen-year-old Oscar de la Hoya was leaving the boxing venue in Badalona having won gold in the lightweight division for the United States, the world now at his feet.

Within four months 'The Golden Boy', as he had been dubbed, was to begin a professional career that yielded multiple world titles and over $500 million in career earnings.

He was accompanied by his entourage as he made his way to his limousine and he briefly stopped and stared at the scene on the narrow side street.

A small group was listening as Phil Sutcliffe, the former Irish

Olympian, was singing Amhrán na bhFiann, all of them close friends of Michael Carruth who, earlier in the day, had won Ireland its first Olympic gold medal since Ronnie Delany in Melbourne in 1956. Thirty-six years before.

The world was passing by, or at least trying to. Cars beeped their horns at the group of Irishmen blocking the street, but the looks thrown at them told them to wait. So, they did.

Phil hadn't been happy with the shortened recorded rendition of the anthem that had been played during Michael's medal ceremony, so called on the group to sing it again – properly this time. It was probably the soldier in him, he, like Michael, was an army man.

Phil's voice filled the air, followed by cheers from the group.

De la Hoya's limousine pulled away.

He and Michael left Barcelona as equals, with gold medals around their necks, but from there their lives were to take very different paths.

• • • • • • •

As a young fella I used to cut out and keep newspaper columns that grabbed me. I had mountains of Con Houlihan's work, there was no-one like him, but there was one I kept from Hugh Leonard that included a line I used for RTÉ when we saw the boxing venue at the 1992 Games: "If Barcelona was having an enema, they'd put the tube in to Badalona."

Badalona was about a 30-minute drive north east of Barcelona and in contrast to most of the venues for those Games, many of them overlooking the magnificent city, it was a kip. Small enough too, with a capacity of around 3,000.

But inside that stadium two Irish fighters won us Olympics medals for the first time since John Treacy came second in the 1984 marathon in Los Angeles. So, a dump it might have been, but the Pavelló Club Joventut de Badalona holds a special place in Irish Olympic history.

The first of the medals was won by Belfast's Wayne McCullough who took silver at bantamweight after losing to Cuba's Joel Casamayor. It was only after that we discovered just how courageous he had been to fight to the end, his cheekbone fractured in the second round.

Wayne was reckoned to be our better hope of gold on that finals morning with another Cuban, the tall and rangy, powerfully-built Juan Hernández-Sierra, firm favourite to beat Michael, their fight taking place within the hour.

After the shambles of the Roy Jones decision in Seoul, the scoring system had been changed with computerised punch counters now being used showing the score after each round.

Michael started brilliantly, winning the first round 4-3, but he was penalised three points in the second for holding, which left the score at 8-8. I was sitting alongside Jimmy Magee in the commentary position and I could feel the tension coming out of him, and from the Irish supporters too, although despite their nerves they roared Michael on the whole way through.

When Michael caught Hernández-Sierra with three hooks in the opening minute of the final round the decibel levels soared, Ireland's first ever boxing gold medal since competing independently in the Olympics in 1924 was within reach. He ran to his corner and embraced his father Austin. It was an incredibly emotional moment.

But even though the scoring system had changed, such was the record of dodgy boxing decisions at the Olympics no-one was taking anything for granted. And Michael himself said later that he knew he had won, but was praying it wouldn't be a Roy Jones moment.

The wait seemed eternal.

Finally, 13-10.

Michael Carruth was Olympic champion.

Pure gold.

• • • • • • •

I think back to the scene in that Badalona side street, Oscar de la Hoya getting into his limo while Michael's pals stood to attention for the anthem. Two Olympic gold medallists who were to have starkly contrasting careers.

While De la Hoya went on to become one of the wealthiest sports people in history, Michael's Olympic success brought no such riches. He turned professional after Barcelona, winning 18 and losing three of his 21 fights between 1994 and 2000, but he was never to experience anything like the high of that August morning in 1992.

A few months after he won gold I went by train with Michael to Cork where I was interviewing him at a conference. He did an interview with a journalist on the way down and I remember his frustration with a line of questioning about the wisdom of him turning professional, the belief among many boxing people being that his style wouldn't suit the pro game.

It struck me how no consideration was being given to Michael's need to earn a living, the focus solely on his sporting career. He was a corporal in the army so the money wouldn't have been that good. Turning pro would give him a chance of making a few quid, maybe enough to pay off the mortgage on the home he had with his wife Paula.

Olympic success changes lives, but it doesn't always bring financial rewards. I can remember Michael talking about signing on for the dole during a later period when he couldn't find work, when most of us might have thought that is something that could never happen to an Olympic champion.

Happily things are better now for Michael, he's coaching in his beloved Drimnagh Boxing Club and working with the Irish Athletic Boxing Association, trying to unearth another Michael Carruth.

• • • • • • •

We had to wait another 16 years until we added to Michael and Wayne's boxing medals, but three in Beijing 2008 – Kenneth Egan (silver), Paddy Barnes (bronze) and Darren Sutherland (bronze) – and four in London 2012 – Katie Taylor (gold), John Joe Nevin (silver), Michael Conlon (bronze) and Paddy Barnes again (bronze) – was an extraordinary haul, considering we had only won seven boxing medals as an independent state from 1924 up to 1992.

And boxing has produced such incredible drama for us all through those years, from the highs of all those successes to many a low too, like Michael Conlan being robbed of victory by the judges in his bout with Russian Vladamir Nikitin in Rio. It was hard to dispute Michael's conclusion that "amateur boxing stinks from the core right to the top."

My own innocence had been shattered after the doping revelations from earlier Games, but athletes being cheated by suspicious judging only deepened that sense of cynicism, the suspension of all 36 of the judges in Rio the following November, while boxing's under-siege governing body investigated, just confirming what a murky world amateur boxing can be.

After he won bronze in London, Michael could probably have made a lot of money as a pro in the following years, but he chose to stay amateur because his dream was gold. It was a massive commitment to go again, but he went to Rio as the World Amateur Bantamweight champion, so his dream looked more than achievable. And in the end he must surely have felt he gave up those four years for nothing. Considering how relatively short the career of a boxer can be, that must have been devastating.

I remember Billy Walsh saying afterwards that he regretted persuading Michael to wait until after Rio to turn professional, he too was convinced he could finish his amateur career with an Olympic gold. And then he was 'robbed'.

Billy, of course, had been a huge loss to Irish boxing when he left to take up a position with the United States team in 2015, there was genuine shock that, after everything he had achieved as head coach, more wasn't done to keep him. But the politics in the Irish boxing world is beyond comprehension for mere mortals.

· · · · · · ·

I've always really enjoyed dealing with our Olympic boxers over the years, so many of them have been such impressive characters, often with fascinating back stories. Like Andy Lee who was born in London, coming from the same traveller community as Tyson Fury, their grandmothers sisters, moving to Limerick in his early teens, boxing helping him settle in to his new surroundings.

I had great time for Andy, our sole boxing representative in Athens, he is such a smart and interesting man. I love listening to him talk about the sport, he gives insights very few others offer.

And then there was Paddy Barnes and his cheeky humour, not to mention his outstanding ability, which made him a big favourite among the Irish team.

I had huge respect, too, for Kenneth Egan for the way he came through such a difficult time after he won his silver at the 2008 Games, admitting himself that he was in a bad place and was drinking far too much. That he turned it all around and is now a qualified counsellor helping others through tough times is beyond admirable. He has always been a very impressive and likeable fella.

Kenneth has talked very openly about that time, how he struggled to deal with all the attention he received when he got home after winning his medal, life just becoming one long drinking binge.

While Kenneth battled his way through it and came out the other side, tragically we lost his team-mate Darren Sutherland who had won bronze at those 2008 Games.

Darren turned professional in October of that year but within 12 months he was gone, found hanging in his flat in London by his manager and boxing promoter Frank Maloney. It was devastating news.

Darren was a bright, handsome, articulate, talented sportsman with, we all believed, a fantastic future. But it was only during the inquest in to his death that we learnt how much he had struggled with the transition in to professionalism, having felt 'supported' in the amateur world.

His father Tony said that Darren wished he'd given up boxing completely after he won his Olympic medal, that he'd lost all his confidence but was afraid of the financial implications if he packed it in. He was depressed, he wasn't sleeping, he was in complete turmoil. It was heart-wrenching to hear what he had gone through, most of us having known him for that beaming smile, that self-belief, that endearing personality.

While Darren's story, and the dreadful, tragic way it ended, is the extreme, I have often wondered about how strange life must be for our Olympians, particularly the ones who come from sports that get little attention in the four years between each Games. And then suddenly they're thrust in to the limelight, we're all over them, they become national figures, and if they're successful at the Olympics they have that heady spell afterwards where there is so much media attention.

Most cope fine, they enjoy the ride and see it for what it is, but for some it must be desperately difficult. They go from almost complete anonymity to being the centre of attention for three weeks, and a few more after if they've medalled, and then most return to anonymity again. The Olympic experience can be life-changing in a positive way, but it can also be cruel.

And for those boxers who turn professional after the Olympics, it must be such a tough, lonely experience. I've seen myself what a close-knit group they are at Olympic Games, how supportive they are of each other and how much fun they have together. There's a genuine family atmosphere in the camp. And then to enter that ruthless world of professional boxing where they must feel so alone at times, especially if their pro careers aren't taking off as they hoped. Brutal.

I often think back to that moment Oscar de la Hoya stopped before getting into his limo on that Badalona side street, Michael's friends standing to attention as Phil Sutcliffe sang Amhrán na bhFiann.

I very much doubt De la Hoya remembers it, but I always will. It's one of my most treasured Olympic memories. I felt lucky to be there.

I knew what it all meant to Michael, how proud he was to have won gold for his country. In the toughest of sports, too.

He was Oscar de la Hoya's golden equal that day.

And in Olympic history, he always will be.

16

Who Does He Think He Is?

'Pat then read out a text, which puzzled him: 'Henson goes into Church after every game'... Pat didn't get the crude joke. He read it again. I said: "Stop!"'

It wasn't until well into the 1990s that I had my first programme on television, *Sideline View*. Once I switched from news to the sports department I had been working solely in radio, which I loved – and still do.

I always preferred the informality of radio over television which, by its nature, has to be much more structured and, therefore, can be quite limiting. I think it's much easier to be yourself on radio, and I've always loved the interaction with the listeners.

I can remember, though, when I had spells filling in as the presenter on *Liveline* and *The Gerry Ryan Show* the producers would say to me, "we don't want this to be about sport." "Grand," I'd say, and then the first call on a Monday would be about a disallowed goal in the hurling the day before or someone throwing a punch in the rugby. And the producers would be tearing their hair out.

There was a danger of *Liveline* and *The Gerry Ryan Show* being turned in to *Sportscall*, angry sports fans deciding I was the one they could vent to, regardless of the show I was hosting.

But lots of opportunities like presenting those programmes, and my own, came my way through the 1990s, the success of the slot with Ian Dempsey on his breakfast show resulting in them opening up. Filling in for Marian Finucane on *Liveline* during the summer of 1993 kick-started it all, leading to my own Saturday morning show *Talk Radio* and, later, taking over from Gay Byrne on Mondays and Tuesdays when he began to wind down.

It was a hugely enjoyable spell, but a difficult one too.

• • • • • • •

I loved doing *Liveline*, loved chatting with the callers and the range of issues they would raise. One of my first calls was from a woman complaining that she wasn't allowed to change her baby's nappy in a restaurant, so that was quite a departure from, say, interviewing Des Smyth about the Ryder Cup. But as a young father of a four and two-year-old I could relate to her, as I could to many of the callers, so I think that helped it work.

Helen Shaw, who later became head of radio, was the producer of *Liveline* at the time and she was determined to take me out of my comfort zone.

At one point she suggested we do a special on Kosovo, Serbia and Bosnia where there was such brutal unrest at the time. I said to her that that was out of my league, but she insisted it wasn't, that I just needed to prepare properly, do my research. So I did, over a week, and then we did the programme. I spoke with people who had come from that region to Ireland, who had survived the atrocities, and got them to tell their stories. It made for really powerful radio and I was grateful to Helen for having the confidence in me that I could do it.

I really enjoyed the experience, I generally have nothing but happy memories from working on *Liveline*, although it did lead to the only occasion I was successfully sued during my time in RTÉ.

A bizarre situation it was too.

•••••••

On Fridays during the summer we'd get a person in to the studio and allow callers to ring in to chat with them and even though I intended keeping away from sport, one Friday we decided to invite Barry McGuigan on the programme. We advertised it through the week and invited people to call in with questions for Barry or with memories from his boxing career.

One thing that wasn't to be discussed, though, was Barry's impending legal battle with his former manager Barney Eastwood. A lengthy battle it proved to be too, Barney suing Barry over remarks he had made about his fitness going in to his title fight with Steve Cruz under the blazing sun in Las Vegas in 1986, a fight he lost.

In the end Barney was awarded £450,000 in libel damages after Barry claimed in a video that he had injuries going in to the fight, and some years later the BBC also had to pay substantial damages after similar claims in an interview with Eamonn Holmes.

I had done a programme with Barney in Belfast a while before, he talked to me about the upcoming case, he argued that whatever anyone said, in Barry's time with him he ended up as a world champion, a wealthy man and finished his career unscathed, and that not many boxers could say that. Barry, though, obviously had grievances about that Las Vegas fight, which Barney felt were baseless, the pair's relationship ending as a result.

All of that, then, was to be avoided on *Liveline*, the intention being that just members of the public would call in to talk to Barry. But then Fr Brian D'Arcy, who had known Barry for years, rang in on the day. Barry was thrilled to hear from him, they chatted away, reminisced about the past.

And then Brian recalled the time he blessed Barry's ankle "out in the desert" before his fight against Cruz because "it wasn't right". We were in trouble.

Barney sued on the basis that it had been suggested on air that Barry hadn't been fit to fight.

RTÉ just couldn't risk going to court, particularly in Belfast, and ended up settling, which I could understand. The amount was around £25,000.

I was raging. It had been an expensive phone call.

• • • • • • •

Meantime, I had also ended up sitting in for Gerry Ryan during the summer.

Initially it started kind of, well, accidentally. I was doing the breakfast show with Ian which immediately preceded Gerry's show, but sometimes Gerry wouldn't make it in for nine o'clock, when his show started, so they created this irregular thing where

I'd do the first hour, from nine to 10, and then Gerry would take over when he arrived. And then I ended up filling in for him in the summer when he was away.

Again, I was a young fella with a young family, I was chatty, so it worked quite well. And they were great people working on the show, including Willie O'Reilly who later became the head of Today FM.

I was nothing like Gerry, of course, he was one of a kind. If ever the description 'larger than life' applied to anyone, it was him. I had great time for him, he was a hugely entertaining man, there literally was never a dull moment when you were in his company.

If Gerry was the biggest star on what is now 2FM, Gay Byrne was the undisputed king back on Radio 1, and without doubt the biggest name in Irish media at the time.

He and Pat Kenny were the best I ever worked with, very different people but both brilliant broadcasters.

I wouldn't have had a close relationship with Gay at all, there were 25 years between us so in that sense we didn't have a lot in common, whereas I did have with Pat, even though there was a gap there too, he's around 11 years older. I had great time for him personally, still do. And even though he's no longer with RTÉ, having moved to Newstalk in 2013, I still regard him as the most knowledgeable broadcaster in the business. Gay's incredible strength was that he understood the mood and soul of the nation.

Pat could laugh at himself too, which is always a plus in anyone's personality. I remember being with him in an open air bar after the 2006 Heineken Cup semi-final when Munster trounced Leinster at the Aviva and the Munster lads were slaughtering him. But Pat was well able for it, and I think some wouldn't think he would be. He enjoyed the banter, loved it.

He probably has a broader knowledge than anyone I've ever met – well, apart from my brother Declan who'd be nerdy too! And he has an interest in everything so no matter what guest he has on he's able to talk to them in an informed way – academics respect him, politicians respect him, everyone does. But when I was on with him, he also wanted to be a blokey bloke – and if there is one thing Pat isn't, it's a blokey bloke.

When I'd come on to do the sports news on his show he'd feel obliged to jump in and show his knowledge on whatever item I was reporting, at times I'd nearly be trying to stop him from interrupting for his own sake.

(There is a famous clip on YouTube of the Monday morning after an Ireland-Wales rugby match. We were talking about one of the Welsh stars, Gavin Henson. Pat then read out a text, which puzzled him: 'Henson goes into Church after every game'. Henson's girlfriend was the singer, Charlotte Church. Pat didn't get the crude joke. He read it again. I said: "Stop!" He read it out loud again. "STOP!" Needless to say, it got a huge reaction on social media).

Gay, meanwhile, would just sit back and let you take over, he didn't pretend to know about sport and that was one of his strengths, and probably a sign of his confidence and security, 'this is your subject, off you go'.

I remember him doing just that when we did a piece on the 40th anniversary of the Munich Air Disaster and among the people we spoke to was Harry Gregg, the former Manchester United goalkeeper who had survived the crash. And Harry spoke so movingly about it all, it was incredibly powerful. It was only meant to last half an hour but Gay let it run, he knew it was great radio, he had a really good sense for that. And he just came in occasionally with a question that he was curious about, leaving the rest of it to me because he knew I knew more about it. And he did that with everyone in a similar situation, he was excellent that way.

In broadcasting you just have to accept that you're not an expert on everything, but Pat would keep chatting away. And he'd start that blokey bloke stuff with me and I'd be, 'ah stop'.

Risteárd Cooper picked up on it all when he did a brilliant sketch on myself and Pat – me, of course, being the gormless eejit (as I always am in sketches – I'm looking at you, Oliver Callan).

It was hilarious, Pat constantly interrupting me when I was reporting on Ireland losing to Wales in the quarter-finals of the 2011 Rugby World Cup in New Zealand. And then he insisted that he, rather than me, would do an interview with Ronan O'Gara by phone – or 'ROG', with a hard 'g', as he called him, rather than 'Rodge'. (Having already referred to Paul O'Connell as 'POC').

"You had given the Irish people a huge lift before bringing them crashing down to earth again," said 'Pat'. "Do you feel you let them down, and all the devastated children who got up at 5.30 in the morning…?"

'I' am sitting there burying my face in my hands.

"Just how disappointed are you? Very disappointed? Extremely disappointed? Terminally depressed? What's the point in anything, that sort of thing?"

At which point ROG hangs up.

It was hysterical. And not all that far from the truth either.

But for all his blokey bloke interrupting, I still loved Pat.

• • • • • • •

As a result of my spells filling in on *Liveline*, which had gone well, I was given my own Saturday morning show called *Talk Radio* which proved very popular. It was really just relaxed Saturday morning chat with guests, shooting the breeze, we'd read out letters from listeners, Michael Holmes would come on and do an item on the origin of well known phrases, like 'the whole nine yards', we'd just have a laugh.

We had Dick Spring and Neil Kinnock and the Dublin Welsh male voice choir in on the morning of an Ireland v Wales rugby match, with a bottle of whiskey in the middle of the table, yarns were told and we had some wonderful singing. It was just light-hearted easy listening on a Saturday morning.

There would have been criticism of interviews I did too, from both inside and outside RTÉ, like one I did with Ruairi Quinn, the then Minister for Finance. I didn't challenge him on the economy, which I wouldn't have been best equipped to do anyway, because the interview was intended to be purely a personal one, looking to find out more about the human side of the man rather than the Government minister. I suppose nowadays politicians would love those kind of interviews, rather than going on *Prime Time*. Lightweight stuff, but I didn't set out to be the king of current affairs.

I was still doing my regular work with Sport through all this, but by then things were beginning to get difficult. Ian Corr, a producer in Sport, was particularly pissed off about me doing these shows. "You want to be a star? We don't have stars!"

Yes, it was giving me a much higher profile, but it wasn't about becoming a star, I was just enjoying the variety of work I was doing, even if sport was, and still is, my first love. I still considered myself a Sport man, I never wanted to leave, but I'd come in on a Monday to do *Liveline* and Ian would ask if I was working in

Sport that day. That should have been sorted out at management level, but it never was, so I was caught in the middle.

I wasn't getting paid a fortune either. Initially it was 200 quid a week extra for doing *Liveline*, by the last summer it was up to 250. That was on top of my wages. But it was having an impact on me in Sport, there was a clear resentment, I could feel it and see it. It wasn't well disguised by one or two. Big star, who does he think he is?

But I *was* being treated differently. I was doing *Sunday Sport*, sport on *Morning Ireland* and 2FM, and they wanted me to do lunchtime as well, which, of course, was denying someone else the opportunity. I wasn't looking to do it, I wasn't trying to hog everything, but they wanted me on it. And there was resentment over that too. I was very conscious of it.

That kind of resentment can bring people down, but I never allowed it to, it didn't bother or intimidate me, I could see it for what it was, petty and mean-spirited.

I'm very independent, I don't need that kind of approval. I'd be irritated by it alright, it could be bitchy, people wanting to do what you were doing and believing they were better than you. But there have been plenty of times when I would look at other people and think I could do a better job than them too. It's a natural thing in broadcasting. Everybody is ambitious. A lot of them would be justified in having egos, some of them less so. It's like any office or company.

Ultimately I made a call to just stick with sport. But not before going through my 'Son of Gaybo' spell.

And trust me, I never once considered myself 'Son of Gaybo'.

17

Disneyland To Saipan

'I remember the then Taoiseach Albert Reynolds arriving and being formally welcomed. But when he saw he us, he said "Howarya lads!" The people around us were mystified.'

Beating Italy on that marvellous June day in Giants Stadium is, of course, my abiding memory of the 1994 World Cup, but another one comes close.

It was in Disneyland in Florida when the small balding man, an Elmer Fudd look-a-like, reached in to his pocket and pulled out some glitter-like substance which he sprinkled all over myself and Gerry Ryan. "Here's some pixie dust to start your day! It's going to be magical!"

And unless you've experienced being showered with pixie dust by Elmer Fudd while standing beside Gerry Ryan, you really haven't lived.

Gerry was a very, very funny man, I loved his caustic, wry wit. I liked him a lot. We wouldn't have hung around together, we had very little in common, but I had great time for him.

It was Ian Dempsey who rang me with the news in April 2010. He wanted to know where I was before he told me. I was walking in Shankill Park. So he told me, Gerry had died. I was simply stunned.

There was such fondness for Gerry. He had a big ego, but there was a vulnerability about him too. He could be brash, but he was brilliant with people, he had a real empathy, which he demonstrated so movingly many times, like the time he spoke with Lavinia Kerwick back in 1993, the rape victim who gave up her anonymity to tell her powerful story. And how Gerry handled such a sensitive story demonstrated not only what a great broadcaster he was, but what a decent, caring man he could be too.

Some of my happiest memories from my time working with RTÉ were from 1994 when it was decided I would be Gerry's radio sidekick for the opening week of the World Cup, spending the first few days with him in New York before we went on to Florida.

I rarely stopped laughing.

• • • • • • •

By its nature, of course, the '94 World Cup was very different from our '88 and '90 experiences, such a vast country being the host this time around. It was, then, more disjointed, but I still loved every minute of it.

I did the show live with Gerry every day that week, with Willie O'Reilly, Siobhan Haugh and Brenda Donohue who were all part of the team. On the day of the Italy match, we broadcast from the lobby of Fitzpatrick's Hotel. I remember the then Taoiseach Albert Reynolds arriving and being formally welcomed. But when he saw he us, he said "Howarya lads!" The people around us were mystified by the informality of a meeting with our Prime Minister.

The Saw Doctors played live on the show one day and later we were all waiting for a taxi outside when Leo Moran took out his guitar and starting playing songs on the sidewalk, with everyone else joining in. Not Albert, I should add, but he probably would have if he was there that day. It was just great fun. New Yorkers passing by, and the Saw Doctors and the Gerry Ryan team belting out 'I useta love her'.

There were bizarre moments too, like the night we were in a packed pub near Times Square when the big ice hockey game was interrupted on the TV by coverage of OJ Simpson in his Bronco being chased by police down the freeway. It was already a big story, we had no idea what was to come.

But after that amazing day in Giants Stadium, when Ray Houghton was once again the hero, that World Cup petered out for us, a defeat by Mexico in the blazing Orlando sun, a grim scoreless draw with Norway back in Giants Stadium, and a knock-out defeat by the Dutch ending the journey.

• • • • • • •

What I noticed changing during the World Cup was that the previously close relations the players had with the media had begun to wane. I think a lot of that was due to the fact that several of the players came from English clubs who were changing their relationship with the media too, with access to players much more restricted.

When I started out you really got to know most of the players and sometimes their families too, like Kevin Sheedy and his father Michael who, like me, was from Clare, so that gave us a bond.

The media would usually stay in the team hotel during Euro 88. I was in the room next to Kevin and Tony Galvin, and often shared the same flights. So much of that has changed. You could attend an entire training session, whereas now you're just allowed in for the first 10 or 15 minutes and then you have to leave. And, generally, it's the FAI that will decide which players are put forward for interview, rather than you being able to just walk up to any of them and have a chat, as it was through the Jack years.

I had a great relationship with Jack, we just hit it off from the start, to the point where he even called out to the house to see Caroline after she'd had Paul. Jack's daughter, 'our Debbie', had her first baby a few months before, making Jack a grandfather for the first time. He mentioned it on *The Late Late Show* and was inundated with presents for the baby, so I'd tell him to pass on his spares. He'd call me mean, I'd say "you're a bit thrifty yourself!" Jack enjoyed all that. And he loved the notoriety of those stories of him being slow to buy a drink for anyone, writing a cheque if he had no way out, safe in the knowledge that it would end up framed behind the bar rather than being cashed. He would chuckle loudly when told half the pubs in Ireland had uncashed cheques of his on display.

It's a big contrast with the relationship Tony O'Donoghue has with Martin O'Neill these days, the tension palpable every time they speak. I really don't understand it, I don't recall Tony giving Martin a reason for being so prickly, but he just seems very sensitive to any questions put to him about a poor performance or result.

Back when I was doing post-match interviews they were very brief, a minute or a minute and a half, so there was just time for a quick reaction to the game. They're longer now so there's time for more in-depth questions, and if the result hasn't gone well that's when tensions can arise.

But in my time covering soccer there were a lot more good days than bad, when you think we qualified for three tournaments in six years, so more often than not there was a party atmosphere about it all and few opportunities to ask, "where did it all go wrong?"

• • • • • • •

Because I developed a good relationship with Jack he asked me to be MC for him at various functions around Euro 88 and Italia 90. That didn't go down well with Eamon Dunphy who, of course, was no fan of Jack or his style of football. Remarkably enough Eamon even turned up in disguise one time at an event I did with Jack in the Cuckoo's Nest pub in Tallaght, 'so not to provoke the great man and his fans,' as he wrote.

The first I knew about it was when he wrote a full-page article on the night for *The Sunday Independent*. Later Michael Lyster told me that he had seen Eamon in make-up in RTÉ having the disguise done, Eamon telling him where he was going, but Michael genuinely thought he was joking.

Anyway, Eamon slaughtered me, mainly for not asking Jack hard questions, so I felt that resulted in him being pissed off with me. I always liked him, and I wish him well after his announcement following the 2018 World Cup that he would be leaving RTÉ. Whether you loved or loathed him, he was a major part of RTÉ's soccer coverage through the years and provoked more heated debates than probably anyone else on our TV screens.

Eamon also has a fantastic sense of humour and was never slow to poke fun at his own football career.

I remember John Giles telling the story of being in his company one night, along with Liam Tuohy, the former Irish manager, and Ray Treacy, Eamon's former Republic of Ireland team-mate. Liam and Ray were picking their worst ever Irish team. Everyone started looking at Eamon.

"Am I in it?" he asked.

"You're the fucking captain," said Liam.

"No, you're only a sub," countered Ray.

Fellas like Liam Touhy and Ray Treacy were part of the reason covering soccer was so much fun.

• • • • • • •

I wouldn't have known Roy Keane well at all, I'd interviewed him a few times but by then, as I mentioned, there was a much greater distance between the players and the media.

Although I do remember meeting him in Manchester after he'd made his home debut for United following his move from Nottingham Forest. A group of us met him in the players' lounge after the game, along with John Givens and PJ Cunningham, sports editor of *The Evening Herald*, who was signing him up as a columnist. Roy was chatty and friendly, a kind and generous host, even making sure we were all okay for a lift back to the airport. He just struck me as a fine young man.

Nine years later I was in Dublin Airport ready to start my journey to Japan for the 2002 World Cup, the first we'd qualified for since 1994, when I read Tom Humphries' interview with Roy in *The Irish Times* in which Roy was hugely critical of the preparations for the World Cup and his team-mates. *Fuck*. I knew there was major trouble ahead. By the time I arrived in Japan, Roy was preparing to leave for home.

If I'd hoped for a fairly relaxed World Cup, I was to be disappointed. It was bonkers. Possibly only Pat Hickey's arrest in Rio in 2016 came any way close to the demands for updates from back home, they couldn't get enough of 'Saipan'. Like with the Hickey story, I ended up co-presenting *Morning Ireland* from Chiba in Japan, the squad having moved there by then in preparation for their opening game against Cameroon.

My own view on it all was that I think Mick McCarthy and Roy could have handled it a whole lot better, there were faults on both sides. I was in a minority, though, most Irish people who took an interest in the story were firmly in one camp or another, it was all so bitter.

I was torn because I really liked Mick as a man, decent and straight talking, but when I looked at those photos of Roy walking his dog back in Manchester, I couldn't but admire him for his mental strength, for giving up the chance of playing in another World Cup because he was sticking to his principles, whether you thought they were right or wrong.

His breaking point appeared to be, as he insisted, Mick accusing him of having 'faked' injuries to miss Irish matches, and you'd guess one thing Roy couldn't tolerate was being accused of faking anything.

There was the theory, of course, that the bad blood between them dated back to an end-of-season run-in in America in 1992 when Ireland were there for some friendlies. Roy, having had a good night out, was late for the team coach, Jack gave out to him and Roy was cheeky back. At which point Mick, then captain, told him he was out of order. Roy, in his own book, said he told 'Captain Fantastic' to 'go fuck yourself'.

You can see how that wouldn't have led to, well, smooth relations between the pair, although I smile at the story, the irony of it – Mick wouldn't have been a stranger to a good night out earlier in his playing days either.

The real problem was, I reckon, that Mick and Roy were such similar characters – stubborn, hot-headed and both damned if they'd back down.

When it all kicked off between them, I doubt there was a mediator in the world who could have got them to patch it up. But I just wish Roy had stayed, I wish he had played in that World Cup.

It was a strange World Cup, too, South Korea and Turkey reaching the semi-finals, so you couldn't but wonder if we could have done the same. There will always be a 'what if?' And while I know Roy will never change his view that he was the wronged party and had no option but to leave, I wonder does he ever think 'what if?' too?

• • • • • • •

It was in later years that my son Paul abandoned his disturbing early Manchester United-supporting tendencies and took Sunderland in to his heart, mainly because of the Irish connection, Niall Quinn having become a good friend of mine. I'm not sure Paul can reflect on it as a wise decision, it's brought him nothing but grief. But I brought him over one year, when he was a young fella, and Mick invited us in to his manager's office.

I remember there was a hole in the wall, around waist high, and I asked him what had happened. He said Sunderland had lost a play-off semi-final to Crystal Palace on penalties and he kept the hole there to remind himself of how he felt. There was a frame around it.

He'd put the hole in the wall himself.

After Mick left Sunderland, my son Paul went back over with a group as guests of Niall Quinn, Niall bringing them on a tour. Niall had by now appointed Roy as manager, and when they got to the manager's office, the first thing Paul noticed was that the hole in the wall had been filled in, and the frame was gone.

But I'm sure there were times Roy came close to putting a hole in that wall too, learning, like Mick, that management can be the most frustrating of businesses.

• • • • • • •

There had been such joy about us being back on the World Cup stage after an eight-year gap. And then Saipan happened. From then the Roy story overshadowed everything, although under the circumstances the team did so well.

There was Matt Holland's equaliser against Cameroon in the opening game, Robbie Keane's wondrous injury-time equaliser against Germany and the 3-0 win over Saudi Arabia.

And then Spain in the last sixteen where it went to penalties, myself and Tony O'Donoghue having an amazing vantage point for it all, right behind the goal. We were doing the 'flash interviews' at the full-time whistle, so for some reason we were put sitting on two seats, literally behind one of the goals. The photographers were kept in the corners of the pitch, Tony and I were there leaning on the advertising hoarding, two yards behind the net. We could have been up the field in Dalkey!

Gaizka Mendieta's winning penalty for Spain proved to be the last piece of action of my spell covering Ireland at major tournaments, it was 10 years before we qualified for another major tournament again, by which time my RTÉ role had changed, taking over the evening version of *The Sunday Game* while, later, doing *Saturday Sport* with Joanne Cantwell.

But I was just incredibly lucky to have been there for Euro 88, Italia 90, USA 94 and 2002 in Japan and South Korea, to have witnessed some of the most treasured moments in Irish sporting history.

18

Brendan

'He was on a life support machine for a few days, but it was just a matter of time before it was switched off. He wasn't going to recover'

I was driving to my brother Declan's wedding rehearsal on a Sunday evening and had BBC Radio on in the car.

It was the final day of the 1995 Ryder Cup, which went down to the wire that year. It was the Philip Walton Ryder Cup, when his win on the final hole over Jay Haas proved so crucial.

The commentators were using terms like 'life or death', 'tragedy', 'disaster', all that. I used similar language all the time too when I talked about sport. Missing a putt, a penalty, a conversion, they were all 'life or death' moments, they were all 'tragedies', they were all 'disasters'.

Much as I loved the Ryder Cup, that evening I just said 'stop'. It's a golf competition. Nothing more. Get a grip.

It just struck me that evening how inappropriate, how careless, how thoughtless talk like that is in the context of sport.

Every time I used that language on radio, which was often, there was somebody listening in a car, somebody coming from a parent dying. Or a wife, husband, son, daughter, brother, sister. Any loved one.

I had just left the hospital where the life support machine had been switched off on my brother Brendan.

I remember vowing never to speak about sport like that any more.

· · · · · · ·

Even in today's Ireland, almost two decades in to the 21st century, it's an unrelenting and often soul-destroying battle for parents of children with intellectual disabilities to get help.

As a patron of the Special Olympics movement in Ireland, I hear these heart-breaking stories all the time. They would fill you with both anger and despair.

But when Brendan was born, in the 1960s, it was impossibly difficult. There was next to no help, next to no options.

Mam already had Brian and myself to look after, and Declan and Pat later on, Brendan arriving in between.

The love of a parent was all that could be offered to a child born with a profound intellectual disability back then, there was no other assistance on offer.

The burden of it all fell heavily on Mam, her love for and tenderness towards Brendan something I will never forget.

I think after what Dad had gone through with his first family, maybe he couldn't take any more?

While both Mam and Dad's families were supportive, she didn't have any sisters or brothers in Dublin, so it was very hard for her.

But Uncle Jimmy, the brother of Dad's first wife, was a genuine help to her. While she was pregnant with Brendan, he helped her with appointments with doctors and specialists, and so on. It just showed what a decent man he was because it can't have been an easy situation for him either.

From early on it was clear Brendan was a danger to himself, often banging his head off walls. There was just no choice other than to put him into specialist care.

It broke Mam's heart, but there just was no choice. Back then the options were so limited. Non-existent, really.

Mam would visit Brendan regularly, but Dad wouldn't have gone with her that often, it was like he shut it all out. She would go off on her own, taking buses across Dublin and back. She'd be gone all day. And she was working part-time too as a nurse, so it must have been incredibly tough for her.

I remember being with Brendan one time and thinking to myself, 'Jesus, he looks so like me'. The guilt thing again. Not that any of it was my fault, I knew that, but it would just make you heavy-hearted.

Thin face. Sad eyes.

He'd look at you and then look away somewhere.

I see his eyes even now.

I remember watching my mother stroking his face.

She was so loving and gentle with him.

Again, you can't but reflect on your own good fortune in life and wonder about fate, all that, wonder why these things happen.

Wonder why Brendan was given a life like this.

• • • • • • •

It was September 1995 when Brendan went in to a coma after falling down stairs where he was in care.

He was on a life support machine for a few days, but it was just a matter of time before it was switched off. He wasn't going to recover.

It was switched off on a Sunday.

We all gathered in Beaumont. Prayers were said, then we left the room.

Declan was getting married on the Tuesday. So that was hanging there. But my mother insisted that the wedding go ahead.

I had to stay behind and formally identify Brendan in the presence of a Garda, which was standard procedure.

It was a week or so after the All-Ireland, I remember the Garda talking to me about the match. Jesus. I remember how wrong it felt. But maybe it was the only way he knew how to handle the situation, I'd guess he meant well.

I had to go from there over to Declan's wedding rehearsal on the Sunday evening.

The machine had just been switched off on Brendan. I remember thinking would it be wrong to turn on the radio? To turn on sport? Would it be disrespectful? My head was in a mess.

But I did turn it on and much as sport is my passion, I just thought in the grand scheme of things, it really doesn't matter.

It's certainly not life or death.

19

Son Of Gaybo

*'People are rising stars one minute and
before long they're yesterday's names.
That's just the nature of it'*

'Cuddly Des'…? Mortifying! I suppose, there are worse
ways to be regarded. But, somehow, that's the image
I ended up with after that spell filling in on *Liveline*
and hosting other shows on RTÉ Radio.

It was only in later years that I learnt RTÉ had carried out
market research to find who might be the preferred choice to
succeed Gay Byrne after he retired from his radio show at the
end of 1998. And I was the 'housewives' favourite' because, well,
I was 'Cuddly Des'. My God!

'Housewives' favourite' sounds so antiquated now, but I can
remember Gay being asked about a fall in his listenership figures
at one point and he put it down to the return to work of so
many women during the 1990s, around 70,000 estimated to
have done so between 1993 and 1995. And women were the
majority of his listenership. There were more of them at home in
those days than men.

Things have changed a lot since then, of course, but advertisers regarded women as their key target market because, they believed, it was women who made most of the decisions about household purchases. Men might have thought they decided who chose the family car, but, so the view went, their preference for a two-seater sports car would be somewhat overridden by the woman asking where would the baby and the shopping go?

So, if you were the 'housewives' favourite', you were also the advertisers' favourite.

• • • • • • •

When Gay began cutting back on his days doing the radio show, after a health scare in 1995, it was Joe Duffy, who had been his reporter on the show, who first took over on Mondays and Tuesdays, with Gay looking after the rest of the week.

Gareth O'Callaghan then replaced Joe, but that didn't really work out, so it was at that point, in 1998, I was asked to do Mondays and Tuesdays. And by calling it *The Des Cahill Show*, rather than me just filling in on *The Gay Byrne Show*, they showed a lot of faith in me.

At first I was filling in for Gay during the summers, and then doing those two shows at the start of the week. I really never enjoyed it.

They decided to send me out to interview people at local festivals, which should have been great fun, but in the summer of 1995 I had a savage schedule heading to festivals all over the country. So on Monday I might be in Donegal at the Inishowen Festival, on Tuesday I could be in Clare, on Wednesday it might be Tramore, I was never off the road and was completely shattered by it all. And I was doing *Sunday Sport* too, so there was no end to the week.

But it was around then that some of the press had started calling me 'Son of Gaybo', tipping me to succeed him on radio when he retired, the whole thing genuinely making me feel uncomfortable.

If anyone was 'Son of Gaybo' I think it was Joe. He'd been a great reporter on Gay's show, they had a terrific rapport and I would have guessed he would have had Gay's blessing to take over from him. But they went for me.

Joe found that difficult, he really hardly spoke to me for the next couple of years, but I always felt he had good reason to feel aggrieved. We got past that, though, we get on well now. He more than survived that spell, he went on to have a far more lucrative career than me.

● ● ● ● ● ● ●

When Gay announced that he would retire at the end of 1998, RTÉ decided to rejig the morning schedule. Marian left *Liveline* to take over the 9.00-10.00 slot, Pat would be on for the next two hours, leaving a gap between 12 and one.

And that was the slot I was offered – five days a week and I would no longer be working in sport. And I would be paid well for it.

Much as I loved sport, it was, of course, tempting. But when I asked what kind of programme it would be, it was obvious they didn't know what they wanted from the slot. They were just choosing me because I was popular at the time – 'just be you, Des – people like you' – without giving any thought to what the show should be. Pat was doing the news interviews, Marian was doing the personality interviews, there was *Morning Ireland* before that, I wasn't sure what was left. Would I just be playing music, as Ronan Collins does now? They didn't know. There was no structure. God help us, they just wanted 'Cuddly Des'.

The more I spoke to them, the more I realised it just wasn't going to work, I really didn't need to be doing this, it would be a big mistake on my part to take it on – and leave Sport.

I loved going to Olympic Games, to World Cups, to Ryder Cups, so many of the great sporting events, and I would be giving it all up. So I said no.

I think it was a brave enough decision, a mature one, I was turning down a very good contract, I would have been paid a lot more, but I knew it wouldn't be right.

And that feeling was confirmed, really, by Carrie Crowley's experience in the slot, Carrie having been offered it after I turned it down. It was shapeless, and it did nothing to help her career. Carrie deserved better than that.

I had a lucky escape.

• • • • • • •

I learnt fairly quickly after joining RTÉ just how fickle a business it can be, people are rising stars one minute and before long they're yesterday's names. That's just the nature of it. I think every area of the media is a bit like that, the search is always on for the next big thing, and when they think they've found it they usually make the mistake of completely over-exposing their latest 'star'.

I think Carrie was one who fell victim to that. The public loved her. She was absolutely charming, with the warmest of personalities, a genuinely lovely and gifted woman. She had burst on the scene and within a couple of years she had presented the Eurovision, she was on several TV shows, she was in every women's magazine, she was totally over-exposed.

I just felt nobody minded or managed her, that she needed someone on her behalf to say no to some things. That's not to say she hadn't a mind of her own, of course she had, but when you're being swamped with requests to do this, that and the other you need a neutral voice to ask, "is this really what's best for you?"

In the end Carrie chose to slip away from broadcasting, focussing now on her acting career. Similar has happened to many others through the years, she was just one example.

I was lucky, after that spell of being flavour of the month, I had sport, my first love, to go back to. Not that I ever left it, but trying to combine everything in that period had proved exhausting, and I felt like I was being pulled in all directions. I loved the variety of the work during that time, I enjoyed the challenge of it all, but in the end I was more than happy to go back to focussing on sport.

I've been at RTÉ nearly 35 years now and you see it all the time – new people come along, the media love them, can't get enough of them, then they get over-exposed, people tire of them, and then they fade away.

But you can come back again. I saw that with Mícheál Ó Muircheartaigh and Jimmy Magee, for example, they probably reached the zenith of their popularity towards the end of their careers. They were part of people's childhoods, their voices lodged in their memory banks, and sport tends to stir the best of memories for people.

• • • • • • •

I had few regrets during that period, demanding as it was, it was a fun time, but one thing I was sad about was having to give up *Sportscall* which Con Murphy took over when I started filling in for Gay.

Initially it was just aired on a Monday night, but it became so popular it was extended to Wednesday and Friday nights too.

RTÉ management loved that programme because you would hear accents you didn't hear on any other programme, from every corner of the country. And usually they were complaining about something.

You'd have some people who'd ring in every night – "Would you go away," we'd say – but then you'd get others who never rang a radio station in their lives, but were so passionate about something that happened they were compelled to. There were plenty of cranks too. And you'd get two people who saw the same incident but you wouldn't think it listening to their description of it. But it could be funny as well, all human life called in.

I remember Keith Wood taking a call from us on every show from a Lions tour in South Africa – for no money. He just enjoyed it. And he gave a fantastic insight to it all. If he'd played the previous day it was, "ah, I'm in bits!", you wondered how he was even able to pick up the phone.

The GAA, meanwhile, hated the programme, regularly complaining to RTÉ about some of the discussions. Like the ones about the lack of women's toilets at venues around the country. I'm not making this up. I was amazed when the programme was dropped, but RTÉ were negotiating with the GAA around that time for rights to cover games. Whether there was a connection, who knows?

Mind you, the GAA isn't the only sporting body that we've crossed swords with. I ended up banned by the FAI after a 2011 discussion on *Saturday Sport* ahead of their AGM in Clare that day.

Chief executive John Delaney's handsome salary of €400,000 was raised in the discussion with Roddy Collins and Damien Richardson, the FAI's subsequent letter of complaint to RTÉ, in which they said the matter was now in the hands of solicitors, objecting to the way I handled the chat and to comments I made during it. I'd mentioned that during a previous interview with John, when I'd asked him about the FAI's finances, he'd said to me "you're only a GAA man".

Soon after we asked if we could speak to Republic of Ireland under-19 manager Paul Doolin ahead of the team's European Championship semi-final against Spain but were told he wouldn't be available for me to interview, but he could talk to anyone else in RTÉ.

As the *Sunday Independent's* Dion Fanning put it, "refusing to talk to Des Cahill is a bit like forbidding your children to read Gentle Ben because playing with bears is dangerous". It was a bit like 'Cuddly Des' all over again.

RTÉ stood up for me, insisting my comments were 'fair and balanced'. But on it rumbled.

Until I got a phone call from Denis O'Brien, who was an important man to the FAI, helping fund the salaries of their senior managers in that spell.

I'd got to know Denis through being a patron with the Special Olympics, with which he was heavily involved.

"What's happening with you and John, you're both my friends," he said, advising me to ring John and talk it through.

So I did. And it was resolved. The power of Denis O'Brien.

I went in to Ryle Nugent, head of sport, and told him it was sorted. "HOW?!" It was over.

That was one of *Saturday Sport's* more eventful days, but usually it's just good conversation about sport and reports from games around the country and beyond.

There's a perception that myself and Joanne Cantwell don't get on, that our relationship is spikey, the texts coming in always suggest that. The truth is that Joanne is definitely one of my closest friends in RTÉ now, even though we have nothing in common. Absolutely nothing.

I wasn't sure about teaming up with her at first, initially she struck me as quite cold and difficult, but I grew to not only admire her as a broadcaster but really like her as a person as well.

The contrast between us is huge. We'd have our panel on *Saturday Sport*. Supposing someone had been in a fight during a game the previous Sunday…

I'd go something like, "so, how are things? How's your family? God weren't Liverpool great last night? Did you watch the rugby this morning?" Seven or eight minutes later, "so, you were in a fight last week?"

Joanne: "You were in a fight last week?"

That's the difference between us.

I ease people towards a tricky issue, Joanne goes straight for it and their heartbeat stops. Then they look at me and I'm just shrugging my shoulders, like 'don't blame me for her ruthlessness'.

Joanne has even less patience for yarns.

She was off one day and I did an interview with Paddy Mulligan, I got so much positive reaction to the interview via text. My God, the waffle that went on.

Paddy went up against Eoin Hand for the job as Irish manager – and he lost by two votes and one of the votes against him was an FAI fella he had once thrown a bun at on an away trip. I thought it was a great story.

But Joanne was like, "it was a story about throwing buns!" We're, well, different.

She'd be in there two or three hours before we go on air. She hates when I come in early because she wants to study the news and research stuff. When I come in I'm just talking. Rabbiting on. She has no patience for that.

She's much younger than me, she has young kids, she doesn't take a drink, so on almost every level we're different. But she always helps me, because I'm involved with the Cuala football team, sometimes on a Saturday we'd have a big game, the programme goes two to nine, she'd facilitate me slipping away to the match.

So we get on really well and we chat about things, which I wouldn't do with most others. I've a lot of time for Joanne on a personal level.

When it became known that Michael Lyster was going to retire from *The Sunday Game* live programme, myself and Joanne talked about it. She asked me if I was interested in the job, but I said I loved the evening show because, journalistically, it was more challenging. But given the newspapers were speculating on the afternoon programme, I was wondering if that's where I really should be.

However, while the papers were saying I was in the running for the job, I never was.

Ryle Nugent, then head of sport, had told me he wanted me to stay on the evening *Sunday Game*, that I was a safe pair of hands for it because most of the controversy comes out of that programme.

To me Joanne was the obvious choice for the live *Sunday Game*. And while it was historic and certainly newsworthy that a woman had been chosen for the job, and I appreciated all that, for me it was just about the best person being picked to take over from Michael.

And that person was, undoubtedly, Joanne.

If Joe Brolly starts telling anecdotes about bun-throwing, he'll regret it.

20

The Sunday Game

'The dickie bow looked absolutely ridiculous, so I said "oh, go for the dickie bow, it looks much better." Tomas is not stupid, he's sharp, but he fell for it'

At the back of *The Sunday Game* studio where all the sets are kept there's a grand piano that is often wheeled out for *The Late Late Show*. One night before going live, Joe Brolly went over, sat down and played the most incredible piece. I was in awe.

And then when the programme started we went, in the blink of an eye, from the peaceful tranquillity of Chopin to a snarling Rottweiler letting rip about some football issue or another.

Life is rarely dull with Joe, or with any of *The Sunday Game* panellists. And it wouldn't be true to say that they're universally loved. I remember Pat Spillane laughingly boasting one time about getting a letter that was addressed: 'Pat Spillane, Bollocks, Co Kerry.' And, he said, "it reached me!"

I was telling the story to a young fella in RTÉ and he said, "sure there was no need to put his name on it, 'Bollocks, Co Kerry' would have found him."

• • • • • • •

I took over from Pat as presenter of *The Sunday Game* in 2009. Michael Lyster had being doing both the live afternoon programme and then the one in the evening, but it was too much.

Pat had been a surprise choice for the job, but by then Gary Lineker had started working for the BBC so it had become the fashion to choose well known former players for presenting jobs.

Pat took it seriously, but it was difficult for him, uncomfortable, because it was almost a case of poacher-turned-gamekeeper, he was now the presenter instead of being one of the lads. I think he might have struggled with that, it was a strange situation for everyone and some felt it just wasn't working. So it was decided that Pat would go back to being an analyst, and RTÉ would find a new presenter for the programme.

I genuinely wasn't expecting to get the job, so when Glen Killane, then head of sport, offered it to me, it came out of the blue. I had been doing *The Road To Croker*, the mid-week programme, and was really enjoying it, but, in my view, *The Sunday Game* was the ultimate job.

I'd always had a reverential respect for the programme. Since it began in 1979, in a much more limited form than we have now, showing maybe just two games instead of them all, it had become an institution.

I have it on good authority that if you're in a rural pub on a Sunday night at half nine and it comes on, the place goes quiet. Everyone's glued to it. And I remember Caroline telling me that after Donegal won the 2012 All-Ireland she was in the Burlington with around 4,000 of her fellow county people (who were in, well, high spirits) when *The Sunday Game* came on. And the 4,000 of them started loudly singing its theme tune, and then it was 'shh, shh, shhhhh'. It was a fantastic image.

When a new season starts, the amount of people on Twitter who say 'this theme tune makes me happy'. James Last's *Jagerlatein*, the sound of summer. Which, of course, is why there was uproar back in 2004 when it was decided to change it as part of an effort to freshen up the programme. They brought it back four years later, they had to, there was no end to the complaints. And not just from Ireland. It had a foreign audience too, if not a legal one at the time.

It was back in the 1980s when a guy in Ireland would record *The Sunday Game* each week, he had a whole bank of video machines, and then he would get on the early flight to New York with a bag of 100 videos. He'd arrive and a taxi would bring him to each Irish pub and he'd get around 200 quid for each video. And all the Irish would come in on the Monday, have a few pints and watch *The Sunday Game*. RTÉ eventually had to sue him.

Happily, with the online streaming service GAAGO, it's a little easier (and legal) to watch the live and evening *Sunday Game* now, no matter where you are. Changed times.

What did make me hesitate at first, though, when I was offered the job was that by then I had been in RTÉ for 25 years and had become used to working across all sports and I really loved the variety, so I was reluctant to give it up.

In the earlier days I could have gone in to commentary in virtually any of the sports, I would have been mentored for that role, and later Glen had suggested there would be a place for me in our rugby coverage, but that didn't materialise once Ryle Nugent replaced him in the job.

But I just never wanted to be restricted to one sport, and Glen took that on board when we talked about *The Sunday Game*.

He agreed that I could continue to cover other sports, so that was that settled.

I was the new presenter, and I was thrilled.

· · · · · · ·

It was probably the 2010 World Cup final in South Africa that made me realise just how much of an institution *The Sunday Game* had become.

It was on the same day that Meath and Louth played in the Leinster final at Croke Park, the game ending on a hugely controversial note when the referee allowed a Meath goal that should have been ruled out. Louth, a point up, had been seconds away from winning their first Leinster title since 1957 – instead they suffered a two-point defeat.

There was uproar. Angry Louth supporters ran on to the pitch at the end and confronted the referee, Martin Sludden, who was jostled and shoved. A bottle was thrown from the stand and hit a steward on the head. The whole thing turned violent and ugly, it was extraordinary.

There was a fair chance that *The Sunday Game* that night was going to get a big audience, as it always does when there's controversy. But we were on after the World Cup final between Holland and Spain and when it went to extra time I began to get a sinking feeling.

It wasn't just going to be the extra 30 minutes, World Cup broadcasters are obligated to stay on air for another 45 minutes after the game ends, so I was pretty sure that with everyone having to be up for work on the Monday morning, no-one would be watching us. Or very few.

In the end I was just grateful to Andrés Iniesta for getting the winner in the 116th minute. If it had gone to penalties we'd have been there all night.

Still, *The Sunday Game* didn't start until around midnight – and the audience, unbelievably, was over half a million. When you think of it, that many people sitting up to the early hours to watch the highlights of a Leinster final, albeit a highly contentious one, hear the reaction from both camps and listen to what Colm O'Rourke and the rest of the panel had to say about it all. It was an incredible figure and it really drove home for me, a year in to taking over the presenting job, what a privilege it was to be involved in a programme that was such a big part of GAA followers' lives.

· · · · · · ·

I've been lucky with the *Sunday Game* team. Television is all about team work, there has to be mutual respect. A presenter could be totally exposed without the production team having his back.

Rory O'Neill is my editor and sidekick. He's a passionate GAA man and we work really well together. We often don't agree, but our friendship is strong. I've had great directors like Kevin O'Connell, who is an expert at reading my body language and sensing where I want to go to, Dave Berry, who is an artist in studio, and Niall O'Flynn who also has great editorial sense. They're like a great comfort blanket.

The Sunday Game highlights programme has long been a big production, but with the significant increase in the number of Championship games since the change in format in both football and hurling, it has become a beast.

On the busiest weekends of the summer, when there might be anything like 15 or 16 football, hurling and camogie games on around the country, it has up to 180 people working on it.

Most of them are part of the three main outside broadcast units, each with a crew of around 40 that includes everyone from directors, camera operators, reporters, floor managers, vision mixers, sound engineers, the BCO's (Broadcast Co-Ordinators hugely important and helpful to me) and so on. Then there would be smaller three, two and one camera OBs at the other grounds.

There are also the riggers who have to build gantries at some of the venues, lifting cameras up to their positions, running cables all around the ground, getting everything set up. It really is a massive operation.

In an attempt to cut down on costs, RTÉ closed its outside broadcast department some years ago, so now uses the private operator that gives the best price for a Championship season. For the 2017 All-Ireland football final, for example, they would have hired a 53-strong OB unit, with another 10 or so RTÉ staff working alongside them. And that's for one day, one venue, just two games, the minor and senior finals. But that's what it takes.

Back in the studio, meanwhile, it's full on for the evening programme, under a fantastic editor, Rory O'Neill. Most of the team are in from about 10am on the Sunday until midnight. We have seven edit suites working through the day, the editors cutting the matches down to the length required. It's non-stop for them, starting with work on the late Saturday games. They don't get a break all day, they just have food brought to them at their desks and they carry on working. It's intense.

We'd often get complaints about the highlights of some of the games being too short, but on those busy weekends, especially since the qualifiers started, squeezing everything in to those two hours is a hell of a challenge. We tried pushing the programme out to two and a half hours but it was too long, the feedback was that finishing around midnight was just too late, people had to be up for work in the morning, so we decided two hours was really the maximum. So it's simply impossible to give every game as much time as it might merit.

The place is buzzing with activity all day, people hard at work in the dubbing suites, the graphics editors doing their thing, it takes a huge effort from them all. There are a lot of highly skilled and really talented people working on the programme.

And the analysts are in around 10am on Sunday too to go through Saturday's games. We go in to a tiny dark room, four of us huddled together watching a match, then another, then we'd split up and watch the highlights of other games. And then there are the live games.

The cost of it all is, of course, huge, I really doubt that any other station would be prepared to spend that much on producing a highlights programme that requires such a big team and so many resources.

It would be far easier just to do two live matches and not go near a highlights programme, but the GAA is very important to RTÉ, as the national broadcaster there is a sense of duty when it comes to covering our national games as broadly and as well as we can.

And a big part of that effort is trying to bring in informed panellists who have strong opinions and who aren't afraid to speak their minds.

In my view the guys on the night time programme should be paid more than *The Sunday Game* live pundits, even if they are regarded as the 'lead' panellists. Their job is a lot easier in comparison. They do what they do well, but the evening analysts have to put in a huge amount of work in comparison, they're still dissecting the day's games long after *The Sunday Game* live lads have gone home.

· · · · · · · ·

I know Donal Óg Cusack found it far more fulfilling working on the night programme than the live one, he enjoyed having the time to do in-depth analysis. And Donal Óg would be one of the panellists who I have the greatest of respect for. A really interesting man, his passion for hurling knows no bounds. He and Brendan Cummins have done brilliant analysis for us. Maybe it's a goalkeeper thing?

Their preparation is meticulous. Brendan would show you something on his laptop in advance of a match, maybe about the puck-outs, something to watch out for. And he'd always call it right. Donal Óg too. The younger football lads, who have only recently retired, Tomas Ó Se, Ciaran Whelan, Colm Cooper and Sean Cavanagh are others, telling you what to look out for in a game. It's fascinating. It's a real privilege sitting with them.

You'd get the odd spoofer who wouldn't put in the work at all before games and would then just try to wing it. (They don't last too long). But then you'd have the likes of Tony Davis and

Anthony Tohill, who have since packed it in, who were both excellent analysts. They would go out of their way to be as accurate as they could be. The amount of notes they would take…and some of the others would snigger. Like they were swots.

And it can be childish at times. I would have great time for Cyril Farrell, his in-depth knowledge of the players is fantastic, he'd be better informed than anyone on hurling. He was helping Davy Fitzgerald with the Limerick Institute of Technology in the Fitzgibbon Cup at one stage so he knew everyone coming through at that level.

Regularly before a programme we'd be sitting around chatting and Cyril would be saying "that fella played wing-back all year with the minors and in college he played centre-back", and so on. And then the programme would start and one of the others would rob his lines. It's always happening. The amount of that that goes on generally, you wouldn't believe, it's schoolyard stuff. But Cyril is a particular victim of it.

• • • • • • •

With a talented, opinionated rogues' gallery featuring the likes of Joe, Donal Óg, Pat and Ger Loughnane, you really need to be on your guard. And that's a challenge when my RTÉ shift has me up at 4.40am on Thursday and Fridays, followed by a long day on radio on Saturday, and then Sunday is a 12 or 14 hour day. But trust me, if you're feeling tired you can't let it get the better of you, with these fellas you have to be at your sharpest.

They're huge personalities, and they're testing you out all the time. Brolly, especially, is always pushing the boundaries. He's the greatest conundrum of a human being I've ever met. Inside there's this unbelievably kind, generous, social-minded person, but he's also the greatest hooer on earth. He's a cranky, whingey fecker. And all of that is rolled in to one.

He makes a lot of people nervous, but I think I'm strong with him, I enjoy the jousting, I enjoy taking him on. We've one or two presenters who like the status quo, consensus – I enjoy conflict, the rows. And there's no shortage of them on *The Sunday Game*. And Joe constantly challenges you. Even when it comes to his appearance.

"Joe, would you straighten your tie?"

Anyone else would want their tie to be straight, but he'll pull it more crooked.

"Joe, could you tidy your hair?"

And he'll stick his fingers in it to make it more tossed.

He'll slouch back in his chair like a bold child. The director would say to the floor manager, "get Joe to sit up straight." "Why would I sit up straight?" he'd ask. "Why should I sit up straight for you?"

"Jesus, Joe."

He's become a brand. He's the most genuine man in the world, but at times he's a complete rogue. Sometimes I wonder if even he believes some of the stuff he comes out with.

It reached a point where I had to put a stop to the lads checking their phones during ad breaks. They were all looking up Twitter to see what was being said about them. And social media can be brutal for all of us.

I can take it, I know already that I'm a fat bastard, and I'm well used to 'Jesus, look at the dyed head on him'. That's a debate that rages on Twitter every time I wear hair gel when I'm on TV. (For the record, I do NOT dye my hair, it's just naturally gorgeous). Half the time the comments are about what the panellists are wearing. Donal Óg started it all with the whole dapper look. My wife would watch *The Sunday Game* just to see what he was wearing. Jesus, it's got ridiculous. A lot of them get suited and booted by a local tailor, then they do their selfies and they go up on Twitter.

When Donal Óg was in his debonair prime, Tomas Ó Se came in and asked should he wear a tie or a dickie bow. A west Kerry man asking that. If his uncle Paudie saw him…

The dickie bow looked absolutely ridiculous, so I said "oh, go for the dickie bow, it looks much better." Dave Berry, the director backed me up.

Tomas is not stupid, he's sharp, but he fell for it.

So he chose the dickie bow and within seconds Twitter blew up. The first ad break Tomas turns to me and says, "you absolute bastard."

• • • • • • •

I remember one of the panellists one time savaging a Roscommon player. Savaged him.

I said, "what the hell was that all about?!"

He says, "do you know his father?"

"No."

"A complete bollocks."

"What's that got to do with your man?! Jesus! What if your son got judged by you?"

Now you see why I have to be on my guard.

21

Suspicious Minds

*'Every inter-county manager wants
to give his team any edge he can find, but
it's incredibly frustrating that one of the
ways they think they can do it is by limiting
access to the media. That will never make
any sense to me'*

It was back in 2011 that Stephen Cluxton captained Dublin to All-Ireland victory for the first time, scoring the point from a free that won the game. Having been MC at the city-centre homecoming, I managed to find myself on board the team's open-top bus the following day as it made its way to his club, Parnells in Coolock, with Sam Maguire on board.

It was around 8.30 in the evening and families were running out of their houses to greet the bus, most of the kids in their pyjamas, clapping and cheering as it went by. The players were having a ball, leaning over the side, waving at the supporters.

The captain, though, stayed in his seat.

"Would you not stand up Stephen, they'd love to see you," I said.

"Na, it's not my thing."

Stephen's only thing is winning matches with Dublin and then going back to his life outside football. He has no interest in any of the rest of it. So we barely know him.

It was a few years later, after he had captained Dublin to another win, in the 2017 All-Ireland final, that he gave one of the most powerful speeches I ever heard from a sportsperson.

I was hosting the players' medal presentation where the only other people in the room were their families. Often these are fund-raising events with supporters allowed to attend, but Jim Gavin, the manager, wanted this to be just for the players and their families; it was their time.

Stephen stood up and spoke for around 10 minutes, mainly about his team-mate Denis Bastick who was retiring. He talked about how Denis responded after he had lost his place in the team. Instead of sulking he just dug deeper, worked harder in the gym, trained even harder, he just drove on, doing everything he could to make himself stronger and fitter to win his place back, while all the time being hugely supportive towards those who were in the team.

Stephen spoke of what an impact his attitude had, how he was an inspiration for everyone on the panel. It was just incredibly moving, the respect and affection he had for Denis evident, and it gave you a real insight to the bond between the players on that panel. And many of them told me after how the speech had the hairs on the back of their necks standing up. I could only imagine the impact a Stephen Cluxton talk in the dressing room before a game would have. You would probably feel unbeatable.

All I remember thinking was that I wished the public saw

this side of Stephen, that they got to know him; instead they've hardly even heard his voice, apart from those brief speeches he delivers in the Hogan Stand after winning All-Irelands. He is one of the leading Irish sportsmen of his generation yet he probably wouldn't even be recognised by anyone beyond those who follow Gaelic football. And that applies to so many of today's great players, to the point where I think many of *The Sunday Game* pundits are better known than them. And that is not a good thing.

In Stephen's case it's his choice, this isn't a media 'ban' imposed by his manager, he's his own man, this is what he wants. He never does interviews, he has no interest in raising his 'profile', he shuns the limelight, it's not for him. And that's a choice you absolutely have to respect, one, I would guess, that was partly influenced by the flak he received from the media, including ourselves on *The Sunday Game*, earlier in his career when his short fuse got him in to trouble, like when he was sent off in a game against Armagh in 2003.

So I understand his attitude, completely, but I just think it's a terrible pity that we haven't got to know him better.

I got a glimpse at that presentation of what an interesting and articulate man he is. It's our loss that we never get to see that side of him.

• • • • • • •

The problem nowadays is that so many of our great players have the same low profile as Stephen when they should be household names. But it's often not because of any choice they make themselves, rather it's because an ever increasing number of managers deny the media access to them. And in doing so, they deny these players the profile they deserve.

It's hugely frustrating because the net effect of it all is that probably most of the greatest players of recent years are barely known to the public by the time they retire; they'd walk by you and you wouldn't recognise them. Quite often we only really get to know them when they become analysts, like some of the Kilkenny greats, Jackie Tyrrell, Henry Shefflin, Tommy Walsh and Michael Kavanagh, for example. All great characters with a great sense of fun, but we don't get to see their personalities at all until they finish playing.

If players want that level of anonymity, as Stephen Cluxton does, they are, of course, perfectly entitled to it, it's their choice, but there are others whose careers could benefit from having the kind of profile their sporting achievements merit. It's in stark contrast to the greats of earlier years who were familiar to us all, and often were able to build better lives because of that, in terms of work opportunities.

Wexford's Lee Chin stands out as one of the few whose profile is high because he engages with the media and we're able to get to know him. He did some really interesting interviews recently where he talked about how he survives without working because he has a good income from sponsors and does ambassador work for various brands. It allows him to be a full-time athlete, to have the lifestyle of a professional sportsman, to fully focus on training and get himself in to the best condition possible for his sport.

He contrasted his own lifestyle with that of the majority of players who wouldn't have the same profile and therefore no additional income, so they have the tough task of combining busy working lives with their inter-county careers and all that involves.

It was fascinating, and a real insight to the life of one of the stars of today's GAA and the disparity that exists between players at that level and all the rest. It was especially interesting because we rarely get insights like that any more, Lee being one of the few to come out and talk honestly about his situation.

Predictably, he got plenty of stick after the interviews, but as soon as he has a poor couple of years he'll be back working again, there's nothing long-term in this. He's making the most of his current situation, like several other players are doing, and I don't blame them for that at all. But just hearing him talk about it was refreshing. He's another bright, capable young man with a compelling story, and because he has been willing to share it, it has helped open up opportunities for him.

And on the managerial front, Davy Fitzgerald is someone who is never shy about opening up. I hugely admire him, I love him. A big personality who's never afraid to speak his mind, even if he ruffles a few feathers along the way. That's such a rarity now. I wish there were more Lee Chins and Davy Fitzgeralds.

· · · · · · ·

Of course every inter-county manager wants to give his team any edge he can find, but it's incredibly frustrating that one of the ways they think they can do it is by limiting access to the media. That will never make any sense to me.

Not that Babs Keating didn't have his own issues with the media in his time, he had plenty of them, but I loved his line some years ago when he was talking about his Tipperary players: "Sure if I can't put them out in front of a few fat journalists, how can I let them out in front of 80,000 people in Croke Park?"

It was a good point. I wish more of today's managers had the same trust in their players.

I remember back in 1996, two days before the hurling All-Ireland final between Wexford and Limerick, I was in Wexford Town doing a live report for *The Gay Byrne Show*. We had a truck up at the back of Dunne Stores and a few thousand people turned out, among them a group of the Wexford players who manager Liam Griffin had brought down to us. I interviewed them all and then Larry O'Gorman sang *Purple and Gold* with the band, the crowd loved it. I remember saying to Liam some years later how times have changed, you wouldn't get that kind of access to players now, especially so close to a final. But he just said he wanted them to enjoy it all, be part of it, understand what it meant to the Wexford people. It was a special time in the players' lives and he wanted them to savour the whole experience. And it didn't do them any harm – two days later they won Wexford its first All-Ireland in 28 years.

Nowadays most times we ask for a player for an interview on the radio, the answer is no. And quite often at the provincial launches for the Championship only the managers will be there, no players, and their interviews from that day have to be stretched out by radio and the papers over the following few weeks because often there will be no more, or very little, access. It's become ridiculous.

And even when players are allowed to do interviews they can sound like they're trained to say nothing. I'd even question the value of doing post-match interviews any more, more often than not they're utterly bland, the sole intent to give nothing away. I'd prefer to give the air-time to our panellists to analyse the games and offer some strong opinions rather than have to listen to banalities.

But while I do think it's getting worse, it's certainly not a recent development. In my own experience it goes back to Kevin Heffernan, the great Dublin manager of the 1970s and early 1980s.

Heffo loathed the media. He would have been one of the first to insist on 'what goes on in the camp, stays in the camp'. His captain Tony Hanahoe would have backed that up very strongly.

In that sense, not much has changed at all. I'm aware of Dublin players today who wouldn't even tell their own families how training was going, about team news, and so on. One asked his brother who would be playing the following Sunday, the reply was "loose lips sink ships". But that's not unique to Dublin. Donegal would have been the same under Jim McGuinness, plenty of other counties too buy in to all that.

Back in the '70s the Dubs became the focus of huge media attention, it had never been that intense before. It was almost pop star stuff. The evening papers, especially, couldn't get enough of them, there was wall to wall coverage of the team – the demand for it was there.

Heffo just didn't like that attention, and he certainly didn't like the amount of it, so from early on he developed a suspicion of the media and did his best to keep a distance between it and his players.

I liked Heffo a lot, he had a real twinkle in his eye, and I was honoured when he asked me to MC the ceremony when he was awarded the Freedom of Dublin. But even in his later years, long after management, when we'd be chatting and I'd ask him something, he'd say: "Why are you asking that?" We'd laugh about it; he never lost that suspicion.

So it's not a new thing – Jim Gavin is by no means the first manager to look upon the media with distrust. And it seems like more and more are becoming the same. If you put it to them that the public want to hear what their players have to say, their response would be "no, they just want us to win an All-Ireland." Heffo felt the same, "what's to be gained here?"

• • • • • • •

More often than not, managers begin restricting access to players after there has been a controversy involving one of them and they're unhappy with how the issue was covered. With Mickey Harte and Tyrone, though, who began a boycott of RTÉ in 2011, one that continues to this day, it was a very different set of circumstances that led to the breakdown in relations.

I'd always got on well with Mickey, one of the most successful managers of his era. Tyrone would use the Cuala pitch for a kick-around when they were down in Dublin for a game and staying in Killiney Castle. He came to a Cuala lunch one time too and even travelled to Mayo to appear on *The Road to Croker*, the television programme I presented. He was always cooperative with us, there was never a problem.

The series of events that led to that breakdown began with a strange decision by Mickey to ask a group of other inter-county managers to sign a letter that was sent to RTÉ Director General Noel Curran asking that Brian Carthy, a friend of Mickey, be given a more prominent commentating role on RTÉ Radio following the retirement of Micheál Ó Muircheartaigh.

The letter was signed by Mickey, Brian Cody (Kilkenny), Mickey Moran (Leitrim), Conor Counihan (Cork), Kieran McGeeney (Kildare), Justin McNulty (Laois), Kevin Walsh (Sligo) and Glenn Ryan (Longford), although Ryan said that he had not given the go-ahead for his name to be included. I was contacted at the time by a couple of people who told me Mickey had phoned them at home asking if they would put their name to the letter, which left them in an awkward situation. "What was I to say to him?" as one asked.

The fact was that rather than replacing Micheál with a single commentator, RTÉ had decided to go with a group of commentators, and Brian was part of that team. While Mickey was perfectly entitled to express his views on the matter, it wasn't his right to tell RTÉ how they should deploy their staff. And RTÉ was correct to stand its ground on the matter.

The situation deteriorated from there and the letter was leaked to the press, which angered Mickey.

And it got a whole lot worse when John Murray did a skit about the situation on his radio programme. Incredibly, in light of the murder in Mauritius of Mickey's daughter Michaela while she was on her honeymoon, reference was made in it to the Dalai Lama who Mickey, a deeply religious man, had gone to hear speak in Limerick after her death. And then it ended with a clip from the song *Pretty Little Girl from Omagh*, a song Michaela used to sing.

I just could not believe it.

Everybody in the sports office was absolutely stunned.

Editorially, it was just inexcusable. I think John quickly realised just how wrong it had been so he spoke with Mickey and apologised.

But I could totally understand Mickey's anger. He already had an issue with RTÉ after the Brian Carthy business, but this made it all the more entrenched and bitter, neither he nor his players speaking to RTÉ since.

The disappointment for the sports department was primarily

that such pain had been caused to the Harte family, but a consequence was that he was taking it out on the department when we had nothing to do with the skit. Even though there was no intention to disrespect Michaela's memory, thoughtless as the skit was, we were genuinely horrified by it, not least because many of us had met Michaela many times over the years and were stunned by her death and the nature of it. I remember her being on *Up for the Match* one year, she just lit up the place, she had an incredible charm and warmth and had great values as a human being.

Her loss, in such circumstances, left Mickey bearing the most intense of grief, I can't even begin to imagine what he and his family endured, and continue to do so. When I travelled up to his home at the time of her funeral to pay my respects, there were literally thousands of people waiting outside. I will never forget the atmosphere, the searing pain and outpouring of sympathy and support for the Harte family and Michaela's husband John McAreavey.

I think Mickey probably just decided there and then that he was done with RTÉ. And that's a huge regret for me.

The interesting thing is that once several Tyrone players stopped playing for their county, like Ryan McMenamin, Philip Jordan, Brian McGuigan and Sean Cavanagh, they were all happy to come on *The Sunday Game*, but while they were part of the panel they were sensitive to Mickey's wishes and loyal to him, so they wouldn't deal with RTÉ at all, which, of course, was their right. But I remember one of their young lads being named man of the match in his first game for Tyrone and he wasn't allowed to come out and collect the award. It would have been such a big thing for him, for his family and his club. To me it was just unfortunate that others were getting caught up in this.

I would never claim to have been Mickey's friend, but we had, I think, a mutual respect. It saddened me that when we would be covering Tyrone games he didn't even want us to say hello, he didn't want to engage with us at all.

I remember once tipping him on the shoulder and shaking his hand. He just turned instinctively and returned the gesture, he didn't realise at first it was me. And I think he regretted even putting his hand out to me.

It's been a desperately sad affair.

22

Three Of A Kind

'Katie, Sonia and Annalise, the last three Irish women to win Olympic medals, have all been inspirational figures in our sport'

I think we've been intrigued by Katie Taylor since we first came to know her. On the one hand she was this painfully shy young girl, uncomfortable with too much attention, humble, quietly spoken, almost to the point of whispering, a devout Christian. To me she was like the girl next door.

And then she'd go in to the ring and transform in to this hugely confident explosive fighter who would, more often than not, batter her opponents. The contrast fascinated people, one Katie was unrecognisable from the other.

That charming humility, I think, is what most endeared her to everyone. It would be perfectly natural if success and fame changed you, as it probably does most people, but it never changed her. That's part of what makes her special. That's why she is so loved.

I remember someone telling me about Paul McGrath doing a press conference after his testimonial at Lansdowne Road and a reporter beginning a question with something like "you were one of the greatest players ever to play for Ireland…" at which point Paul, quite genuinely, said, "who, me?"

There is a lot of that about Katie too.

She has been an award winner at the *Irish Times'* Sportswoman of the Year awards just about every year since it started, winning the overall award in 2007, 2008, 2012 and 2014, which gives some indication of how long she has been at the very top of her sport. And she's still going strong.

It's always been so interesting to see the impact she has on the other award winners each year, all women who have achieved extraordinary things themselves. They all want to meet Katie, have their photo taken with her, but they're often too shy to approach her, so many of them are just in awe. I'd say, "did you get the photo with her?" and they'd be "ah, I didn't want to go over". And Katie is genuinely completely oblivious to this, she's busy being in awe of the likes of Nina Carberry, Rena Buckley and Leona Maguire.

So, I started getting them all together before the ceremony so they could chat and then have photos taken. And when the ice is broken they all start bringing their mothers and fathers over to meet her. Katie still has no idea that they feel this way towards her. She doesn't put herself on any pedestal, and never has done, but there is that incredible respect and admiration for her from her sporting peers.

• • • • • • •

I get to MC a lot of events, but I'm not sure I ever enjoyed one as much as Katie's homecoming in Bray after she won gold in

London 2012. It was by the seafront on the most beautiful of days, the sun was beating down, the sea was an azure blue, the sky cloudless, there was music and singing, and a crowd of around 20,000, who had come from every corner of Ireland, were there waiting to greet her.

I could see from the crowd that day just how much joy Katie's success had brought. It was another example of how someone can transcend their sport and just make the country feel good about itself.

She was genuinely overwhelmed by the reception, but I remember sensing that her overall emotion at the time was just one of relief. Exhilaration of course too, she had, after all, achieved her dream, but there was enormous pressure on her going in to those Games. She was the poster girl for women's boxing, she more than anyone was responsible for it finally being introduced to the Olympics Games, and nothing less than gold was expected. And that was an enormous weight to carry.

And she must have felt that pressure even more when she walked in to the ExCel Arena for her final that day, the place thronged with Irish supporters, the atmosphere electric, the chanting and singing and roaring simply deafening.

It was a nerve-wrackingly tight final, too, against Russia's Sofya Ochigava. I was sitting alongside Jimmy Magee at his commentary position, for what proved to be his final commentary on an Irish gold medal, and although I'm no expert in boxing, even I knew Katie was really up against it.

It was 2-2 after the first round but she trailed 4-3 after the second and I remember us all feeling sick with worry. The final two rounds seemed to last forever, but she dug deep and used all her class and experience. She was 7-5 up after the third and when the referee raised her arm in triumph after the fourth and final round, Katie having won 10-8, there was an explosion of pure joy in the arena.

I'd known Katie since her early days in boxing and we'd always got on well. I think when you've followed someone's journey closely from when they started out, it adds to the emotion of the moment when you see them achieve their dream. And I rarely felt as emotional as I did when I saw her on that podium kissing that gold medal, and then standing to attention for the anthem.

I headed back to the Olympic Stadium after, a journey that proved close to interminable, to watch Usain Bolt in the 200m that evening, but my head was buzzing all night from having watched Katie Taylor win gold. It was magical.

• • • • • • •

In many ways, Katie and Annalise Murphy's Olympic journeys went in opposite directions, Katie left heartbroken by her experience in Rio having reached the highest of highs in London, Annalise left devastated by what happened to her in 2012, and then making up for it all in Rio with a silver medal.

Although they're from very different backgrounds and there really couldn't be a greater contrast between their sports, the two also have a lot in common. Annalise can be kind of shy as well, and she has that same humility. They're both bright, warm and engaging. But like Katie, she's teak tough when it comes to her sport.

And they both gave interviews after their Olympic anguish that made such an impression, Annalise left shattered and in tears after finishing fourth in her sailing event in London, when a medal had been in sight, Katie looking ashen-faced in her interview after losing to Finland's Mira Potkonen in her opening bout in Rio. Her pain was palpable.

They were both hard to watch, not least because you knew how much work both women had put in in the four years leading up to the Games.

The redemption for Annalise in Rio, as she saw it herself, was a wonderful thing, you couldn't but feel overwhelming happiness for her when she won that medal, that and the O'Donovan brothers' silver in rowing the highlights of a fortnight that was partly overshadowed by events surrounding Pat Hickey.

Annalise has managed to maintain her profile since, partly through her involvement in the Volvo Ocean Race, even if her sport doesn't enjoy quite the same profile. But her personality and lovely sense of humour give her that likeability factor, and I suspect there's a lot more to come from her in her sporting career.

• • • • • • •

Annalise's story, while again so different in many ways, had echoes for me of Sonia O'Sullivan's Olympic experience in that both women showed incredible resolve to come back from huge disappointments and finally get their hands on an Olympic medal.

While what happened to Sonia in Atlanta was a huge story in itself, it was overshadowed to an extent by what was happening with Michelle Smith. Going in to those 1996 Games, Sonia would have been our main medal hope, so outstanding had her form been, and I wondered at the time if Michelle's medal haul at the pool heaped more pressure on her. Sonia confirmed as much in her *Irish Times* column a couple of years ago.

Everyone thought what she achieved in the pool would take the pressure off me, when actually it probably added to the expectation. After all, I was the world champion, fastest in the world, so all I had to do was turn up and collect the gold medal. Nothing could have been further from the truth.

In the end, Atlanta was a desperate let-down for her, she failed to finish the 5000m final, complaining of a stomach upset, and was clearly unwell when she came second last in her heat for the 1500m.

It was after the 5000m final that her father John uttered the immortal line: "Lads, nobody died tonight…she'll be back."

Perspective. Which we all tend to lose at times like that. But everyone was devastated for her. She was one of the greatest runners in the world and whatever happened, she was left physically incapable of reproducing the form she had shown all the way up to those Games.

The incident before the 5000m final, when she was made to change her running gear in the tunnel because of a dispute over kit sponsorship, only added to the frustration – and was met with no little anger over her being treated in that way. But her father's prediction was accurate – she came back. And in some style.

Between Atlanta and Sydney, Sonia enjoyed enormous success, most notably at the World Cross-Country Championships and the European Championships, before taking time out in 1999 to give birth to her daughter Ciara.

We greet every one of our Olympic medals with joy, but I'm not sure many would have been celebrated with as much elation as Sonia's silver in Sydney.

I'll never forget the sight of her coming around the bend chasing Gabriela Szabo in the 5000m final, certain that she would catch the Romanian and take gold. And there was a moment when you really thought she was going to do it, she seemed to have so much strength left in her legs. But Szabo, somehow, held her off to win the race by less than a quarter of a second.

Still, Sonia had her Olympic medal and all you could do was marvel at not just at her brilliance, but her guts in coming back from that desperate low in Atlanta.

And when you look back on Sonia's remarkable career you know that her medal collection would have been even greater if it wasn't for opponents who cheated. She would have had two more World Championship gold medals but for Chinese runners we now know were part of systematic doping within their country. And while Szabo never failed a test, suspicion hung over her too when a car driven by a family friend was seized by French border police and a performance-enhancing product was found inside. It proved nothing, but it left us all wondering.

• • • • • • •

For Katie, of course, life changed utterly after Rio when she turned professional. I was worried for her when she did. I worried that she was in a bad place, she was heartbroken by what had happened. There were family issues too, Katie parting ways with her father Pete earlier in the year after he had coached her from the very start. And she lost at the World Championships for the first time in 11 years just three months before Rio, so the build-up couldn't have been more difficult.

I think everyone just wanted to hug her after her defeat, it really was heart-breaking to see her so distraught, especially when she had that personal upheaval in her life too. I didn't know what to do after the fight. I would text her every now and then as she was preparing for fights, wishing her well, or congratulating her after victories, on the good days. This was a rare bad day, but I just didn't know what was the right thing to do. In the end I felt she just needed space so I left her alone.

But since she turned pro, she's experienced nothing but good days again in the ring.

We tend to view the world of professional boxing as one inhabited by sharks, so I worried that she wouldn't be looked after well. She would be dealing with very different people to the close-knit community of the Irish amateur team that she had been part of for so long.

But so far her professional career has gone perfectly, all that saddens me is that because all her fights have been in the UK and the US and have only been on pay-per-view television, we're losing the connection we had with her. She's in such a different world now.

All I hope is that she earns enough money to get out of it when she feels the time is right, and that she's secure for the rest of her days. It's the least she deserves.

When I saw that spectacular Lucozade Sport television ad that she did in 2011, I smiled thinking back to when I helped her get her first sponsorship deal. It was during one of her early interviews she mentioned having a banger of a car, so I had a word with a couple of friends involved with Spar, exchanged numbers, and soon after they began sponsoring her. It wasn't a fortune, I'm sure, but it was a help.

Her life has changed so much since then, huge companies like Toyota and Adidas signing her up to promote their products, but even now that she's in the professional world it strikes me that she's still the same Katie.

Back when I would ask to interview her in those early days you'd hear a sigh and an "oh God", so uncomfortable was she doing media work, but even though it's become increasingly part of her life, she still doesn't look completely at ease with it, even if she just accepts it's a requirement of the job. If those promoting her professional bouts were hoping she'd start trash-talking opponents and engage in all the usual stuff we hear from that world, they've been disappointed. That's not Katie.

• • • • • • •

Katie, Sonia and Annalise, the last three Irish women to win Olympic medals, have all been inspirational figures in our sport. Boxing, running and sailing might not have a whole lot in common, but the three women certainly do. And apart from their talent, I think the fact that they all bounced back from experiences that would have floored most others is what I admire most about them.

Katie picked herself up after Rio and embarked on what has so far been a hugely successful professional career. Sonia and Annalise chose not to give up on their Olympic dreams after shattering experiences, and got their just rewards in the end.

And despite all they have achieved, they all retained the most charming of qualities: humility.

23

Changing Times

*'I'd never be slow to describe the performance
of a sportsman as 'brutal', but I know I'd
be much more hesitant to do the same for
a sportswoman'*

I was looking through old newspaper clippings a while back and I came upon a report on the 1982 women's All-Ireland football final which, as it proved, was the first of Kerry's nine-in-a-row. 'Great Display Wins For Kerry Girls,' read the headline, followed by a report that would make you cringe:

Kerry's lady footballers did the county proud at Nenagh on Sunday when they avenged the men's defeat at the hands of Offaly by decisively beating the ladies from the Faithful county in a very entertaining All-Ireland final.

... Seldom have I experienced such heavy rain and full credit to the ladies for the entertainment they provided. I have often seen men's games being postponed in conditions not nearly as bad.

This was my first time seeing a ladies GAA game and, frankly, I was amazed at the skill level, especially from the Kerry girls… And the girls weren't afraid to get stuck in either. There were quite a few un-ladylike comments after the tackles!

Offaly, in particular, employed quite a few hatchet-men (or hatchet-women to be more correct) and a couple of Kerry girls came in for rough treatment… the top scoring honours went to Del White of Austin Stacks, one of only two married girls on the Kerry team (Margaret Lawlor is the other). The powerful Mrs White was also very good in the air.

You'd wonder if the person who wrote it would feel mortified if they read it now, 36 years later.

Well, I can confirm that they do.

It was me.

• • • • • • •

I could only imagine Rena Buckley's reaction if she read it.

Actually, I'd be afraid of Rena Buckley's reaction if she read it, although she might argue that the tone in the coverage of women's sport hasn't changed enough in the intervening 36 years.

I was doing a panel discussion in Cork last year with Rena, former Kerry footballer Tomás Ó Sé and Cork hurler Damien Cahalane.

By the time she announced her retirement from inter-county football and camogie in May 2018, Rena had become the most decorated player in the history of Gaelic games with a phenomenal 18 All-Ireland medals across both codes for Cork and 10 All Star awards. We'll probably never see her like again.

We were discussing the enormous growth in coverage of women's sport in recent years, and I found Rena's views on the nature of it fascinating.

While she's pleased with that growth, she dislikes the tone of a lot of it because, she said, she finds it to be generally fawning. Maybe not quite at my 1982 'aren't they great girls?' level, but not a whole lot beyond it. What she wanted was proper analysis and criticism when it was merited, just as men's sports get.

I said to her that if, say, I criticised Cork's camogie corner-back when I was on television, and she might be a 17-year-old, people would say "you bastard, how could you slate a young girl like that?"

Rena was having none of it, so long as it was honest and fair she would have no problem with critical analysis. In fact, she'd welcome it.

I was looking forward to being able to say to her at some point after a game, "God you were brutal", but I never got the chance with her retirement.

But I thought about what she'd said when I watched RTÉ's coverage of the women's Rugby World Cup in 2017, which proved to be such a let-down for the Irish team.

And I know, instinctively, my response to their disappointing performances would have been along the lines of 'hard luck, they gave it everything'. Exactly the kind of response that would drive Rena mad. But the panel of Fiona Steed, Rosie Foley and Lynne Cantwell, all former internationals and pioneers of the women's game in Ireland, weren't going down that route at all, they skewered the team for some of their displays, Fiona in particular – if she was the prosecutor in my trial, I'd give up, I'd just plead guilty.

It was, of course, honest and fair, but I remember being taken aback by it because I'm not sure we had heard Irish women's sport so frankly analysed in that way before.

The players themselves would always have been their own harshest critics, but I think there was a definite reluctance on the part of those covering their sports to be as critical. I'd certainly include myself in that. I'd never be slow to describe the performance of a sportsman as 'brutal', but I know I'd be much more hesitant to do the same for a sportswoman. And I still think a lot of people would be uncomfortable with that level of criticism. Maybe it's a generational thing, a kind of old-fashioned chivalry, which, I see now, is probably deeply irritating for the likes of Rena or any top-level sportswoman who wants their performances to be analysed in an honest and serious manner. It's something I am much more conscious of now.

And it's the players themselves and former players who are driving that change of tone. It probably makes it easier when it's initially coming from them, others can then more comfortably follow their lead. It's interesting, and it's a good thing. It's all part of the evolution of women's sport and how it's covered. It's certainly a step forward from 'the powerful Mrs White was also very good in the air'. (Still mortified).

• • • • • • •

There have been enormous changes in the media since I started out all those years ago and coverage of women's sport has been one of the biggest. In that time many of our highest profile sports people have been women, from Sonia O'Sullivan and Catherina McKiernan in my earlier days, through to Nina Carberry and Katie Walsh and their achievements in horse racing, on to

Katie Taylor and Annalise Murphy with a host of other names emerging through that spell.

I suppose our most successful individual sportswomen, not least our Olympic medallists, have always received recognition, as any story of success does, but probably the most significant increase in profile has come in team sports like Gaelic football, rugby and soccer. Before, the likes of camogie, hockey and basketball would, I think, have been the team sports where women got most coverage.

Women's Gaelic football has come an incredibly long way in recent years, on every level – from the quality of the games, to the skills and fitness of the players and their professional-like commitment to their sport.

Back in the 1980s, when I started covering women's All-Ireland football finals they weren't even held in Croke Park, the first, when Kerry made it five-in-a-row against Wexford, not staged there until 1986.

The crowds were modest in those early years, so for those who have battled away trying to promote women's football it must have been a special moment when the attendance was announced at the 2017 final between Dublin and Mayo – 46,286, the biggest ever crowd at a women's final and the highest attendance at any women's sporting event across Europe that year.

That's remarkable progress and, if it can be maintained, a huge boost in terms of making more companies sit up and recognise the commercial possibilities in a tie-in with the women's game, as Lidl did when they began sponsoring women's football in 2016. That's not to say that outside of the finals the crowds are good, generally they're not, and there's still the issue, as many of the players talk about, that not enough of their fellow county people support them as they do their men's teams.

I'd like to think that is beginning to change. I remember being blown away by the size of the crowd when I went up to Monaghan to watch the Cuala women's team play Corduff in the All-Ireland junior semi-final in late 2017. I took a photo of the banks and banks of people on the opposite side of the ground and whenever I showed it to anyone they assumed the game was a curtain-raiser for a men's match. It wasn't.

And that's where it needs to start, people supporting all their club teams, regardless of their gender. And then they need to follow that through with their county teams.

But the growth in women's football in particular has been incredible. And the young girls who have been taking it up in their droves have had brilliant role models to look up to. The Cork football team that won 11 senior All-Ireland titles in 12 years, between 2005 and 2016, breaking Dublin hearts in four of those finals, were one of the finest teams we've ever seen. I was thrilled when they won the 2014 RTÉ Team of the Year award which, most importantly, was voted for by the public. That might have been the first time a women's team received that level of recognition in Ireland, although I'm not sure that particular team got quite the credit it deserved overall.

I think in her later years playing for Mayo, the phenomenal Cora Staunton might finally have begun to get the recognition she had long since earned, her brilliant career taking a twist in 2017 when she joined Australian Rules club Greater Western Sydney to play for them in their league. To take up a new sport and a challenge of that magnitude at the age of 34 was remarkable, but GWS's decision to sign her for a second season was an indication of what a success she had been.

• • • • • • •

One of my favourite memories is from St Patrick's Day in 2013 when, after surviving working on the parade for RTÉ, I headed to Mulligan's pub on Poolbeg Street to watch the Irish women's team win the Grand Slam in the most miserable of weather conditions in Milan.

Ireland had never finished higher than third in the Six Nations before that year, their first ever international only taking place in 1993, and they'd battled through the toughest of times when there was little support and next to no recognition for the women's game.

For the likes of Joy Neville, now a top class rugby referee, Lynne Cantwell, Nora Stapleton and Fiona Coghlan, all of them trailblazers in women's rugby, that final whistle in Milan must have been especially emotional. I'm sure when they all started out playing rugby such a day was unimaginable.

There were fantastic characters on that team, impressive, articulate, inspirational women, many of whom have featured on our *Saturday Sport* panel. Sophie Spence and Jenny Murphy are two more players who have really stood out for me over the years as people who were so dedicated to promoting their sport and encouraging more girls to get involved. It wasn't just about them and their own careers. They were – and remain – powerful role models, and I think their legacy will be a lasting one.

What I've always loved too is their sense of fun, as you so often see between them all on Twitter, social media really giving you a sense of their personalities. And what always strikes me is how supportive all these sportswomen are of each other, across sports, there's a real sense of sisterhood.

I'm sure there are big-headed, cocky sportswomen out there, but you don't meet them very often. And that's honestly not just a sweeping generalisation, it's my experience and that of most people I ever talk to about it. Our elite sportswomen are grounded and humble, almost without exception.

That humility makes it all the more forceful when they take a public stand on an issue within their sports. As many Gaelic footballers and camogie players have done when they felt they were being treated poorly by their county boards or governing bodies, over issues like poor training facilities or clashing football and camogie fixtures. Or our international soccer team when they spoke out about their treatment by the FAI. Or Ruth O'Reilly when she opened the lid on Ireland's less than ideal preparations for the 2017 Rugby World Cup. More rugby players have followed since, speaking of their unhappiness about how the women's game is being run, and citing examples like the IRFU rejecting an offer from Rugby Australia to host a three-test women's series as a double-header with the men's internationals in 2018.

You always get the sense that they're reluctantly speaking out, but feel they have been driven to it, so while we might have grown accustomed to professional sportspeople in particular complaining about minor things, when these women take a public stand you know they've been pushed to breaking point.

And I hope they continue to do so, and I hope the public get behind them, as I think most did when the soccer team revealed how they had been treated.

Even to the point of having to change out of their Republic of Ireland tracksuits in airport toilets because they had to return them.

Simply unbelievable.

• • • • • • •

One of my favourite days of the year is the *Irish Times'* Sportswoman of the Year awards, for which I am the MC.

It's a really special occasion with a lovely atmosphere, and one of the aspects of it that I enjoy the most is watching the stars of today getting to meet so many of the women who paved the way, like Olympic gold medallist Mary Peters, the extraordinary all-rounder Maeve Kyle and the one and only Rosemary Smith, the pioneering rally driver. Incredible characters and personalities, all of them in the awards' Hall of Fame.

And I love the interaction between the likes of Rosemary and today's sportswomen, very different generations with nothing but mutual respect and admiration, the younger women full of questions about what it was like when they were competing, the encouragement and praise from the older women. It really is lovely.

Maeve, of course, had a remarkable career, representing Ireland in hockey and athletics, making it to the Melbourne, Rome and Tokyo Olympic Games. And she was more than a little useful too at cricket, tennis and swimming, to name but three.

That's actually a feature of the careers of so many of today's leading sportswomen, that until they had to focus on one discipline they tried their hand at several.

Sarah Healy, for example. She's another sporting all-rounder who I took notice of early on because she played with Cuala. She's also a very talented hockey player, but really hit the headlines in the summer of 2018 when she won gold in the 1,500m and 3,000m at the European Under-18 Athletics Championships in Hungary, an incredible achievement.

And it turned out to be a really fantastic summer for Irish athletics, with Rhasidat Adeleke winning gold in the 200m and Sonia O'Sullivan's daughter Sophie winning silver in the

800m at the same event. And days later at the World Under-20 Championships in Finland, Ireland won silver in the 100m relay, through Molly Scott, Gina Akpe-Moses, Ciara Neville and Patience Jumbo-Gula, while Donegal's Sommer Lecky took silver in the high jump.

We were dizzy from all this unprecedented success.

And the presence in and contribution to those Irish teams of Adeleke, Akpe-Moses and Jumbo-Gula really reflected today's Ireland, these young immigrants, or children of immigrants, now playing such a major role in our sport.

I always remember Seán Óg Ó hAilpín, the former Cork hurler and footballer, talking about moving to Ireland having been born in Fiji before living in Australia for a while. He was around 11 when his family came to Ireland and at first he found he had nothing in common with the other kids. It was tough, really tough, for a young fella in a situation like that to adapt.

But what helped him do it was his involvement in sport, and I'm sure today's young immigrants find it similarly helpful. Moving from Dublin to Carlow and then Kerry is hardly the same journey as Fiji to Ireland via Australia, although some might argue that the cultural differences in my move were even greater (I wouldn't, I promise). But I learnt too how sport helps you integrate and become part of a community when, at first, it can be difficult because you're an outsider. Sport has endless value on so many levels. This is another hugely important one.

• • • • • • •

What I would love to see is these young women being backed by companies, instead of those potential sponsors spending their budgets on, say, bringing clients to Old Trafford, Wimbledon or Twickenham.

That need for backing, of course, applies to young sportsmen as well. Regardless of gender there is a depressing lack of financial help for our young sportspeople, but I think for women it has been a longer and harder battle.

Rarely has the issue been highlighted so dramatically as it was during the Irish women's hockey team's remarkable run at the 2018 World Cup in London, their first appearance in the tournament in 16 years, when they reached the final after taking on and beating nations ranked well above them who were either professional or semi-professional.

It was only around a month before the World Cup began that the team acquired a sponsor, having struggled for so long to get one on board to help fund their high performance programme.

And look at the reward SoftCo, a Finance Automation Software Provider, got for backing the team – their name on the players' shirts in all those photos on the front pages of our newspapers and on RTÉ television for the knock-out phase and final of the tournament. How much would similar exposure have cost in advertising?

We learnt, too, that up until two years before the World Cup the players actually had to pay an annual €550 levy each to help keep the high performance programme going. So, effectively, they, or their parents, had to pay so that they could play for Ireland. That, in itself, is scandalous, but there is the obvious danger that when that happens in any sport that it becomes elitist, that only those who can afford to pay such levies can progress.

But while I passionately agree that government should put more in to sport, not least because of its health benefits, I wish the private sector would step up more too to take a punt on all this talent, to give people like these hockey players a chance to realise their potential.

I had the pleasure of hosting the team's homecoming in Dublin from the World Cup. I've hosted many a homecoming in my time, but this one was special, largely because the success had been so unexpected and the joy of the players unconfined. And, again, the humility shone through, despite what they had achieved.

Second in the world with the most meagre of support.

Just imagine what sportswomen like them could achieve if they got the backing they deserved.

24

A Tale Of
Two Great Men

*'I could see him dropping his head to avoid
the glare of the lights. It all just felt like
exploitation. I decided to end it there, so
someone came and wheeled him away'*

One of the many privileges my career has afforded me over
the years has been the opportunity to meet the most
extraordinary of people, both from inside the sporting
world and beyond.

If I had to draw up a list of icons who I most admired and
who I believed had the greatest impact during their lives, Nelson
Mandela and Muhammad Ali would, undoubtedly, be at or near
the top. Two men who played an immeasurably huge role in
black history, the presence of both of them in Dublin for the
opening ceremony of the 2003 Special Olympics World Games
making the occasion all the more spectacular.

The great Irish sports photographer Ray McManus took a
wonderful photo of Mandela and Ali meeting in a Dublin

hotel during the Games, the pair squaring up to each other boxing style, Mandela, a boxer himself in his youth, throwing a 'straight left' to Ali's face. Ray described it as the meeting of the greatest sportsman who ever lived and the greatest statesman. That it was.

But while I was fortunate enough to meet both men, they were very different experiences.

• • • • • • •

It was 2009 when Ali returned to Ireland, the notion being that he had come to look in to his family roots here, his great-grand-father Abe Grady said to have been born in my own home town of Ennis before emigrating to the United States in the 1800s, although it was later disputed that he had been born in Ireland at all.

Ali's schedule for the trip included a visit to Ennis, fundraisers in Dublin and Dromoland Castle, and a visit to Lansdowne Road. It was insane.

It was probably in 1996, when we saw him light the Olympic cauldron for the Atlanta Games, that we first became aware of his frailty having been diagnosed with Parkinson's Disease 12 years before.

It shouldn't have come as a surprise, then, that come 2009 his condition would have seriously deteriorated. But even so, I was still shocked by just how fragile he was, assuming that having been brought to Ireland and given such a busy schedule that he'd be able for it.

The trip had been organised by Pearse Lyons, the Dundalk-born businessman who had started up a hugely successful animal feed business in Kentucky called Alltech. Through Alltech, Lyons had set up the Muhammad Ali Center Global Education and Charitable Fund, so that was the connection between the two men.

I had been asked to MC the fundraiser in a Ballsbridge hotel and it was, by some distance, one of the most uncomfortable nights of my life.

It was a Who's Who of Ireland in the room, then Taoiseach Bertie Ahern among the guests, over 300 people attended, paying €650 each.

Both Ali's wife Lonnie and Lyons spoke, and then Ali was wheeled out to rapturous applause. People were standing and cheering and whistling, there were cameras flashing everywhere and he was wincing with discomfort. I was horrified by it. And then I was supposed to chat with him when it became quite obvious that he was in no condition to do so.

I tried saying a few things to him and he just nodded, he wasn't really able to speak. It was awful. I just didn't know what to do. I could see him dropping his head to avoid the glare of the lights. It all just felt like exploitation. I decided to end it there, so someone came and wheeled him away.

I really don't know why he was there, why his people had brought him. I don't know if he needed the money – you would think not, but you just never know in these situations.

As a thank you for MCing the event I had been invited along with Caroline, Paul and Amy next morning to a breakfast at which Ali was supposed to appear.

I wasn't sure if I should go after what had happened the night before, but I was doubtful Ali would be there so we went along.

There was a small group at the breakfast, and next thing Ali is wheeled in again.

And again the cameras started flashing.

There's a photo of Caroline, myself, Amy and Paul with Ali, but again he was wearing dark glasses and wincing.

"Stop this," Amy whispered to me.

And Paul was just sick, he was so upset about it. The photo is hidden away at home to this day, we would never put it on display.

• • • • • • •

A photo myself and Caroline will always treasure, though, is the one of ourselves with Nelson Mandela in his Cape Town home, some years after his retirement from the presidency of South Africa.

I had done some work with Niall Mellon and his Township Trust, a charity that built houses in South Africa's townships using Irish volunteers, many from the building trade. Niall did trojan work with the charity, and there were some wonderful people among the volunteers.

I'd taken Paul there as a labourer on one occasion, to the Imizamo Yethu Township, just outside Cape Town, and he did really well. The builders, on the other hand, thought I was useless; twice I won the Softest Hands award. I just wasn't made for manual labour. That's my excuse anyway.

It was through that connection with Niall that myself and Caroline were invited to lunch at Mandela's home, along with Niall and his family, Mandela being a big admirer of the Township Trust and the generosity of the Irish people who gave their time to work for it.

It was an awe-inspiring experience, just laying eyes on the man was like looking in to the face of history.

He was so natural, so relaxed, and made us feel that way too.

We talked about his time on Robben Island, a place I had visited and was overwhelmed by. It can't but have a profound effect on you.

He explained how every prisoner was given the task of educating a fellow prisoner – so you might have a teacher who wouldn't be good with his hands being paired with a carpenter, and they would exchange skills and knowledge. They called it 'Each One Teach One'.

And we talked about the often-made comparisons between the ANC and the IRA, Mandela insisting that the ANC had much fewer civilian casualties during their campaign, their chief tactic the sabotaging of government property like power stations or telephone exchanges. He was very aware of the IRA campaign.

It was at that point Caroline said, "I'd like to give you a little gift, if I may?"

Her mother Eileen recently passed away – it was a desperately sad time for the family, who are very close.

Caroline's father Paddy worked in the ESB but with 14 kids he had a second job, as caretaker in the local convent, to keep things going financially. And Eileen used to knit Aran sweaters and scarves to help out too. A fella would arrive with a couple of bags of wool and when she'd be cooking the dinner she'd be knitting, when she watched telly she'd be knitting, all to get the extra few bob.

The last thing she knitted before she died was a scarf, and Caroline decided to give it to Mandela.

He genuinely seemed moved by the gesture.

He asked about the pattern on the scarf. The history of it is, of course, much disputed, but we grew up hearing that each pattern was unique to a family so that if fishermen were lost at sea their bodies could be identified by the pattern on their Aran jumpers. He was fascinated by that. And by the fact that Caroline's mother came from such a big family.

"Oh my God!" he said when he heard she was one of 17 children.

He and Caroline really connected, their conversation so warm.

We were with him for a couple of hours and he put us so much at ease you would almost have forgotten who this extraordinary man was.

If our experience of meeting Muhammad Ali was one we want to erase from our memories, our afternoon with Nelson Mandela is one we will never, ever want to forget.

And we won't.

25

The Games People Play

'It's all limos, guards, people rushing to serve them, it reeks of privilege, power and wealth. And from there for Hickey to this savage humiliation'

By the time I went to Rio in 2016 as part of the RTÉ team I honestly thought nothing could surprise me any more in terms of, well, unexpected developments at Olympic Games. I had, after all, been in Athens when showjumper Cian O'Connor won gold, Ireland's only medal that year, only for him to be later stripped of it after his horse Waterford Crystal tested positive for banned substances.

I remember when I got a call to tell me about it I actually thought it was a joke.

What followed in the months after was, as so many suggested at the time, Dick Francis stuff, although even he might have struggled to persuade a publisher that the plot was believable. There was a portion of the horse's B sample stolen from a laboratory in Cambridgeshire and there was a break-in at the Irish equestrian federation offices. It got more bizarre by the day. And even now there are still so many unanswered questions.

Cian, of course, went on to win bronze at London 2012, but I think it was overshadowed partly by the boxing that year, but also because of what had happened in Athens.

So, 12 years later, heading for Rio, I was certain nothing could shock me.

And then Pat Hickey was arrested.

• • • • • • •

On the sporting front, Rio proved to be a mixed bag for Ireland. The boxers had gone there with high hopes of several medals, but even before they got started news came through that Michael O'Reilly had failed a doping test, so his Games was over before it had even begun. He later received a four-year ban.

It went from bad to worse for the team with shock defeats for Katie Taylor, Michael Conlan and Paddy Barnes, making Rio the first time since Athens in 2004 that we had failed to win a boxing medal.

Our successes came out on the water with Annalise Murphy in sailing and the inimitable rowers Gary and Paul O'Donovan whose interviews made them overnight celebrities. 'Pull like a dog' and 'Shteak and spuds' even started appearing on t-shirts, the lads should have demanded royalties.

I thought RTÉ's Joe Stack was terrific with them, I'm not sure some other interviewers would have got their humour and been relaxed enough to let them ramble on, they'd probably have tried to get them focussed and back on track. But as a Kerryman, and

Dublin's Alan Brogan showing his three arms at the city's homecoming after the 2015 All-Ireland. In the background, with his hands in his pockets, is my Cuala club mate, Michael Fitzsimons – a top quality young man

(Above) Over the years, Cuala was a great club for a party – with Vinnie Holden and Karl Schutte back in the '80s. (Left) The Sunday Game crew call into McCoy's pub on the 'Fair City' set. Ger Loughnane, Pat Spillane, Jackie Tyrrell and Ciaran Whelan

(Above) Joanne Cantwell and I have become great friends through many long hours doing Saturday Sport in Studio 10. (Right) 'Up For The Match' with Gráinne Seoige has become an integral part of All-Ireland final weekend

Another Open champion! Darren Clarke was always great fun when we did Q&A sessions with the public at the Murphy's Irish Open

Pádraig Harrington's homecoming party after he won the Open Championship in 2007. I was in tears when he collected the trophy!

I know he has a reputation for being cranky on the golf course, but I found Colin Montgomerie to be great craic! He tried really hard on behalf of our team in this Pro-Am at the Irish Open

Amy and Caroline were with me at the JP McManus Golf Classic – we shared a table with Ian Poulter and his family. Caroline thought he played for Arsenal

Denis Law – a Manchester United legend who has a wonderful roguish sense of humour

The greatest manager of all-time? Sir Alex Ferguson fascinated me because he was such a straight talker, and he could tell a good yarn too!

If you didn't know better, you'd think George Best was trying to hang out with me on a night out. What a shame that such a unique talent could also be so vulnerable

(Above) Martin O'Neill raises a laugh as he and Michael O'Neill shared the Philips Sports Manager of the Year award in 2015 after both the Republic of Ireland and Northern Ireland qualified for the European Championship finals. (Left) I honestly don't remember why I was showing former Taoiseach, Bertie Ahern, a pair of Speedos!

The RTE Radio commentary team at the Champions Cup final, after Leinster's famous win in Bilbao. With Michael Corcoran, Donal Lenihan and Bernard Jackman – I always enjoy working with them

I love this photo because it was full on laughter. Apart from being one of Ireland's greatest sporting talents, Ronan O'Gara is also a very funny man

(Above left) The 2009 Grand Slam night in Cardiff couldn't have been more dramatic. At the homecoming the next day, I reckon Paul O'Connell and Donncha O'Callaghan were the only two players who had any sleep! (Above right) I'd like to think I didn't look star-struck when Paul O'Connell asked me how I was getting on in 'Dancing With The Stars'

My God, he's tall...! Interviewing Brian O'Driscoll and Leo Cullen after their last game as Leinster players. They contributed so much to the remarkable growth of the Leinster brand

Back covering the General Election in South Kerry in 2016, and a pleasure to meet up with the men I soldiered with more than 30 years earlier – Don McMonagle and the wonderful Donal Hickey

Katie Taylor – the most loved woman in Ireland. And I don't think she realises it…

(Below) with two of the Cuala lads, Con O'Callaghan and Conor Mulally the morning after the 2017 All-Ireland final. John Small and Brian Fenton are jumping in. If I look like I hadn't had much sleep, it's because I hadn't!

I love this pic (above) of my Downs Syndrome Godchild, Cameron McNamara water-skiing. (Right) The Special Olympics involvement gives so many people something to look forward to in their lives. The medals are a wonderful bonus!

(Left) I was MC when President Bill Clinton spoke in Limerick. That's me far left. Unlike the President, I had no bullet proof glass in front of me

With Tiger Woods at Adare Manor

(Right) One of my favourite photos: Caroline presenting Nelson Mandela with an Aran scarf knitted by her mother, Eileen, just before she passed away

Talking through the running order with Pele before an interview in the Mansion House

Another great man. The legendary Jimmy Magee at his last All-Ireland final. He loved All-Ireland final day

The smiles hide the nerves just before we went on air in Week 10. With Aidan O'Mahony, Denise McCormack, Aoibhínn Garrihy and Dayl Cronin

Taking part in 'Dancing With The Stars' at my age was the most daft, frightening but wonderful experience. Karen Byrne was a little diamond who worked so hard to improve me...and went on to win it the following year

One of my favourite moments was when John Sheahan of The Dubliners turned up at our rehearsal

The Dessie Swim. (There are no words...)

A night out when I was given the Radio Hall of Fame Award. With brothers Declan, Brian, Pat, my nephew Colm and Caroline. (Above right) A cup of tea with my mother at the allotment

Proud of Paul for all the wrong reasons. He somehow got a horse and rode it through the square in Poznan at Euro 2012

(Above) The day we stopped at a gathering on the Florida Keys and I ended up as Grand Marshall of the St Patrick's Day Parade

Una's family parties kept us going for 30 years! With my mother, Brian, Eileen, Pat and Declan

a fellow Munster man, Joe got it, he fed them the lines and let it run, and it was the best of fun. I think Joe was a big part of it working so well.

But once the news came through about Hickey's arrest, much of my time in Rio was spent covering that extraordinary story, so it became a challenge to squeeze in much sport at all. I call it my nocturnal Olympics, and not because I was partying through the night on Copacabana. Honest.

• • • • • • •

There was already drama in Rio when Sports Minister Shane Ross flew out to meet Pat Hickey, president of the Olympic Council of Ireland and the European Olympic Committee, because of a controversy surrounding tickets for the Games. An Irishman, Kevin Mallon, was arrested for ticket touting, most of the tickets seized from him allegedly part of the OCI's allocation.

Any of us who have had dealings with Hickey over the years wouldn't have been all that surprised to hear Ross say that Hickey "ate him for breakfast" when they met. But I think for many it was a first insight to just how powerful a man Hickey had become in his Olympic role, even to the point of feeling comfortable dealing with a government minister in that manner.

So, when news broke of his arrest, and that extraordinary footage emerged of him naked at his hotel room door when the police arrived, then being taken away in his bath robe, there was plenty of glee among people with whom he'd had run-ins over the years, especially in the media.

Hickey had powerful allies, but he had made a lot of enemies too. In one moment he had gone from being this enormously powerful figure in the Olympic movement to this vulnerable older man. It was humiliating.

If you attend any Olympic Games you see how the people running the movement are treated, quite literally, like royalty. It's all limos, guards, people rushing to serve them, it reeks of privilege, power and wealth. And from there for Hickey to this savage humiliation. And I have to say I was shocked by the release of the footage, just on a human level I thought it was an appalling way to treat anyone.

I'd had a mixed relationship with Hickey. Outside of Olympics business, I enjoyed his company, but we'd had our run-ins and angry words were exchanged at times. I always disliked how he tried to control coverage of issues relating to the OCI, but you couldn't help but be impressed by his politicking powers. And he was a consummate politician, I doubt there is anyone in the current Dáil who has his 'vote management' skills. Any time it looked like he might be toppled as OCI president he gathered more than enough votes to ensure he survived. He was, without doubt, a brilliant operator.

•••••••

Ireland was consumed by the story, to the point where I started co-presenting *Morning Ireland* with Cathal Mac Coille. Cathal from Dublin, me from Rio. Just as we had done for Saipan, a story we probably thought would never have a rival. But here we were.

It was a strange one for me because, of course, I had gone to Rio to cover sport, but for the last week or so I'd had to become a news reporter again.

After *Morning Ireland* I would often break in live to Sean O'Rourke's show with updates from Rio, there was a new twist to the story almost every day. We had a great translator out there who helped us with the court proceedings, and an Irish journalist living locally was invaluable to us too.

I was working through the night in Rio along with an editor from *Morning Ireland*, Vincent Murphy, who was brilliant journalistically, and a sound engineer called Andrew Kane.

It was a tough slog. We'd finish at 5am local time, get the 6am bus back to the hotel, get there around 7am, I'd sleep to about 10 or 11am, and then get up again – otherwise you wouldn't get to see any of the sport.

But I loved every minute of it, even if the sleep deprivation was intense. For a journalist, though, there was a great buzz working on a story of that magnitude, particularly one that was so fast-moving.

I remember on the last day myself, Vincent and Andrew going out for a few drinks in Copacabana, we were like giddy children who had been set free. We didn't have a lot in common, and we hadn't known each other well in RTÉ, but working together that closely through the nights gave us a kind of a bond at the end of it all. We enjoyed those few drinks.

The one break in the middle of it all came on a Saturday night because there was no *Morning Ireland* the next day. It was the only night I was out in Rio apart from that last one.

I was in great company. Jacqui Hurley, Hugh Cahill and Evanne Ní Chuilinn brought me to a Mexican restaurant, but we were there on our own. The place was completely dead. "This is crap," we all agreed.

Everyone was outside on the streets watching the Olympic football final, Brazil v Germany, on big screens. The match went in to extra-time, then penalties, Neymar scoring the winner for Brazil. And the whole city erupted. It was the one gold they wanted more than anything.

In no time the restaurant went from having just the four of us to the place being completely crammed with ecstatic Brazilians. There was a Mexican band playing, we were the only non-Brazilians there, we became part of the celebrations, it was just fantastic.

Jacqui, Hugh and Evanne were up dancing on the tables too, but I opted to stay in my chair.

For, well, health and safety reasons.

• • • • • • •

So I eventually learnt to always expect the unexpected when I went to Olympic Games, and that so often sports stories become major news stories, dating back to my first Olympics with that Ben Johnson failed test.

But I really was blessed to have been at the Seoul, Barcelona, Atlanta, Sydney, Athens, Beijing, London and Rio Games, it was such an incredible privilege. I could never pick out a favourite, because there wasn't one. They were all unique experiences, if united by the sheer thrill of attending an Olympic Games.

There was something magical about Athens, for obvious historical reasons, some of the venues – like the archery which was overlooked by the Acropolis – simply breath-taking.

But when, in later years, you see those photos of rotting unused venues, the sheer definition of white elephants, you have to conclude there's a certain obscenity to the money countries as economically weak as Greece put in to hosting these Games.

Then there's the doping, the cheating, the corrupt judges, and all that dark side to it all, and you could very easily let cynicism overwhelm you and stop you being thrilled by it all.

But I don't, because in the middle of all that darkness you find the most uplifting of stories, many of them our own, like Michael Carruth, Sonia O'Sullivan, Katie Taylor, the O'Donovan brothers and Annalise Murphy, to name but a fraction of the people who have provided us with utter joy over the years.

And it's not even just about the medal winners. One of the most powerful images from Rio was of our modern pentathlete Natalya Coyle after the final discipline in her event, the 3.2km run combined with shooting. She had collapsed with exhaustion at the end of it, stretched on the ground.

She had given literally everything she had. She finished seventh, that placing later upgraded to sixth after a Chinese athlete failed a doping test. She might not have got the headlines our medal winners did, but she gave no less.

· · · · · · ·

I've been lucky enough to see some of the greatest Olympic athletes of all time in the flesh.

Curiously, Michael Phelps' achievements in swimming didn't get me hugely excited. I watched him in Beijing winning a marginally ridiculous eight gold medals, by the time he retired he'd collected 28 medals in all, making him the most decorated athlete in Olympic history. But because he became so dominant in his sport, there was a predictability about his success, which lessened the drama of it all.

Contrast that with the raw excitement of Anthony Nesty

winning a gold medal for Surinam in the 100m butterfly in Seoul, prompting us all to rush to find out where Surinam was. A population half the size of Dublin, we learnt. It's not Michael Phelps' fault that he was so relentlessly brilliant, but I suppose it's stories like Nesty's that really grab you.

Mind you, Usain Bolt had phenomenal success too, and I never tired of watching him in action. Absolutely thrilling.

I wouldn't put him on the same iconic level as Muhammad Ali, as some people did, but I think he had a similar charm and charisma, he was brash and cheeky, but when he was boasting he was smiling. And that made us smile too.

I also got to see some of the greats of basketball in Barcelona, Magic Johnson, Larry Bird, Karl Malone, Charles Barkley and the man himself, Michael Jordan. The Dream Team. One of the most ridiculous episodes in Olympic history, these multi-millionaire professionals allowed to compete in the supposedly amateur Olympic Games. But it's carried on since, tennis and golf among the sports now allowed to send its richest professionals to take part in the Olympics, which is farcical.

The Dream Team that year played eight matches, won them all, their narrowest margin of victory 32 points over Croatia in the final. Madness. In their opening game they beat Angola by 68 points, and you sensed they were taking it easy.

I got to see Jordan and the rest, which was a thrill, but you could only sigh.

• • • • • • •

You can take the GAA out of the man, but…

In Athens I skipped the end-of-Games party to get home in

time to see the All-Ireland football semi-final replay between Fermanagh and Mayo. I had my ticket booked to go home on the Monday but I just felt if Fermanagh were going to win and get through to an All-Ireland final, I wanted to be there to witness this slice of history.

I paid a fortune to change the ticket to get home for the replay, it took about three days to do it.

I got there.

And Fermanagh lost.

So, that went well.

Meanwhile, one of my fondest memories from London 2012 was being in a pub close to our Premier Inn hotel, which was next to the London Eye and looking across to the Houses of Parliament, a stunning location. Donegal were playing Kerry in the All-Ireland quarter-finals so I sought out a pub that would be showing it.

It was a small pub, not many there. When I went in there were two elderly men speaking Irish to each other and watching the match. I could have been in Glenties.

There was a Scottish woman behind the bar. She stared at me. Then, after a moment, she said, "you're the guy off the telly."

At first, I thought someone had put her up to saying it, but she explained that with *The Sunday Game* on every week on the telly in her pub, she couldn't get over how important it was for the Irish emigrants.

It was another reminder of how special it is to be involved in a programme that means so much to so many Irish people, especially to those far from home.

26

Proud Role

*'He told the room about how much I loved
and cared about the Special Olympics, and
that I was just emotional about it... and
then he started crying himself. So there were
now two big fat fellas crying on stage...'*

O ne of my great regrets over the years is that I haven't had
more time to give to Special Olympics Ireland, having
been honoured by being named as one of the patrons of
the organisation.

I've been involved with them for a long time, and my heart
is very much with them because of the marvellous work they
do, but between work and family I just haven't been able to
contribute as much as I would have liked.

The real heroes of the Special Olympics movement are their
volunteers who quietly work away in communities across the
country, week in, week out. And they don't get anywhere near
the recognition they deserve.

I feel very strongly about the use of volunteers generally to avoid
funding sport in Ireland to the level that it should be funded

for a host of reasons, not least for physical and mental health. But without those volunteers who help those with intellectual disabilities, and give their families some relief, there would barely be any kind of support network at all.

The Special Olympics is not about the elite athletes who make it to the World Games, it's about, say, the 40-year-old man or woman with an intellectual disability who is living with a parent who might be in their 80s.

And a volunteer might come every Monday evening at 7.30 to collect them and take them bowling. And the gear bag will be ready and sitting in the hall from 6.00. It's a break for the parent and an outing for their son or daughter.

That's what the Special Olympics movement is really all about, it's those little nights out around the country, the importance of them to so many families, giving them some comfort and a sense that they are not alone.

• • • • • • •

I think opinion was divided when Ireland hosted the World Games in 2003.

Many felt that for the nine days the spotlight would be shone on the athletes and their families, everyone would say "aren't you great?" and then when the show left town they would all be forgotten about again, sent back in to the darkness. With only those volunteers left to help.

There was truth in that, there remains a shameful lack of support for these people and their families, but my feeling was that the Games here could only help. It was about awareness and the education of the public, and I do think it helped on that front, even if there is so much still to do. The alternative was just to do nothing, not to host the Games at all and carry on as we were.

And I think the whole event was extraordinary, particularly through the use of host towns which led to communities everywhere feeling involved.

If a kid from, say, Venezuela won a medal they'd go back to their host town and there'd be huge celebrations. It was brilliantly done.

But it was a struggle to get the funding to stage the Games. Padraig O'hUiginn, former Secretary General at the Department of An Taoiseach, who is also a patron of Special Olympics Ireland, played a major role in getting government funding for the Games, but plenty was required from the private sector too.

I remember MCing a fundraiser at the Berkeley Court where corporate tables were sold for a lunch at which Van Morrison had agreed to play for nothing. It was hosted by Denis O'Brien who was chair of the organising committee for the 2003 Games.

He asked me to really sell the event when I was up on stage, that we needed to explain to everyone what the movement was all about and encourage them to give generously. Many of Ireland's wealthiest people would be in the room.

So I got up and started speaking about the movement, the athletes, their parents, their day to day battles, how they rarely get a chance to shine, how even children with severe disabilities would get a chance to compete, and the more I talked the more emotional I became, until I began to cry.

It was awkward in the room. People were looking down at their feet. I could see Denis O'Brien looking at me, like 'what are you doing?'

I was trying to take a deep breath to compose myself and get through it. But it was disastrous – my voice was getting higher, I was gulping.

So Christy O'Connor Jnr, a great big lovable man and a huge supporter of the Special Olympics, who was sitting at a table in front of me, came up on stage beside me and gave me a hug. He told the room about how much I loved and cared about the Special Olympics, and that I was just emotional about it…and then he started crying himself.

So there were now two big fat fellas crying on stage.

I looked down at Denis and he had his head in his hands.

Christy was, by now, so emotional, recalling the tragic death in a car accident of his son Darren, it made me think 'my God, I better get this back on track'.

Which I somehow managed to do.

There was a sports car there that someone had donated – half the room bought it and gave it back so we could auction it again. It was a massive success. A seven-figure sum was raised, all of which helped make the Games become a reality.

• • • • • • •

There is still so far to go, though, much as I do believe the 2003 Games helped.

And I worry about some more recent developments. It had become easier for kids with intellectual disabilities to be accepted in to ordinary schools, for example, but more and more I am hearing about parents complaining about these kids being disruptive and wanting them separated from the mainstream system again.

So there are issues around that, they're hugely difficult to resolve, but I think it's critical that people with intellectual disabilities are integrated to regular day to day life as much as possible, particularly in the education system and the workplace.

And still we are so dependent on volunteers, the state leaving so much of the burden on their shoulders. They are people who would help regardless, but they deserve – and need – so much more support.

My own daughter Amy began volunteering when she was around 15 with Bray Lakers, a sports and recreation club for children and adults with an intellectual disability, her experience there helping her decide that she wanted to do intellectual disability nursing. She's terrific with kids especially and the experience really made her see it was the path she wanted to take. She later went to the Games in Greece as a volunteer.

I saw first hand with the Lakers the brilliant, patient, loving work that is put in to make the lives of these kids and adults that bit better, and to give some relief to parents who must desperately struggle to cope at times.

And I know from experience how great the reward can be. I'm Godfather to a Special Olympics athlete, Cameron McNamara, son of Ciaran and Susan, two of my closest friends. He's just a bundle of energy and fun and brings laughter everywhere he goes. A huge character who gets away with everything because he's so funny and cheeky. Even in a few moments in his company he gives me more than I have ever given him.

● ● ● ● ● ● ●

2003 was the first times the World Games were held outside the United States. Since then they have been hosted by China and

Greece before they returned to the US in 2015 when Los Angeles was the host city. In 2019, the United Arab Emirates will stage them.

I think the Games remain hugely important for the raising of awareness about the challenges people with intellectual disabilities face, but it's vital that more of the bigger nations show an interest in staging them, like Britain or Germany or Australia, to help really boost that awareness.

I was fortunate enough to travel to Shanghai for the 2007 Games for RTÉ, which was another enriching experience.

One of my favourite memories from there was having dinner with a group of around 20 people which included Fergus Finlay of Barnardos and his family. Among them was his daughter Mandy who would know my own daughter Amy through their involvement in Bray Lakers.

Mandy, who is in her 40s now and has Down Syndrome, is a remarkable woman who has achieved so much in her life, including representing Ireland at the 1995 Special Olympic World Games in Connecticut.

Mandy, though, overestimates my fame. We were in a rooftop restaurant in Shanghai in the evening, Mandy was sitting opposite me. My back was to a door, it opened and everyone was looking at who came through. I looked back and it was this stunning woman, I half recognised her. It was Bianca Jagger.

"Oh my God, you're beautiful," Mandy cried.

"Oh my God, that is so nice," said Bianca.

"Do you know Des?" asked Mandy.

I discovered from Bianca's blank expression that she doesn't watch *The Sunday Game*.

But Mandy can add that to her list of achievements – she introduced me to Bianca Jagger.

27

Cuala Man

'Cuala has been an anchor for me right through my life, the place where I have made so many treasured friends'

I was flicking through the channels one evening recently and up popped a replay of the 1983 All-Ireland football final between Dublin and Galway. My son Paul had dropped in to the house so I called him in to have a look at it. As a fan of Gaelic football today I'm not sure he would ever have seen anything like it. It was carnage.

Three Dublin players were sent off and one from Galway, and even though I'd been at the game I'd forgotten just how filthy some of the tackles were. There were digs going in everywhere.

And that's how most GAA supporters would remember the 1983 final, the ugly side of it. If you were from Dublin they were 'The Twelve Apostles', if you were from outside Dublin they were 'The Dirty Dozen'.

I remember the final for a different reason, though.

All through the match I would glance down at the programme on my lap and focus on 'Mick Holden (Cuala)'.

One of our own.

I can't begin to describe how proud I was of Mick, the first Cuala man to play in a senior All-Ireland final, and how elated I was for the club that has been such a major part of my life since I was a young fella back in the 1970s.

Back then Cuala was just a tiny GAA enclave in south county Dublin at a time when playing Gaelic Games in that part of the world was just about the uncoolest thing you could do.

We could never have imagined one of our own going on to have a career like Mick enjoyed with Dublin, and we certainly could never have envisaged the success Cuala would go on to experience in more recent years.

It's been the stuff of dreams.

• • • • • • •

The local GAA history dates back to 1918 when it was founded by a group of men whose roots were in hurling, some of them having taken part in the 1916 Rising and ending up interned in England, starting up the club on their release.

It's been a long and winding journey since then, with several mergers with other local clubs taking place through the years, until the club's final reshaping in the early 1970s when Cuala Casements – a juvenile club in Dun Laoghaire and Sallynoggin, merged with Dalkey Mitchells.

Tom Holden – father of Mick – was one of the founders of Cuala Casements.

I've been involved with Cuala, which is based in the village of Dalkey but has roots too in Blackrock, Dun Laoghaire and Shankill, in a number of capacities since I first joined up, playing for them for several years, joining the committee in 1978 as a young fella, becoming PRO during my time doing journalism in Rathmines, helping out with some of the teams, and having a spell as chairman.

But my contribution to the club pales next to that of men like Tom Holden, Mick Dunphy, the Sheanon family, Maurice O'Callaghan, father of Dublin players Con and Cian, Peter Dunne, Damien Byrne, Willie Braine and Tony Bass down through the years. And I could list dozens more who have helped make Cuala the club it is today, not only a successful one but, more importantly, a vibrant, thriving part of the local community.

I remember Vinnie Holden, son of Tom and, like his brothers Mick and PJ, a Cuala stalwart, saying once in an interview with *The Irish Times* that Cuala used to be "a gathering of fellas who loved playing hurling and enjoyed a few pints". And that's how it started out.

Now? It's one of the biggest clubs in Dublin and while we have achieved our greatest success in hurling, Cuala contributes players to the county panels, men's and women's, in every code.

I remember 2015 in particular, it was dizzying, the club reaching 17 hurling, football and camogie finals, winning 12 of them.

Back in the 1990s the club membership was around the 300 mark. In recent years it has mushroomed to over 1,800, much of the credit for that growth going to Damien Byrne, the former Dublin hurling goalkeeper.

He was like our Pied Piper. Sometimes I'd be walking through Dun Laoghaire with him and every kid we'd pass would say "hiya Dayo", they all knew him from his work for the club in the schools in the area.

Damien was a postman, he'd work the early shift and then on an entirely voluntary basis would go to the national schools in the area, some of them with little or no tradition of GAA, and get the kids involved. He started leagues between the schools for each age group and the kids loved it, there were summer camps that were hugely successful, and from then our membership gradually began increasing.

Damien didn't have any official title like 'development officer', but that's effectively what he was; he was ahead of his time. Maurice, myself and John Sheanon, the current president of the club, pushed for him to get paid a few bob for the work he was putting in because it was invaluable.

Willie Braine and Ken Fitzgerald then followed Damien in the role, and Cuala continued to go from strength to strength. Former players helped with coaching the coaches. It was slow but very steady progress.

It probably took 15 or 20 years for it all to bear fruit. I thought it would happen in five, some of the kids joining us were so gifted, but you really need a second wave of fresh talent to come in, and another one after that, before you see the results. You need all those waves to push each other to a higher level. And that's what happened. Back then we'd never have dreamt of having Dublin minors; now we're just throwing them out.

I talked earlier in the book about the growth in popularity in Dublin of Gaelscoileanna, where education is done through Irish, the schools' excellent academic reputation making them the preferred choice of so many parents now for their kids.

And, of course, Gaelic Games have strong roots in these schools, so that has contributed too to their growth in popularity, particularly in parts of Dublin, like Dalkey, Blackrock and Dun Laoghaire, where rugby or soccer would always have been the more popular sports. I'll never get over just how cool Gaelic Games have become in those areas

• • • • • • •

Mick Holden was our hero. And with his blond hair and orange Fiat Ritmo, you couldn't miss him.

He was more of a hurler than a footballer, a classy one too, his love of the game coming from his father Tom who was a Kilkenny man. One of Tom's proudest days was when Mick, Vinnie and PJ all played on the same Dublin minor team in the 1969 Leinster final…against, of all people, Kilkenny.

But it was in football that Mick enjoyed that unforgettable success with Dublin in 1983, one that elevated him to legendary status with Cuala.

By then he had started selling insurance door to door, like Tom had also done. He'd collect a couple of quid from people who were saving for their funerals, that kind of thing.

One of the great yarns told about him was when he brought the Sam Maguire cup to a school in Sallynoggin after winning the 1983 All-Ireland.

"Do you know who this man is?" asked one of the teachers.

"Yes miss," replied a little girl, "it's me nana's insurance man."

Mick was a firm favourite with Kevin Heffernan, not just because of his playing ability but because of his rogue-ish personality too. Heffo loved him.

Before one All-Ireland final with Kerry, the Dubs had a Saturday morning training session and meeting in Parnell Park. Before they left, Heffo asked them if anyone needed a sleeping tablet in case they'd struggle to nod off that night.

Mick put up his hand.

"Jesus, Mick," said Heffo, "you're the last fella I thought would be struggling to sleep."

"Oh no, it's not for me," said Mick, "it's for my mother."

• • • • • • •

Mick was a Cuala man to his core, going on to coach the young hurlers at the club. It's hard to describe just how loved he was. So, his death from a heart attack in 2007, at the age of just 52, was devastating.

Con Houlihan had a typically beautiful line in his tribute to Mick when he died. Speaking about the work he had put in at the club with the youngsters, he quoted an old Roman proverb: 'The good peasant plants and tends the vine even though he may not live to drink the wine'.

It was a line that could have been equally applied to one of Mick's team-mates from the team that won the club its first Dublin Senior Hurling Championship in 1989, Brendan 'Batty' Ryan. And like Mick, Batty died tragically young, in his late thirties. They had so much in common. Both were warriors as hurlers and footballers, but hurling was their passion.

Batty played once for Dublin and it happened to be the time their shirt sponsor was Kaliber, Guinness's non-alcoholic beer, so when Guinness put posters of that team up in every pub in Dublin, there was Batty staring out at us from the front row. Batty loved his beer, but not of the non-alcoholic kind, so he got endless ribbings about it.

He used to say he knew his playing days were done when he turned up for a Dublin game one day and there was no linesman.

"Batty, you do linesman," said Lar Foley, the manager. And he had always been in trouble with referees, so becoming part of the officiating team was not for him.

He was a successful man having set up his own company selling alarms. He was one of a kind. He'd read the *Sunday Tribune* and *The Irish Times* at the weekend but he'd keep it quiet, it wasn't good for his image. He'd be whispering to you about a really good article he'd read.

He was diagnosed with cancer and became very ill just about the time his wife, Orla, had their first baby, Liam. Around 12 of us were invited to their home for the christening. Liam was brought in to Batty in the bedroom and was christened there. I went in then to chat with him before heading home.

It was around three or four in the morning that I got a call to say Batty had passed away.

Liam is playing now for one of Cuala's underage teams.

That he never knew his dad, and what a magnificent character he was, is one of life's great cruelties.

• • • • • • •

Sport has a habit of making me emotional, but few, if any, occasions had quite the same impact on me as the one on March 17, 2017, the day Cuala won their first senior All-Ireland Club Hurling title when they beat Ballyea in Croke Park.

It was beyond our wildest dreams.

We'd had so many great days already, like when the under-21 football team I helped out with beat Kilmacud Crokes to win the Dublin title on my 50th birthday.

Kilmacud would have been packed with Dublin players, senior

and minor, we were complete underdogs. Jesus it was fantastic. That morning at O'Toole Park is one I'll never forget. It was magical.

But St Patrick's Day, 2017 – and a year later when we retained the title – was an extraordinary day that saw an outpouring of emotion from everyone connected with the club.

The greatest thing about it was that only two of the players had not come through our juvenile system. Here was a bunch of our own young lads, shining in Croke Park. So many of their mothers and fathers had played for Cuala – indeed the grandfathers of the O'Callaghans, the Schuttes, and the Sheanons had all played a huge part in the fledgling Cuala club. There was a very significant input from Galway – Mattie Kenny had taken charge of the team, and along with Greg Kennedy they nurtured the talented youngsters and turned them into All-Ireland winners. I haven't a doubt they would be hugely successful at inter-county level.

What a day. And all we could think of were the people who had gone before and had helped Cuala become what it is today.

Tom Holden, especially.

Unlike the funeral of his son Mick, who had been taken so young, our farewell to Tom turned in to a celebration of his life, as Irish funerals often do when the person gets to live to a good age.

I had been over MCing a Q&A event at the Clanna Gael/ Fontenoy club in Ringsend, one that had been organised by Niall Quinn. Niall had assembled a panel that included Nicky English, Ray Houghton, Chris Nicholl, the former Northern Ireland international, and Bobby Saxton, Peter Reid's assistant manager at Manchester City where Niall was playing at that stage. And then Eoin 'Bomber' Liston ended up joining the panel too after ringing me to say he was in Dublin and wanted to call in to Mick

Holden to pay his respects after the death of Tom. Mick would have marked Bomber In many a Dublin v Kerry encounter, the respect between them immense despite those bruising battles.

Nicky wanted to come out to the house too to pay his respects, he lived out that way and knew Tom, and Niall's link was through his mother who used to play cards with Tom.

Ray, Chris and Bobby were to go to a local pub and wait for us, but it was closed and they couldn't get in, so they ended up following us to the Holden family home. It was after midnight. Ray, Chris and Bobby had never been at a wake. They were horrified to see the coffin open in the middle of the living room, with a hooley going on around it, fellas leaning on it holding cans and singing with their eyes closed.

I only stayed 45 minutes, I had to be in work at 5.30 next morning, but the mood of my three visitors relaxed, and one of the highlights of the night was Ray Houghton, around three hours after I left, singing a song at the coffin of a man he didn't even know.

It was like Tom was part of the hooley going on around him.

He would have loved it too.

● ● ● ● ● ● ●

It was in 2011 that Michael Fitzsimons became the second Cuala man, after Mick Holden in 1983, to win an All-Ireland football title. Just as I had been with Mick, I was so proud of him. I dropped down to the Burlington that night to congratulate him and found him outside chatting with some of the Cuala lads, which I thought was lovely.

And in 2017 Martha Byrne became the first woman from

Cuala to win a senior All-Ireland football title when she was part of the Dublin team that beat Mayo in front of a record crowd of 46,286. She has now been joined in the squad by Jennifer Dunne – her granddad, Pete, would be so proud.

The incredibly talented Con O'Callaghan, Conor Mullaly and Mark Schutte joined Fitzy in the senior football squad, while the Dublin hurling squad has been backboned by Cian O'Callaghan, Oisin Gough, Paul Schutte, Sean Moran, Colm Cronin, Jake Malone, David Treacy and others. Con and Mark Schutte would be automatic choices on the hurling squad if they weren't tied up with the footballers.

The Dublin camogie panels now have a bunch of Cuala girls who are coming through from Donal Murphy's squads.

Older members of the club like me will never take these successes for granted because they all seemed so unlikely back in the day, but for the younger people at Cuala you can see the confidence flowing through them now, girls and boys. Winning, as they say, is a habit, and this younger generation have seen the club enjoy so much success in recent years they just believe anything is attainable now.

I have been involved with the senior footballers for the last 10 years. While the hurling team is obviously seen as the main team in the club, it's a remarkable feat that the football team has TWO All-Stars – Michael Fitzsimons and Con O'Callaghan.

We have progressed every year, winning the Intermediate Championship and consolidating ourselves as a strong Division One team in the strongest league in the country. It's incredibly competitive in Dublin.

Of course, from a point where most everyone else was applauding us becoming the first Dublin team to win a senior All-Ireland hurling club title, our continued success means everyone now wants us to lose. Did I ever think I'd see the day? We've come a long way, then, from the days people didn't even know how to pronounce our name ("Koo-a-la?"), we're a relatively young club but we now have a tradition and a history.

Cuala has been an anchor for me right through my life, the place where I have made so many treasured friends.

To this day, there is nothing I love more than going to one of our games, football, hurling or camogie.

And I never fail to think of Tom, Mick, Batty and all those who have since left us but not before helping make Cuala the special place it is.

28

Gaelic Life

*'I went a whiter shade of pale. I think
my heart stopped. "You didn't?" "I did!"
I could just see the headline:
'RTÉ'S DESSIE FLOGS ALL-IRELAND
TICKET TO TOUT"*

T he squad car was driving slowly behind me as we walked
up the road. Caroline, Amy and myself had just been on
Portnoo beach on what was a glorious day, it was like
God had kissed Donegal.

The mood about the place was euphoric. The day before, the
county had beaten Cork to reach the 2012 All-Ireland football
final, their first since 1992 and only their second ever at that
stage.

And for a county like Donegal, that has suffered huge levels of
emigration and has gone through relentlessly tough economic
times, it was a rare moment of collective joy.

For me the most memorable days in sport aren't necessarily
about their scale or magnitude, they're more about what they
mean to the people involved. And so days like Donegal reaching

an All-Ireland final are the days I love the most. Because for counties not accustomed to that level of success, they bring nothing but exhilaration.

A moment of madness struck after the final whistle blew in that semi-final. I was doing *The Sunday Game* that night but decided when I was watching the interviews afterwards and seeing just how much this meant to Donegal, I wanted to be up there. So I rang Caroline before we went on air, told her I'd be home at midnight and then we'd set off for Donegal.

"Imagine the buzz?"

If she thought I'd lost the plot, she didn't say – as a Donegal woman herself she wanted to be there too.

So we set off and arrived in Ballyshannon at around three in the morning.

We headed for a local pub, which was magically still open, but when we got inside there wasn't a person you could have a conversation with, they were so drunk.

There were lots of hugs. And a few double-takes.

"You were on the telly five minutes ago!"

Time flew.

It hadn't gone quite as planned.

So next day we go for a spin and end up in Portnoo.

It was when we were walking along the beach we first spotted the squad car. It went away and then came back packed with Gardai. It struck me as odd.

And then they started driving behind us.

Eventually they pull up beside me, one of them gets out and says, a bit gruffly, "we're doing a search."

Searching me?

"Yes."

I was taken aback.

"What's the search for?" I ask.

"All-Ireland final tickets," says your man.

And the squad car began shaking with the laughter inside.

• • • • • • •

It would not be correct to say that I coulda been a contender. The closest I ever got to playing for Dublin was when I made the minor panel in 1977. I was number 17 against Kildare in Navan in the first round of the Championship, but never got on. We lost. I'd love to claim it would all have been very different if I'd played, but I doubt it.

That was probably the end of me playing football seriously. Once you start doing journalism you're rarely free at weekends, so even if I'd wanted to carry on it wouldn't have been possible.

But I loved my years playing football, with Cuala and Clann Coláiste Mhuire in Dublin, Éire Óg in Carlow and Dr Crokes in Killarney. And as I talked about before, it wasn't just about the enjoyment of playing the game, it was about being part of a club that helped you feel part of the community. And in Carlow and Kerry, especially, that was so important to me and helped the blow-in become accepted.

Gaelic Games have been a thread right through my whole life, from playing the game as a young fella, from travelling the country with Frank Dargan following the Dubs, from reporting on games right from the start of my career in journalism, through to being the presenter of *The Sunday Game*.

I was especially lucky to have been living in Kerry at a time when they had one of the greatest teams in the history of Gaelic football, with legends like John Egan, Mikey Sheehy, Jack O'Shea and Bomber Liston, arguably the best full forward of all time, and having the privilege of watching them train, play for their clubs and their county.

There's been many a heated debate in recent years about whether the current Dublin team would top that Kerry side in the all-time list, but the game is so different now they really are impossible to compare. I'd be fairly sure, though, these Dubs would destroy the winter version of Kerry back then because most of them would have been on the beer.

In those days, there was less pressure on the players, they could have a life outside football. That's a lot harder now. Between club and county it's almost getting to be an all-year game, with incredible demands on the players in terms of fitness. If Kerry were meeting the Ulster champions in the semi-finals back in the '80s, they could nearly time their run – and fitness – for September, Ulster not being so strong in those days.

The one edge you could give this Dublin squad is their strength in depth. There was very little change in the Kerry team for a long period and age eventually caught up with them. Mick O'Dwyer stayed loyal to his players, understandably because they were producing the goods, but the team then went suddenly to having to make eight or nine changes in one go. With today's Dublin you barely notice the changes because they happen so gradually, the team evolves. Jim Gavin has been able to bring in the likes of Brian Fenton, huge impact, Con O'Callaghan, huge impact, and, in 2018, Brian Howard and Niall Scully – huge impact.

There is, of course, some resentment towards Dublin's success, the sense that it's not a level playing field. And I understand that, I completely get the frustration – and a lot of Dublin people don't. How do the smaller counties compete with the level of funding and sponsorship Dublin has and the size of the county's player pool? It's very hard to see how it's possible. And, of course, there's the added disadvantage of, probably, the majority of counties having players based in Dublin because of their studies or work, and that makes it hugely difficult for them. There are so many players in that position, having to put their careers on hold if they want to play at that level, and that's an enormous sacrifice. The travelling back and forth to their home counties must be wearying.

And so few get the rewards they deserve.

I remember after the 2011 All-Ireland football final, when Dublin won for the first time since 1995, myself and Ciaran Whelan running out of Croke Park on the final whistle to meet a car that was taking us back to Montrose for *The Sunday Game*.

Ciaran had joined the Dublin squad not long after that 1995 win, and quit just before their 2011 victory – in between he was the best midfielder of his day.

As we ran alongside each other, Ciaran considerably more athletically than me, I decided not to start talking. I could sense his brain was processing the whole thing. He was elated about Dublin winning, but he had to have mixed feelings too.

I really felt for him.

It can be a cruel game.

• • • • • • •

With the quality of the hurling Championships in recent years, not least in 2018 when we saw some truly phenomenal games, the semi-finals just spectacular, it's been a struggle for football to keep up.

I think hurling is by far and away the more entertaining game to watch, a much better spectacle, and I'm not sure anything in sport compares to one of its great encounters.

Football, of course, tried the Super 8s in 2018, with mixed reviews. I'm sure they'll keep on tinkering with the format in the coming years but it won't be easy to get it to the point where everyone's happy, the need to allow enough space in the year for club football making it nigh on impossible to avoid the All-Ireland Championship being condensed too tightly.

It's all getting so big and so complicated, the club standard now is so high, I'm not sure what can be done to accommodate everyone.

The chief worry is that the demands on the players have become too unrealistic, especially players who get to the latter stages of All-Ireland Championships with their counties. They could lose, experiencing a massive low, and then they're getting a text from their club saying 'hard luck, we're training Tuesday, it'll be great to have you back'. Some of the players tell me they find it so hard to get their head around going back to their clubs.

They're still their best friends, and they will be for life, but they need a bit of time to recover, emotionally and physically. But the club is waiting for them to return and transform their fortunes. When the player comes back he or she is taking the place of someone who's been playing away, filling in for them, which they're uncomfortable about too. The GAA gets a whole pile of criticism, and often it deserves it, but in this I have sympathy for them. I genuinely don't know how they can resolve a situation where counties and clubs have competing demands on time.

But, ultimately, however it's done, the players' welfare has to be put on top of the list of considerations.

• • • • • • •

While unrelenting excellence, produced year on year, whether by the Kilkenny hurlers or the Dublin footballers, is always a thrill to watch, it's the underdogs winning out that captures my heart every time.

I think back to that spell in the 1990s, between 1994 and 1998, when Offaly, Clare and Wexford won those five All-Ireland titles between them, with Limerick reaching the final twice in that time. It was a barren spell for the kings of hurling, Kilkenny, Cork and Tipperary, but it was a wonderful time for the underdogs, the excitement and enthusiasm of those years infectious.

And from that spell, it was the 1995 Munster final between Clare and Limerick in Thurles that I remember with the most fondness. Myself, John Givens, brother of Don, and Davey Hudson and Brendan 'Batty' Ryan from Cuala went down together on the train to witness Clare win their first Munster title since 1932.

I'm a Dub, but I was born in Clare, home to both my parents, so neither eye was dry come full-time.

And I'll never forget the sight of Davy Fitzgerald racing up the field to score a penalty, the mad determined face on him, and him punching the air with joy on the way back.

We ended up missing the train back to Dublin but we were offered a lift by a Good Samaritan, stopping off in Morrissey's of Abbeyleix on the way home. And inside was a bunch of Clare people, including businessman Martin Donnelly, who ploughed a fortune in to sponsorship of Gaelic Games, among other sports, over the years, and Tony Garry, the former chief executive of Davy Stockbrokers. I'll never forget the pure emotion of them all – and it wasn't the booze, honest! But I just saw how much it meant to them all, they were overcome, most of them not even close to being born when Clare last won Munster.

The wait since Clare last won an All-Ireland was even longer, interminable, it was 1914.

I brought my mother to the final, as well as Paul, but Dad was too frail by then and said he wouldn't be able for the steps. I met Liam Mulvihill, the GAA president, a few days later. "Your father must have enjoyed that, Des," he said. I told him he didn't go. "Jesus, Des, you know we would have looked after him, brought him down the tunnel."

I was raging I hadn't thought to contact Liam, and I always regretted it. But Mam was there and she had the time of her life, loving meeting up with all the Clare crowd.

About an hour and a half after Clare's victory we were walking across the pitch when we met Pat Fitzgerald, Davy's father, who was coming across with the Liam McCarthy. We got a photo of Ma, Paul and myself with the trophy. Mam was in heaven.

Afterwards we headed out to the Leopardstown Inn to meet Mam's brother Sean. There was a gang of bikers there, big hairy fat 40-year-olds. I remember my mother going up to them, her spirits high after a couple of celebratory jars, and saying to them: "Boys, wasn't that a wonderful day!"

They had absolutely no clue what she was talking about.

• • • • • • •

There have been so many more days like that one, where the underdogs prevailed, and they always make for the most magical of stories.

Like Leitrim winning Connacht in 1994, when the only other time they had done it was in 1927.

I was doing *Sunday Sport* that day, I'll never forget Micheál

O'Muircheartaigh's commentary when he talked of Leitrim people watching it all "from the veranda of heaven."

They lost the semi-final against Dublin, but just the sight of them running out on to the pitch, and the roars that greeted them, was spine-tingling. There were more Leitrim supporters in Croke Park that day than lived in the county, it was an incredibly emotional day for them all – including my good friend Ciaran McNamara from Annaduff. Or 'Up the Duff', as he regularly cries.

When Annaduff won their intermediate championship Ciaran asked me to go up and MC their awards night. I agreed, but I just didn't have the time to prepare for it, when I would usually have looked up facts on the club and their championship success. So, as I was ushered on stage, I asked if the club had any local rivals.

"God yeah, Bornacoola, we hate them."

So I go up on stage and I congratulate them and say, "I certainly wouldn't have come up if Bornacoola had asked me."

I'm such a chancer.

The roof nearly lifted off with the cheering.

I could have dropped the mic and gone home there and then.

That was a Saturday night. Come Monday lunchtime I was in Croke Park MCing the club of the year awards. There was a winner from a club from every county. It came to Leitrim.

"And the winner is......Bornacoola!"

So the chairman and secretary come up.

And as they pass me…

"We heard what you fucking said about us the other night."

• • • • • • •

Donegal winning their two All-Irelands are among my favourite GAA memories. But my least favourite comes from 1992, when they won their first. Caroline's family is huge, and every one of them thought I could get them tickets for the final. And people always assume I get an endless supply when, in fact, I don't – I haven't asked the GAA for tickets for the last 10 years at least.

But that time I wrote to Croke Park to look for four. I sent a blank cheque because you didn't know what stand they'd be in. So I got the four and over the next couple of weeks I asked around for spares. Very, very luckily, I ended up with around 20 tickets, and come the Sunday morning I was handing them out to the Donegal relatives.

But they all thought I'd got them for free, when I'd paid for every one of them, so nobody was handing me any money. And, between everything, I had no money at the time, but had spent a fortune on the tickets – all the time assuming I'd get it back from the relatives. Caroline was aware that I was less than happy, she was mortified.

When the game was over I went to meet her and the family in town. She came running up to me and gave me a big hug.

"Everything's sorted – I sold a ticket to a tout for 400 quid!"

OH MY GOD. JESUS CHRIST.

I went a whiter shade of pale. I think my heart stopped.

"You didn't?"

"I did!"

I could just see the headline: 'RTÉ'S DESSIE FLOGS ALL-IRELAND TICKET TO TOUT'.

Caroline couldn't understand what the problem was.

"Jesus, you're killing me when you didn't get money for them, now you're killing me when you do."

It was a while before my heart started beating again.

29

Sport For All

*'Most of the patients were looking forward
to the game, especially 'the old men', so
when they were told they wouldn't be able to
watch it, they were crestfallen'*

The media landscape hasn't just changed since I started out in journalism with *The Irish Press* in the 1980s, it's simply unrecognisable from back then.

For the newspaper and broadcasting industries the challenges have been immense, not least for RTÉ who, when I joined in 1984, had no national rivals in Ireland at all when it came to covering sport on radio and television.

It was, then, effectively a monopoly and as a sports broadcaster it was a dream. We had access to just about any event we wanted to cover, at home or abroad.

It is, of course, a very different picture now, particularly in television, with TV3 (or Virgin Media Television, as they are being rebranded) a seriously big player when it comes to competing for TV rights. And Sky Sports, too, has become a competitor on the GAA front, with eir Sport another rival on the scene.

TV3, backed by the powerhouse that is Virgin Media, has been especially successful winning rights to major events in the last few years, one of its biggest coups getting the Six Nations rugby which they showed for the first time in 2018 – and with Ireland winning the Grand Slam, it was a hell of a debut.

Its loss was a huge blow to RTÉ, there is no denying that, as was TV3 winning an even bigger slice of Champions League coverage for three years starting in 2018-19, including exclusive rights to the final. RTÉ now has just 16 matches on Tuesday nights, having always had games on the Wednesday as well.

In the face of that level of competition, there are major challenges ahead for RTÉ's new head of sport, Declan McBennett, and difficult decisions to be made.

And, as ever, it's about balancing the effort to be competitive in the battle for these rights while weighing up the fact that RTÉ is funded by tax-payers' money, so you can only take that battle so far.

The BBC, like most state broadcasters, finds itself in much the same situation, having lost a host of major sporting events in the last decade or so to Sky, ITV, Channel Four, BT Sport and others.

That's just the nature of it now, there is enormous money in sport, most of it earned through the sale of broadcasting rights, and while RTÉ has lost out on many fronts, I think the viewers have too when the winners have been pay-per-view channels.

• • • • • • •

I remember Amy ringing me in a panic a couple of years back when she was on a work placement in a hospital in Donegal. She was asking me if there was any way of getting Sky Sports in the hospital, even illegally, because Donegal had a Championship match that weekend and it was only on Sky. Most of the patients were looking forward to the game, especially 'the old men', so when they were told they wouldn't be able to watch it, they were crestfallen.

I told her there was nothing they could do, a public hospital certainly couldn't afford to get in Sky, so they just wouldn't be able to see the game live.

I know people who defended the GAA's deal with Sky Sports dismissed those kind of anecdotes as just emotive stuff, that the GAA was entitled to maximise its revenue, which would ultimately be ploughed back in to their sports, and we had to live with it.

I didn't – and still don't – think those stories are just about being emotive at all. They were simply true accounts of how the deal impacted GAA supporters around the country who had no access to Sky, in most cases because they simply couldn't afford it.

Speaking on *The Sunday Game* last year Michael Duignan made a similar point when Sky had had exclusive rights to the Waterford v Kilkenny game that weekend.

"The Sky deal is so wrong on so many different levels and this isn't just because I'm in RTÉ working for The Sunday Game. My father is 83 years of age, a savage hurling man. Why should he have to go to the pub to watch a match? He doesn't go to the pub. The GAA have enough money; how much money do they want? What about the people that supported the GAA all of their lives? I think it's disgraceful."

I agreed with Michael. I think it was absolutely the wrong

thing for the GAA to do. And I don't say that because I'm an RTÉ man. I would have had no problem if, for example, TV3 had retained the rights they had before Sky entered the fray, or any free-to-air channel.

The GAA is an amateur organisation that depends hugely on volunteers, and a lot of them are people who might have lost their jobs or are retired, and so have the time to help out at their locals clubs. You meet them in every corner of the country, they are the lifeblood of the GAA. And they're generally not people who could afford a Sky subscription.

It's all very well claiming that one of the purposes of the Sky deal was to promote the games beyond these shores, but you have to give consideration too to the community at home that have contributed significantly towards making the GAA the organisation that it is.

I remember someone tweeting a photo of a scene in Balla, Co Mayo, during Mayo's All-Ireland quarter-final against Donegal in 2015, which was on Sky. It was captioned 'the only house in Balla with Sky' and showed people crammed in to a small living room to watch the TV, with 10 or more standing outside staring through two windows to try and see the game. On the face of it, it was funny, but when you thought about it, it was actually sad. It was probably a representative snapshot, from just one village in rural Ireland, of the impact of the Sky deal on people who wanted to watch their county's game live on television. From kids to the elderly and everyone in between.

So, for me, it was just wrong. Naturally the GAA wants to bring in as much revenue as possible to fund the development of its games, but I think you have to draw a line at the point where you're hurting the very community to which you belong.

I have no issue at all with Sky's actual coverage. I think it's good and they have some top class analysts, like Jim McGuinness, Peter Canavan and Jamesie O'Connor. Their viewing figures so far, though, have generally been poor enough, and they've barely impacted on RTÉ's audience when we've been up against each other for semi-finals and finals. RTÉ, for example, averaged an audience of 925,000, peaking at 1.2 million, for the 2016 All-Ireland football final, compared to Sky's 9,000 which was just a 0.7% share of the audience.

But from their point of view the deal probably still makes sense because they wanted that Irish link to boost their efforts to get a bigger share of the market here for their wider operation. Littlewoods, who couldn't be more English, did something similar when they became a GAA and camogie sponsor.

The GAA renewed its deal with Sky in 2016 which gave it the rights to 20 championship matches a season between 2017 and 2021, 14 of them exclusive to the channel, while RTÉ got 31 matches with, again, both channels showing the semi-finals and finals.

The renewal was welcomed by some, lamented by others. I still belong to the latter camp.

• • • • • • •

I know there are those who object to RTÉ using as much of its licence fee income as it does on covering sport, particularly on major events like the Olympic Games and World Cups which are hugely costly and are a big chunk of the annual expenditure when they arise.

As a sports fan, of course, I see it differently.

If you look at the list of the most watched programmes in

Ireland in 2017, sport on RTÉ produced four of the top five and seven of the top nine. Only the beast that is *The Late Late Toy Show* and a news bulletin about Storm Ophelia got in the way of a sporting clean sweep.

The All-Ireland football final between Dublin and Mayo was second behind the *Toy Show* on the list, followed by the second leg of the Republic of Ireland's World Cup qualifying play-off against Denmark, the result of which I'd prefer not to talk about. Both programmes had audiences of over a million, over a fifth of the population, which is just extraordinary.

After then there was the hurling final between Galway and Waterford, Ireland's World Cup qualifier against Wales, and then three of Ireland's Six Nations matches.

We love our big sporting occasions and we tune in in our droves. They're communal experiences. They're part of what and who we are, as the saying goes. And they are the days when even those with only a casual interest in sport are watching too because they are national events.

If any of these games had been on pay-per-view television, the audiences would have been a fraction of the size. And in the workplaces and schools the following morning there would have been much less buzz and chat, that experience shared by only a relative few.

Instead, these games were available to everyone, thanks to the licence fee, including those patients in that Donegal hospital and all the people of Balla. There was no need to stand at a window to try and catch a glimpse of the television screen inside.

And I would say the same for TV3's coverage of the 2018 Six Nations, it was free for viewers too, and over 1.3 million of them were watching when Ireland won the Grand Slam in Twickenham. That's just a fantastic figure.

That's why, then, that I believe it's so important that these occasions remain free for everyone to watch. They're special days that we should all be able to share.

And I think that applies especially to our national games, Gaelic football, hurling and camogie, the rights to which the national public service broadcaster should always battle to keep. Winning the rights to soccer and rugby, especially, will become increasingly difficult, but I think it's vital that we continue to fight to retain our coverage of Gaelic games.

Ryle Nugent made the point when he stepped down as head of sport at RTÉ in 2018. "RTÉ Sport's relationship with the GAA is the single-most important relationship that we have," he said. "It's the core of what I believe RTÉ, the national broadcaster, should be about to be at the centre of the biggest matches our national games has to offer."

And I absolutely believe that too, as does Declan, Ryle's successor. It's not just about sport, for me it's critical on a cultural, social and community level too.

· · · · · · ·

The cost of watching so much sport now on TV is increasingly proving beyond people's means. When TV3/Virgin Media Television won the bulk of the Champions League rights for 2018-19 and the following two seasons they announced that they would charge up to €20 a month for access to their Wednesday games, the coverage on TV3 having been free until then.

The estimate at the time was that if viewers wanted the full range of live soccer games on offer in various competitions, across all pay-per-view channels with rights, they could end up paying around €170 a month. Over €2,000 a year. That's some money. You really have to wonder about the wisdom of slicing up the rights in that manner.

But there was an inevitability about soccer going that way, although so far RTÉ has managed to hold on to the rights to live coverage of Republic of Ireland competitive games. That for me too is critical. There was no way we could carry on competing for rights to, say, English Premier League highlights, which we lost in 2013, but I think it would be a desperate shame if our national team's key games ended up on pay-per-view.

So I think that's what RTÉ will continue to prioritise as it tries to compete in these markets – our national games, our national teams and major events like the Olympic Games.

● ● ● ● ● ● ●

There have been big changes too on the radio front with the emergence of the likes of *Off The Ball* on Newstalk and *Second Captains* on their podcast and weekend shows on RTÉ through the summer.

Both have built a very good brand and they've done it really well, they have extremely talented teams and do some brilliant interviews.

It's very different, of course, to how, say, myself and Joanne Cantwell would do our *Saturday Sport* show. Often with *Off The Ball* it's a conversation among themselves, whereas we would usually have someone in with us, we'd put questions to them and they'd do the talking.

I think back again to Ian Corr shouting down my ear if I started offering my own opinions, "NOBODY WANTS TO

KNOW WHAT YOU THINK!" That was drummed in to me from my earliest days in RTÉ, so it's stayed with me. Your role is more about facilitating a conversation or a debate rather than necessarily being one of the chief contributors to it.

So there is a big contrast in how we all do it, but I think they do sport well and I think we do too. There's room for us all and there's a market for us all.

I think journalism has generally gone that way, in every field, it's becoming more and more about opinion now. And I enjoy listening to or reading strong opinions as much as anyone, and we welcome them from our analysts and panellists on *The Sunday Game* and *Saturday Sport*, but I think there has to be a balance. Journalism primarily has to be about facts and reporting too.

I think, though, the newer breed probably look at us like we're old fogies.

I remember meeting one of the younger radio sports guys a few years back and offering him my mobile number in case he ever wanted to ring me about anything. I wasn't doing the big fella, it's just something I'd often do if I met someone new, or relatively new, to our world.

"Why would I want to ring you?" he asked.

He didn't take my number. I thought it was rude – he could have just taken it and torn it up! – but the message was clear enough. The likes of me, and RTÉ sport in general, are the establishment and completely uncool. They're the cool kids, probably with a disdain for how we do things.

I'd seen it before. When Ian Dempsey and Ray D'Arcy were getting huge figures on Today FM, RTÉ Radio 1 wasn't cool, 2FM wasn't cool, RTÉ was just plodding along. And the national broadcaster will never, ever be the cool place. It will always be seen as an out-dated dinosaur, that goes with the territory.

The irony is that when I started doing sport with Ian on 2FM, it was viewed as being new and fresh and ... cool. I know, me ever being cool, even very briefly, is unimaginable.

But these things go in cycles, the bottom line being that despite the emergence of these new rivals, RTÉ still pulls in enormous audiences. Over 200,000 listen in to *Saturday Sport* most weekends, a programme RTÉ had considered dropping less than 10 years ago because the listening figures had gone way down. But Donagh McGrath, deputy head of Radio Sports and News, said no, stick with it, bring in a panel, have some good discussion, so we went with that. And it has worked.

We're still not cool, we're still not a brand, but huge numbers of people tune in, still way more than listen to Newstalk.

And I'm proud of our coverage; I think we do it well.

• • • • • • •

In many ways I think RTÉ and the GAA are viewed in similar ways by the public, both part of the 'establishment', they irritate, they irk, but the odd time they do something that makes people go, "ah, that wasn't bad".

The national broadcaster will always get stick, that's not unique to Ireland, the BBC would get much the same. RTÉ gets an awful lot of criticism. It's a bit like getting pissed off with a family member, an annoying uncle who has embarrassed you, but you'll stop short of disowning them. Because they're family?

And RTÉ, because of its public service remit, has to cover lots of things that make no sense at all commercially.

I talked to someone recently who said they were always bemused by RTÉ broadcasting *Mass on Sunday*. Why would they do that?

Then their elderly mother became too weak to walk down to the local church, so for someone with a deep faith in that fragile condition, *Mass on Sunday* became a lifeline. Something hugely important to them. And it's RTÉ's duty to cater for just such people.

It would make more commercial sense for us to buy in more programmes, as TV3, for example, do, or play automated music instead of having Lilian Smith connecting with an audience late at night.

RTÉ put out programmes for the blind, the elderly, the infirm, they have special foreign affairs reports, investigative work, none of it making any commercial sense, all of it adding to that licence fee expenditure.

But, in my view, all of it is essential, all of it part of the state broadcaster's duty. Not everyone will agree, but I think we do it well. Not least, sport.

Even if the annoying uncle, or embarrassing mother, leaves you exasperated at times.

30

Paul And Amy

'Life hasn't been easy for her and it will always have its challenges, but nothing, absolutely nothing, dampens her spirit'

My son Paul was born in 1988, my daughter Amy in 1990. Miraculously, considering how busy both those sporting years were, I managed to get home for both their births. Caroline, though, has to take almost all the credit for how they've turned out – two good kids, not a bother on them – because I was away so much, particularly in the early years.

And there were times when my parenting skills fell a little short of the desired levels.

Like when I was in the bar at the back of the Cusack Stand after an All-Ireland final and Mary Harney, the then Tánaiste, joined us. She was a big GAA fan. "My God," she said to me, "isn't that dreadful? Imagine someone bringing their child in here and just leaving him in the corner reading a book while they're off drinking?"

"I know," I said.

(But Paul was enjoying the book).

Somehow he forgave me and hasn't held any of it against me over the years. He has a very good manner, he's quieter than me, which wouldn't be hard. He's a good lad. He has shown rascal-ish tendencies occasionally, which he obviously inherited from his mother, while his sister Amy's good looks were clearly inherited from me. There's a lot more to Amy, though.

• • • • • • •

Amy was around five when she was diagnosed with dyspraxia, Caroline having already sensed there was something wrong, like Amy being slow to develop basic skills like crawling.

Very little was known about dyspraxia then, so the diagnosis was frightening because we just had no idea what the implications would be for Amy.

Dyspraxia, which is known as Developmental Coordination Disorder, is a condition that affects the motor coordination of children and adults, sometimes given the less kind tag of 'Clumsy Child Syndrome'. It can cause a range of problems, including poor balance, general difficulties with coordination, difficulty with reading and writing, speech problems, obsessive behaviour, and so on, all of which can lead to low self-confidence and struggles to fit in socially.

Not everyone with dyspraxia suffers from all those problems, and Amy's condition is relatively mild, but it was tough for her growing up, she struggled to fit in among her peers. She was always the outsider because of that coordination, balance issue. She couldn't do ordinary things. She couldn't play the games the other kids were playing, difficulties with throwing and catching a ball, riding a bike, hopping and skipping all part of the condition.

If there was a game going on, no-one wanted her on the team. It isolated her.

But what was most striking through it all was what a happy kid she was, her spirit was incredible. If she got knocked down she'd just pick herself up and battle on. And she is still that way today, nothing holds her back.

Many people with the condition will never be able to learn to drive, for example. That knowledge made Amy even more determined that one day she would. And she did, she passed her test. And then she rang her first driving instructor, who had told her she would never learn to drive, and gave him the news.

I laughed so hard. That's my girl.

• • • • • • •

One of Amy's passions in life is horses, she's been fanatical about them since she was a kid. I used to take her out of school on the Tuesday of Cheltenham so she could watch the opening races at home. She'd have *The Star* in front of her with the list of runners and riders. She loved it.

She was mad about JP McManus's brilliant horse Istabraq. She did loads of projects on him in school. When Istabraq retired she bought about eight angels with pins on them to put on clothing, to give as Christmas presents to her Granny and the family. But she gave one to Noreen, JP's wife, to put on Istabraq's blanket, to keep him safe. She made a big impact. Sometimes a simple, but thoughtful gift can mean a lot.

We worried when Amy took up horse riding, in case of injuries, and she had plenty of falls – she broke her arm at one point – but she was tough as old boots; she'd just get back up again.

I think my single biggest regret in life came after she was given a gift of a wonderful old pony called Storm by friends who knew about Amy's love of horses, but also were aware of her condition. Storm, they said, was 'bombproof', calm and relaxed, so he would be safe for Amy.

There were stables up at the back of Shankill where we live and the livery to keep Storm there was 100 quid a week. I could easily have afforded that, but I came from a background where you'd be embarrassed to say your daughter had a pony, that it would make you look like you thought you were a big shot, so instead of paying the 100 quid I chose the half livery, 50 quid, which meant the stable got first use of Storm. Amy would only be able to ride him when they weren't using him for other kids.

And it turned out, as we'd been told, Storm was brilliant with kids, so gentle. That meant that when Amy went up there every afternoon, and at weekends, she'd hardly ever get to ride him because he was being used for lessons. When I think back on that, I'm just ashamed of myself. I had the money, that wasn't the issue, I was too busy worrying about how it would look for me. I honestly can't think of anything in my life I regret more.

After a while a good friend of mine from Arklow, Pat Corcoran, came to have a look at Storm and said he was being worked too hard for his age, which was round 26 or 28, so he went in to retirement in stables down in Arklow.

Storm died soon after. The land was later sold to a major retail chain, so I told Amy that Storm was getting a fabulous headstone.

"Ah, that's so sweet," she said. "What will it say?"

"Dunne Stores."

"Daaaaad!"

• • • • • • •

Harry Conway runs the Irish Dyspraxia Association. The man is a saint, a legend. He's the first port of call for most parents after their child is diagnosed with the condition, he makes them feel that they are not alone.

Harry invited Amy to speak at a talk on dyspraxia in the Clarion Hotel in Liffey Valley one time. I was nervous for her, I just couldn't imagine her getting up to speak to a large group of people, but she did and she was absolutely brilliant. I was blown away.

There were parents there from all around the country, the room was jammed. The first speaker was a young woman with dyspraxia who had got an honours degree in Cambridge University. She was, then, brilliant academically, but she talked about her struggles socially, how she found it hard to mix and make friends.

Then Amy stood up and talked about how all she ever wanted to do was nursing, specialising in intellectual disability, but it had been a real battle to get in to it. But her perseverance is paying off.

She spoke unbelievably well, the purpose of her speech to reassure parents about the future. When their kids are young they can suffer from bullying and there's always the worry that there's a lifetime of that ahead, it can be so dispiriting. But she told them things can get better, their kids would always have challenges, but they could also lead happy, fulfilling lives too, nothing should hold them back.

I was so proud of her, she's a remarkable young woman.

She would love to work for the Dyspraxia Association, to go around the country to talk with youngsters and their parents, and she would be great at it. It's a very lonely place for the families and for those youngsters in particular, so having someone like

Amy tell them "look, life hasn't been a doddle, but I've got places – I even got my driving test!" would be so uplifting and encouraging. But, as with so many of the services in this country, the funding isn't there to make it possible.

I hope, in the longer term, it can happen, or something along those lines. Amy has a lot to give. She has so much empathy, she cares deeply about people in these tough situations.

Life hasn't been easy for her and it will always have its challenges, but nothing, absolutely nothing, dampens her spirit.

• • • • • • •

Paul hasn't been without his challenges either. I've lost count of the number of injuries he picked up while playing Gaelic football, rugby and soccer – he has had three cruciate operations and three shoulder operations.

Most memorably, though, he broke his front tooth.

It was around four in the morning when the phone rang at home.

Paul had been away inter-railing for a week or two, he was in Germany at that stage, so when you get a call like that in the middle of the night, your heart sinks.

I grab the phone. It's Paul.

"Da, do you know any dentists in Dusseldorf?"

And then the line went dead.

What the...?

I'm trying to ring him back, but his phone has gone dead. I was sweating. Was it a fight? Had he been knocked out? Was he down a lane at 4am in Germany? Why would you ring your Da in the middle of the night to ask him if he knew a dentist in Dusseldorf? I'm awake all night, I start ringing his friends non stop, five numbers, and I eventually get one of them at 7.30 in the morning. I woke him. "Have you seen Paul?"

"No." By now, I'm feeling physically ill.

Finally, at around 9.30, Paul rings me.

There had been no fight or mugging; he'd been in a karaoke bar, singing and an American lad beside him was swinging his microphone when it hit him in the mouth. And broke his front tooth. He eventually went to A&E in the early hours and they crowned his tooth in the dental hospital for 50 quid.

But in such high spirits had he been, he just thought he'd give me a quick ring at four in the morning to check my knowledge of dental services in Dusseldorf. My nerves at the end of it all were a little like his front tooth. Shattered.

• • • • • • •

Paul was born during the 1988 Tour de France. I managed to get home for his birth, before having to return to the Tour. There was a running joke among the commentators there that he should be named after the stage winner on the day of his birth.

There was a breakaway that day, at one point I wondered how I'd go about suggesting to Caroline that our first born should be christened Dag Otto Cahill. Because Dag Otto Lauritzen led the group. In the end, though, Jean-Paul van Poppel won the stage. I decided not to ask Caroline to name our boy Jean-Paul Cahill, but he ended up with 50 per cent of the name.

It was four years later that I was at the Barcelona Olympics. Caroline had taken Paul to Donegal to be with her family while I was away. I called her and Paul came on the phone.

"Hello Daddy," he said, in the strongest Donegal accent. He sounded like a baby Daniel O'Donnell. The drawl. I couldn't believe the accent out of him.

I said to Caroline: "Jesus, you need to take him home."

Paul and myself are very close, unusually so for the age gap. I'd know his friends, he knows mine, we have a great relationship. And, like me, he's sports mad.

He could be a right messer as a young fella (I wonder where he got that?), so I smile now when I see him on the sideline taking charge of Cuala's third team with Seanie and Shane. It's gas. My little fella.

After all those injuries he can't really play sport any more, which is a shame, but it's great to see him staying involved with Cuala where, like myself, he played.

I tried to put him off going in to sports journalism because I think it's such a tough game to be in now. There are hundreds of journalism graduates coming out of colleges every year, but there are so few jobs. And the ones that are out there generally pay very poorly. There are lots of outlets now, lots of websites, but I'm not sure how many of them are making money.

And there are so many bright young journalists working for such low pay, which you can do for a while when you're young, it makes sense to do it to gain experience, but when you get older and want to settle down, buy a house, how on earth do you manage? Where do you go if there aren't jobs?

I've been so lucky. When I went to Rathmines you were effectively guaranteed a job by the union, there was a security of sorts back then and much better money. And I was so lucky too to get to Olympic Games and World Cups and so on, but there aren't many who are that fortunate.

So I urged Paul to consider PR, or something along those lines, an area that might offer better opportunities in the longer term, but sports journalism was what he wanted to do, so that's the path he chose.

He had been freelancing these past few years, working for a number of outlets, including 98FM, and he came back in to RTÉ for the 2018 World Cup as a sub-editor before getting a staff job with TV3 Sport as an assistant producer later in the summer. I was delighted for him.

He's really good with digital media, cutting and mixing clips and putting them to music, and he's made some excellent sports-related videos, including one on the history of Cuala.

It's a tough business to be in now, staff jobs with any degree of security a rarity, so I do worry about the long-term prospects for today's young journalists.

But Paul is bright, talented and determined, and the TV3 job is a great break for him. I think he'll be okay.

• • • • • • •

My favourite photo of Paul was from Euro 2012 when he and his gang were in Poznan. It shows that he has the same type of spirit as me, of that 'messer' kind.

He's sitting on a horse in the middle of the town square, holding up a pint and wrapped in an Irish flag. And you're looking at it and asking: "Paul…where did you get the horse?"

He saw a fella with one down a lane and offered him a fiver if he'd let him ride it in to the square. Your man agreed. So he arrived on horseback, the crowds cheering and clapping; he felt like a king. I laugh out loud every time I look at it.

There's a certain 'like father, like son' quality about it.

31

Dancing Dessie

*'Des Cahill and a lady were grinding on
each other on RTÉ, and not even after the
watershed. The RTÉ One Twitter account
can call it 'The Dessie Swim' all they like.
We know it was grinding'*

y family's enthusiastic response when I told them that
I had been invited on *Dancing With The Stars* was
moving. I could tell they were giddy with excitement
about it.

This is an actual extract from our WhatsApp exchange when I
broke the news:

Me: I've been asked to go in the Irish version of *Dancing With
The Stars*...
Amy: Oh Jesus Christ.
Paul: That would be the final straw.
Paul: I'm changing my name!
Me: Your mother said: They always have a joke figure, don't they?
Amy: Haha, brilliant Mam.

Meanwhile, my mother and sister Eileen were horrified by the prospect of me going on the show. Horrified. 'Good Lord, what are you doing, you've built up a reputation and now you're going to destroy it by doing this?!' was the gist.

I have to say, my initial reaction to the invitation was along similar lines.

When the production company, Shinawil, first rang me about it, I genuinely thought the call was a wind-up. "Are you serious, the state of me?! Absolutely no way." They asked me to think about it, they'd ring again, but I said "no, not interested."

I had never danced in my life. I'd head straight to the bar at weddings when the music started up. I never once watched *Strictly Come Dancing* or its international version, *Dancing With The Stars*. Not once. I was old, fat and unfit. I'd always been game for a laugh and up for a challenge, but this was ridiculous. *Dancing With The Stars*? No. Not a chance.

• • • • • • •

Some time later, the headline on Joe.ie: 'Des Cahill grinding on Dancing With The Stars has changed Ireland forever'. The full article read like this…

All changed, changed utterly. A terrible beauty is born. On Sunday night, sports broadcaster Des Cahill pulled some moves on the dance-floor that could full well get you thrown out of even Coppers.

Performing in what seemed to be an Austin Powers costume, Des lay on the ground while his dance partner pressed her hips to his and sort of locked her legs with his arms. It was like something out of the Kama Sutra. It was eye-opening.

Basically Des Cahill and a lady were grinding on each other on RTÉ, and not even after the watershed. The RTÉ One Twitter account can call it 'The Dessie Swim' all they like. We know it was grinding.

Whatever about the birth of a terrible beauty, my life changed, changed utterly for the 10 weeks I somehow survived on the show.

• • • • • • •

I blame Caroline. When I got home I told her about the invitation and after we laughed about it initially, she then thought about it and said it would actually be good for me, it'd be great exercise and I'd lose some weight.

I wasn't convinced, but when they rang back I asked them what would be involved. I told them I was overweight, my knee was knackered, from my footballing days, and I had a problem with my heel. Apart from that I was perfect.

They just asked me to do a trial and to see how it went. So next thing I find myself in a dance studio with Karen Byrne and her dance school partner, Wojtek Potaszkin, and Karen's trying to teach me the Waltz. Her efforts went on for two hours. She had to send a video of the session to the production company and on the back of that they wanted me in. I'd guess it was because I showed such spectacular promise as a dancer.

By now I was thinking it might be a laugh and at the very least, as Caroline said, it would be good for me. I'd last one week on the show and then I could return to normality. That was around October, the rehearsals were starting in December and then the show was kicking off the following month, January 2017. They kept the line up under wraps until mid-December, I just got wind there'd be a Kerry footballer on it, so the guessing games started. Joanne Cantwell reckoned it would be either Paul Galvin or Kieran Donaghy, but I had heard it was 'a very fit' player, so I had a hunch it might be a player who had a habit of taking his shirt off after some matches to reveal a ripped body. I told Joanne to Google 'Kerry player with shirt off after match'.

"Aidan O'Mahony!"

"It'll be him," I said. It was too.

And then the full line-up was revealed. There were the comedians Katherine Lynch and Des Bishop, the actresses Aoibhín Garrihy and Denise McCormack, my RTÉ colleague Teresa Mannion, the model Thalia Heffernan, HomeTown singer Dayl Cronin, Hughie Maughan, who had finished runner-up in Big Brother in the UK, Dr Eva Orsmond, the ripped Kerry footballer and the oldest and by some distance heaviest contestant: me.

Paul took to Twitter, over my promo photo for the show: "I'm just glad @sportsdes is doing this after I left school, because I definitely would have been beaten up."

By now I don't know who was more nervous, me or my family.

• • • • • • •

My biggest worry going in to it all – a genuine worry – was that because my dance partner was Karen, people would think 'big fat dirty Dessie with a young one'. I really did feel that. I mean, I was holding her, and as I got better (at the very, very, very end) I was lifting her. Jesus. And you would be so close physically. But, to my relief, nobody took it like that. Or not many anyway.

I got on so well with Karen, we had the same sense of humour, we had a good laugh. I was thrilled for her when she won the second series of the show with the singer Jake Carter. She told me Jake was so determined he would train until midnight, whereas I'd do an hour and half and then we'd go to SuperValu in Palmerstown for a roll, a coffee and a chat. Then I'd say, "me knee's sore, we'll have another coffee."

And Wojtek was brilliant. When Karen was getting thick at me – and I gave her plenty of reasons to over the weeks – he was calm and patient. They were great teachers and their School of Dance in Palmerstown is hugely successful, they've got the best kids in the country there.

Karen got slaughtered on social media when we appeared on *The Late Late Show* together, there was loads of slagging of her Dublin accent. It was cruel, as social media often can be, and it upset her, she was new to that kind of thing, but she moved on from it, she is so competitive she kept her focus on the show.

And everyone on the show was competitive, even me. You just wanted to stay in there, and you got more determined as the weeks went by.

Myself, Aidan and Dayl became really close. After Hughie and Des Bishop were eliminated early on, the three of us ended up sharing a dressing room and we got on great. Dayl is less than half my age and we had absolutely nothing in common, but we became good friends. He'd be showing me how to work Snapchat, we'd be talking about the boy band stuff, and chatting with Aidan about Kerry football, the Dubs, and Cuala. Aidan's wife Denise was to have a beautiful baby, Lucia, before the series ended, so we had lots of pregnancy talk as well.

We'd be in at 7.30 on a Sunday morning for rehearsal and we'd be there all day until the show started. The others would often head off to a nightclub after the show, but Dayl and Aiden would always come to my local pub, Brady's in Shankill, for a pint afterwards.

I hit it off so well with Denise too, and really got to like Thalia after initially having my doubts. We'd all be standing around talking and Thalia would be telling everyone they were gorgeous and how brilliant they were and I just thought this was insincere world-of-modelling luvvy stuff. But after a few weeks I saw that she is absolutely that person, she's just warm and generous and real, the loveliest young woman. She had a good word for everyone. I told her mother she was a credit to her.

The show was filmed in a huge studio in Bray, a really professional set-up. They put in a catwalk for the promo that we had to dance down while looking in to the camera. Aidan and myself were panicking, we hadn't done anything at that stage, and now we had to dance in costume. He started doing these high kicks out of panic. I hadn't a clue. I was wearing a tuxedo so Kai Widdrington, one of the pro dancers, whose father Tommy played for Southampton in the Premier League in the 1990s, just told me to be cool, fix my cufflinks, like James Bond. James Bond? Kai was trying to turn water in to wine.

So I did my 007, and finished it off by doing a little bunny jump, kicking my feet in the air. Like Morecambe and Wise, only higher. The catwalk was probably 40 yards long; it felt like seven miles.

It was so hard learning the routines. It took me three or four weeks to learn the first one when we did the foxtrot to Van Morrison's *Moondance*. It was gruelling. Well, it was gruelling if you were old and unfit. And fat.

I couldn't describe how nervous I was before each show. I can speak to a crowd of 1,000, not a bother, I'm completely relaxed for live TV, but my breathing would actually be affected by the tension of the dancing. I didn't expect the experience to last very long, though, but to my amazement I survived the first vote, Hughie getting eliminated first.

I was getting hammered by the judges almost all the way, your man Brian Redmond especially was giving me a real hard time, he was doing an Eamon Dunphy on me. Julian Benson and Loraine Barr were a little kinder. Julian would be saying, "you're such a lovely man, Des..." and you sensed a but. "But..."

And Loraine, who was highly respected because she was a world class dancer (unlike Brian), liked me. "I'm doing my best for you here Des..." and you sensed a but. "But..."

There were no buts from Brian, he skewered me. The laugh was, though, that the bigger the bollocking I got from him, the more the public seemed to say 'aw, poor auld Dessie'. So people started voting for me more.

In the second week we danced the Paso Doble, which, until then, I would probably have thought was a Uruguayan footballer. I waved a cape around quite a bit, pranced around like a matador, and threw Karen across the floor. I got a standing ovation. Safe again. The first couple of weeks the pro dancers were all going 'Dessie, Dessie, Dessie' out of sympathy, week three: nothing. They were mystified: I was getting the votes.

• • • • • • •

The Dessie Swim was the night Twitter melted down.

Many a person has since said to me that they will never be able to unsee me as Austin Powers in my satin suit, 'humping and grinding' my way through the routine. And Karen straddling me and me grinning at the camera. As the singer Niall Breslin tweeted that night, 'what Des just did there is illegal in 267 countries'.

I was going to wear the Austin Powers teeth and wig too, but for copyright reasons you must have three things that are different from the character you're portraying or you could be sued. So the public was at least spared that. So, I was Austin Powers, I was meant to be rescuing the woman. She was to swim to safety with me. In the middle of it she straddles me, Jesus it looked pure sexual. Bressie was probably right.

The big part of the routine was when I was shot and I had to fall to the floor. I said: "I can't fall on the floor, I'm too heavy, I'll break something."

All week, Karen: "Fall on the floor!"

But I continued to fall very, very slowly, putting my hand down first to ease the impact. "You can't do that, you've been shot!"

In the final rehearsal I did everything really well…except fall like I'd been shot. In the actual dance, I did everything wrong… except fall like I'd been shot.

I mistimed the routine at the start, so I was two steps behind the whole way through. Nobody noticed because they were laughing so hard. I got a really stern look from Karen that said: 'You feckin' eejit'.

We had this thing perfected where we were back to back, arms intertwined, I'd bend forward, she'd go up in the air, feet first. And she had it perfected so that when she bent forward she would lift me in the air – and it looked extraordinary for such a little thing to be lifting me.

But it was all about timing and you had to be tight up to each other, back to back. I got that wrong as well. I made a mess of it. Everything was a disaster.

But when it came to the bullet, I fell to the floor like I'd been mowed down. Because I was so bloody terrified of her. By now I think she wanted to shoot me for real.

So, *splat,* I threw myself on the floor. She said she nearly fell out of her shoes when she saw me.

But I got it wrong again between that and the end bit.

The judges didn't really know where to start. "I need a stiff whiskey after that," said Julian, "after that last bump'n'grind...I can never look at you in the same way." I don't think they viewed it as memorable in a good way. We got two fives and a four. But as I walked off, I was told the internet had just exploded. And I survived, again.

By now I was fairly sure Paul had changed his surname.

And Amy too.

• • • • • • •

The reaction was hilarious. I was on the front page of a pile of newspapers. And the strangest thing started to happen; I began getting recognised wherever I went by people who wouldn't have known me from Adam from doing sport.

It was kids especially, six and seven year olds. I was in town with Caroline one day, I had to collect a costume in Capel Street. And the costumes, which were looked after by Monica Ennis, were fantastic the whole way through. A Pakistani family was walking towards us and I could tell from 20 yards that the kids knew me, their eyes widened and their mouths dropped. The father stops and he's like, "it is SO nice to meet you!" We chatted for a minute, they were lovely.

And I started getting a pile of letters, mainly from kids telling me they were supporting me. One of the producers said I was cornering that market, with older women too, because I was the jolly fat man having some fun. The granddad who had, well, a unique way of dancing.

I was expecting to get slaughtered by the 20-something-year-old blokes, but they were like "fair play to you Dessie!" In the Cuala WhatsApp group I was getting messages from the most unlikely of lads, telling me they were getting their Mas to vote for me. They wouldn't admit to voting for me themselves, mind. Young fellas admitting to watching *Dancing With The Stars*, never mind voting for the contestants, would be a bridge too far.

Joanne Cantwell was mortified for me, but Evanne Ní Chuilinn was loving it, sending me supportive texts. Evanne did dance to a high level, she'd be brilliant on the show, but if she was traumatised by my performances she very kindly didn't let on.

You'd have older people calling you aside and whispering: "I gave you a vote." It was like it was a general election.

The demand for tickets for the show was unbelievable so they started bringing people to the rehearsal show. Roisin Ingle, *The Irish Times* journalist, was there with her daughters. I was standing at the side waiting to walk on when someone taps me. "Good luck, I wrote you a letter," said one of Roisin's young girls. She did too. By now I was getting very emotional about the reaction, it really was lovely.

The one thing I had a big problem with was the cost of voting. The kids from Karen's school and some of my friends and neighbours' kids were voting for me repeatedly – and each texted vote cost 60c. Karen's kids were so loyal to me, they were showing me their phones and how many times they'd voted, I was mortified. Initially we had been urged to seek votes, but I didn't want to because of that. I had a huge issue with it.

Obviously not everyone was impressed by Dancing Dessie, you'd have people perfectly reasonably asking how the fuck I was still in it. "He's brutal!" And some of the people left on the show as the weeks wore on were very accomplished dancers, ones who should have stayed in it, but it clearly was a personality thing too.

A lot of people were just enjoying it and thought it was a good laugh. So because of that I was getting a lot more votes than I deserved based on my dancing efforts. Including my Viennese Waltz, to the strains of The Marino Waltz, which I love. When they brought the man who wrote it, the legend that is John Sheahan of The Dubliners, in for our rehearsal, I was teary-eyed.

• • • • • • •

The problem was that through it all I was still doing my regular work for RTÉ Sport. It was mad.

Doing an early morning shift on the radio meant getting up at 4.40am, and then there was the all-day Saturday programme, as well as everything else in between. I'd be out at rehearsals at 7.30 on the Saturday morning, I'd go on to work then leave at 4.30 or 5.00 in the afternoon to go back out and do the last rehearsal, and then the show, all day Sunday. That meant not finishing until 11 at night. And there were all the other days you had to work on your routines, as well as having to get costumes fitted. It caught up on me.

I hadn't needed to go to a doctor for 20 years, I'd been very lucky, but in the middle of it all I dropped in to a neighbour who is a doctor and he said: "I was expecting you." I said: "Why?" He told me he'd been watching the show the night before and said to his family, "Des isn't well."

It was a bit of everything. I had conjunctivitis and a sinus infection, and my knee was giving me trouble. But it was mainly just exhaustion, I was absolutely shattered. He just told me I couldn't keep doing it all.

The reaction to the news I might have to drop out was incredible. It was even front page news in a lot of papers, which was hysterical. My phone never stopped ringing – and it was all the gossip and showbiz writers, which was a new one for me.

I went to see Dr Conor O'Brien who had been team doctor to the Irish Olympic team in 1996 and the Leinster rugby team for a while, so he was used to dealing with finely tuned athletes like me.

My knee was swollen and he gave me injections so that I could carry on – I wouldn't have got through it but for him. He was great. He was just laughing about it all and ended up watching the show.

"I can't believe I'm wasting my Sunday nights watching this," he said. I hope he voted for me.

• • • • • • •

In those last three or four weeks I felt like I was improving at the dancing. I started out being a million miles behind the others, now it was only a thousand. I'd closed the gap. There were even a couple of dances towards the end when I was throwing Karen up in the air and there were huge cheers. I felt like Popeye.

But then I lost the run of myself. I said to Karen: "It's all very well the crowd liking me, but I have to do more dance steps."

She said: "What?"

I said I need to do more – the judges want more. She went

quiet. I knew she was annoyed. But an hour later I said it to her again, I need to get more content in.

"Just leave it Des," she said.

"What do you mean leave it?"

"DES! IF YOU COULD DANCE, I'D HAVE YOU DANCING!"

I was mortified. I had actually started to believe that I could dance.

"Trust me," she said. "I would like if you could dance. I'm having to choreograph routines that will bring out your personality with what talent you have...and it's not much."

I was embarrassed. We laughed. It was time to accept my dancing limitations.

• • • • • • •

Paul, meanwhile, continued to be supportive on Twitter.

'Week 9, and we're still here. 8 weeks more than expected.'

'I'm not there tonight. He invited all the other Cahills, but he said my laughter would be distracting.'

'The last time I saw him on his toes as much, he was trying to sneak past mum after coming in from the pub.'

'Keep the dream alive. Vote Des C to help keep a man nearly 60 with a bad knee in a dancing contest.'

But the dream – or in the judges' eyes, the nightmare – was over come week 10 when it was myself, Aidan, Aoibhín, Dayl and Denise left. When I ended up in a dance-off with Aoibhín and Vitali Kozmin, who were both brilliant, that was that. The whole audience was 'aw', even before the dance-off started, they knew I was finished.

We still had 'aaaaaaand we'll be back after the break with this dramatic dance-off!', but there was nothing dramatic about it. There was no way I was going to survive this one. No-one felt I should go through. Including myself.

We were at the side of the stage waiting to go back on. There was just silence. Karen was saying nothing. So I said: "You know, I'm going to miss all the mornings and the coffee and chat." And she burst out crying.

So I got teary-eyed too. I'm sure people were thinking 'why is the big fat fecker crying?', but it was because she had been so good to me, and really cared how I did on the show. She had put in so much work to it, she had dragged me, sometimes literally, to that point.

And that's the strange thing, a lot of the people who appeared on the show found it really hard after. Caroline and Amy said I was like the anti-Christ for a while.

The downside of it, and I didn't realise it at the time because Caroline was hugely supportive, was the number of women who were saying to her, "do you not mind him with that woman sitting up on top of him?" She was going "no!" They were looking at each other like she was stupid. She didn't tell me at the time, she only mentioned it afterwards. It was tough on her, people can be weirdly thoughtless.

But she was thrilled with the positive effect it had – I changed my whole lifestyle, I stopped drinking apart from a pint on a Sunday night, I stopped eating shite, and I lost over two stones. It was so good for me. Especially posture-wise. I hadn't even thought about that before, I would always have sat slumped at a desk. But Karen kept telling me to stand up straight – and I do now. Well, at least a bit straighter. But you notice that about the kids at her dance school, who are all stunningly athletic and just so healthy looking – they have perfect postures. If I had young kids now I would definitely send them to dancing, or gymnastics, it's incredibly beneficial.

I'm definitely going to go back to it soon. Michael Flatley needn't worry, his crown is safe, I'll only be doing it for health reasons. And the fun of it.

Speaking of fun. As a result of *Dancing With The Stars* I was asked to do a pantomime the Christmas after. I said I'd love to, I was dying to do it. But Ryle Nugent said: "Oh no you're not!"

I think he might have feared that what little was left of my reputation after humping and grinding in my satin Austin Powers suit might evaporate completely if I next turned up as Widow Twankey. It was probably a reasonable concern.

The week before I was knocked out of the show I went to see Pete Dunne, a long time stalwart of Cuala and a dear friend. Pete was very ill at that stage, but he told me that he loved watching *Dancing With The Stars* with his family because he couldn't believe how ridiculous it was that I was in it.

Pete passed away on March 9 and the day after my elimination from the show I went to his funeral in Killiney.

I was talking with his wife Mary and their children, Louise, Derek and Adrian. People were coming up to commiscrate with the family. "I'm so sorry, I'm so sorry."

And then they were turning to me and saying, "I'm so sorry, I'm so sorry – we all voted for you, how did you not get through? You're as good as that Aidan O'Mahony."

The Dunnes laughed out loud. I think Pete might have been laughing too.

32

Good To Talk

*'When Pele arrived he was like, "hey Des!"
Everyone around me was, "how the feck does
he know you?" "Ah, me and Edson Arantes
do Nascimento go back a long way..."'*

There was a group of us hanging around outside chatting before a dinner where I was to introduce Irish rugby great, Moss Keane, as a speaker. I asked Moss how many caps he had won for Ireland.

"How many caps? Jesus, what does it matter? You journalists and your bullshit questions. I never judge a man by how many caps he's won, I judge him by the fight in him, by the passion in him, by the fire in him, when you're in trouble in a ruck and he has your back, that's how I judge a man. Not by how many caps he has! Bullshit!"

I'm on stage soon after. "Now ladies and gentlemen, I have an Irish sporting great to introduce to you, he's a legend of Munster and Irish rugby, he won 25 caps for Ireland..."

Then a voice boomed from the side of the stage –"Fuck off – I've 52."

I could fill several books with memories of the great characters from a host of sports who I've been lucky enough to have met or interviewed over the years. There really was no-one like Moss, though, as anyone who ever knew him would tell you.

When he became ill there was a golf day held for him at the K Club and President Mary McAleese turned up at it. Her husband Martin had shared a flat in a house in Dublin with Moss when they were students and by the sounds of it, Moss was a house-mate like no other.

Mary recalled Martin inviting her back to the flat to meet Moss and when she arrived she was mystified to see a long plank of wood in the hall leading in to the living room where Martin led her. And there was Moss sitting by the fire, nudging the plank in with his foot as it burned.

"Sit down there Mary," he said, our future president dumbstruck, possibly noting that fire regulations needed to be enforced a touch more stringently in her boyfriend's home.

It was some years later she was visiting Jack Lynch and his wife Maureen at a time when the former Taoiseach was very ill.

While Mary and Maureen chatted, Jack was drifting in and out of sleep. At one point Mary said that her husband Martin used to live across the road years before, that he had rented a flat with Moss Keane.

Jack woke up on hearing Moss's name and recounted a story about a difficult night he'd had in the Dáil.

He got home at about half past midnight, he had a lot on his mind, so he went in to the front room to have a nightcap and think things through.

Jack was standing at his window when he saw a flurry of activity in a lit room across the road. The window was up and he saw a very large object of some kind was being placed on the window sill. And then, suddenly, it came flying out the window and landed on the lawn. It was a wardrobe. And from inside it emerged Moss Keane. To that day Jack didn't know why Moss was inside a wardrobe that fell from a window sill. But Moss being Moss, these things happened.

I had so much fun with the fella. His brother had once marked me in an East Kerry junior final, I was full forward, he was full-back, so we had that link. And like most people from the Kingdom, he was bemused by the fact that I worked for *The Kerryman*.

Before concentrating on rugby he had played under-21 and junior Gaelic football for Kerry and was on the team that lost to Wicklow in an All-Ireland junior final. Wicklow! "Kerry football's greatest shame," as he described it. So whenever I introduced Moss at a function, I would always make sure to mention it. "You're some fucker," he'd whisper to me.

As Con Houlihan put it after Moss died in 2012, he was "a man of few airs and many graces." I really don't think I ever met a character quite like him. He was a wonderful man.

• • • • • • •

I've MCed countless events over the years, some professionally, when you're paid to do conferences and the like, but I would never take money from clubs when they ask me to host an event for them. That, of course, makes you even more popular because word gets around, and I genuinely always find it hard to say no, regardless of my schedule. Although I've been cutting back of late, it all got too busy.

I do some after-dinner speaking too, it's really just about telling stories, or making someone feel at ease when you're interviewing them. Generally people would be comfortable with me, so it usually works well. I'm totally at ease speaking publicly, I was always comfortable in myself, although if I stopped and thought of all the things I should be uncomfortable about on stage – I never look in a mirror and go, 'God, you're looking fine and handsome and slim' – I wouldn't get up there. So I don't think about it.

But through that work I've had the chance to meet some really interesting people, at various stages of their careers. I remember, for example, chatting to the leading amateur at the 1998 Irish Open, a young fella, when I was MCing. I was interviewing him in front of a corporate audience, I don't think any of them had ever heard of him. I asked him how he passed the time in the evenings during tournaments and he said he just liked playing his PlayStation. He didn't have the latest version, though, him still being an amateur he couldn't afford it, so I asked Murphy's, the sponsors, to get it for him as a reward for him finishing as the leading amateur. So, they did.

A year later he won the Irish Open, his first victory on the European Tour after turning professional. Seeing as his career earnings are now close to $50 million, I'd imagine he's able to keep his PlayStations up to date. His name? Sergio Garcia.

· · · · · · ·

I enjoy golf (on a good day I'm only average, on most days I'm bad) and play when I can with a group of friends at Woodbrook in Bray, among them Barry McGann, the former Irish out-half. I did a piece once for *The Irish Times* where I said the group was a mixture of Cranky, Whingey and Moany, so when I met them the following week each was sporting an A4 sheet with one of the adjectives assigned to themselves. I cracked up.

In the professional world of golf cranky, whingey and moany are probably the adjectives most often used to describe Colin Montgomerie, a man with whom I struck up an unlikely friendship.

I went through a phase of being invited to play in Pro-Ams and was paired with Monty. Because of his image I hadn't anticipated the experience as being enjoyable. A lot of the players take the pro-ams very seriously, using them to prepare for tournaments, getting to know the course, yardage and so on, they focus on themselves, there's very little interaction with them. I played with Retief Goosen one time and he was cold – very polite, but wanted to do his own thing, he wasn't up for chatting with the rest of us. Then others would be great fun, like José María Olazábal and Paul Casey. But I wasn't expecting Monty to be one of them.

The first time I met him was back in the 1980s when I was in his group for an Irish Open pro-am. We teed off around seven in the morning which meant I had to do a live call with Ian Dempsey for his *Breakfast Show* from the course. And we know how Monty feels about phones on golf courses.

I nervously told him about the call and held my breath. "No problem," he said, "do you want me to talk to your colleague?" And he did. He was brilliant. "How's Des playing?" Ian asked. "Very well," said Monty. Which wasn't true at all, I was rubbish.

We just got on like a house on fire, he was great fun. We chatted away, he was big into football, he was raised in Leeds, he'd heard about my ABU (Anyone But United) thing, so that bonded us. After another tournament I asked him what he did after a day's golf and he said he just went to his hotel and stayed on his own.

I told him I had to head in to RTÉ and he agreed to follow me in. He did an hour's phone-in. No money, no manager, no nothing. He just did it.

I can see why he has a terrible image, he hasn't always helped himself, but when I asked him about it he said that when he was out on a golf course during a tournament he was just trying to perform to his very best, so he had no patience for people doing stupid stuff, like not turning off their phones, shouting out at the wrong time, all that. If that made him look grumpy, so be it.

But his reputation never helped. I remember standing beside his first wife Eimear during the play-off for the 1998 Irish Open when he was up against David Carter. Monty hit a poor shot and there was a massive cheer. It was just the classic Irish thing of being up for the underdog, allied to Monty's image. But Eimear became tearful. "Why are they doing this?" Monty lost, he was furious. He signed his card and left in a helicopter.

* * * * * * *

One of my favourite Monty experiences was at a JP McManus event in Adare Manor. I was there with Nicky English, Niall Quinn, Bomber Liston and a few others. Nicky was saying, "oh Dessie's always going on about how he and Monty are good pals."

"We are!"

Rolly eyes.

So Monty is arriving by helicopter from the European Open and everyone is going: "Ha, we'll see if Monty knows Dessie."

Amy was with me. "Dad, why do you always get yourself in these situations?"

Monty walks in to this packed bustling bar, the whole place

goes quiet, he goes bright red, he looks around and goes: "Oh, hello Des!"

Big cheer!

Not that my best golfing buddy was always kind about my golf.

"Thanks very much for your patience given I'm not very good," I said to Monty after The Druids Glen pro-am.

"Not very good? You're shit," he said. "But at least you're quick and shit." That might have been the warmest tribute ever paid to my golf.

• • • • • • •

I had a similar experience with Pele, incidentally. I MCed two events with him in Ireland in the space of a week, and when he arrived for the second he was like, "hey Des!"

Everyone around me was, "how the feck does he know you?"

"Ah, me and Edson Arantes do Nascimento go back a long way."

Meanwhile, Patrik Sjöland, the winner of the 2000 Irish Open, was left befuddled by the crowd at a pro-am in Foto Island in Cork consistently likening me to a German golfer.

"I do not understand this, why are they saying you are Bernhard Langer?" Patrik asked.

It took me an age to explain to Patrik why cries of 'Des, you langer!' had nothing at all to do with Bernhard.

• • • • • • •

Padraig Harrington is another character who I've become very fond of over the years, I have great time for him. When he won his first British Open I was teary-eyed and so emotional about it I wrote him a congratulatory letter that night and dropped it in his front door, his house was just around the corner from me.

I've enjoyed hosting few events more than his 'home-coming' on the Monday night which was held in Dermot Desmond's casino in Dublin. Although I remember Paul, who had come with me, being almost more excited when he saw a figure standing at the back of the room.

"It's Jimmy Fallon!"

"Who?"

The Jimmy Fallon who went on to become one of the biggest names in American television, now hosting *The Tonight Show*. He happened to be in Dublin at the time and as a big golf fan he was invited along. I still laugh when I look at the photo we had taken with him. Paul was told he had to wear a jacket if he wanted to come in to the casino so someone gave him one that was around five times too big for him, his hands barely visible when he put it on. So, he's standing there with Jimmy in his oversized jacket, with his bleached blond hair, and to this day I say "what were you like?"

I always found Padraig fascinating to interview, he gives such an interesting perspective on his sport. I did an *'In Conversation With…'* type event with him one time in the College of Surgeons and it was brilliant. I could listen to him forever.

I was thrilled when he did so well in RTÉ's *Ireland's Greatest Sporting Moment* series, the public really love him.

His first Open win only lost by one per cent in the end to the Italia 90 penalty shoot-out. What upped his vote so much was how engaging and warm he was talking about that famous day, especially about his young fella Patrick wanting to put ladybirds in the Claret Jug.

And I think so many of our great sports people are similarly likeable and interesting characters, usually with a great sense of fun too, most of them not taking themselves too seriously. Ken Doherty is a good example, a great fella, and Ronan O'Gara too, an absolute rogue. I love their company. But, as I said, if I was to list all the sports people whose company I have enjoyed, this book would be longer than War and Peace.

• • • • • • •

My MCing, I should confess, doesn't always go smoothly. I've tried to erase it from my memory, but I can't – that time I was MCing an event where I was asked to host a Mr and Mrs-type competition. So a woman came on stage and I began asking her if she had known the last woman in her husband's life before they'd met.

There was a stony silence from the crowd.

"Did you ever meet her?"

Silence.

"Ah, come on now Mary, what did you think of her? Was she a rip?"

Silence.

It turned out that the last woman in her husband's life was his previous wife who had died around a year before. *Jesus.*

"I didn't know!"

The organiser of the event accepted my defence.

"That was so bad you couldn't have fucking known."

33

Just A Matter Of Opinion

'He'd know an ad break was coming up so he'd launch in to a tirade just before it knowing there wouldn't be enough time for me to balance it. He'd look across at me, the eyes, 'gotcha"

Colm O'Rourke and Pat Spillane started out as analysts on *The Sunday Game* 20 years ago. I just remember them having huge spectacles – Colm looked like Deirdre from Coronation Street, and Pat looked like his sister.

It was unusual to have players come on back then, most others from that era would have chosen not to. The analysis was good, but there wouldn't have been as much criticism as we have these days. The nature of it has changed completely since then, it's generally all about criticism now and examination of games and incidents in forensic detail. You'd imagine former players would have an empathy or sympathy for current players, but I'm not sure that some of them do.

Colm does, I think because he's a school principal and the father of a recent inter-county player, Shane.

But sometimes I wonder if some of the others are nearly competing with each other, and I wonder if that leads to them showing little or no empathy at times towards the people they're slating.

I don't think we're pushing them to be controversial for the sake of it, I think a few of them on occasion have chosen to be that way themselves, which I wouldn't welcome.

• • • • • • •

Pat and Joe Brolly would be among the least shy of our analysts when it comes to dishing out a slating.

The pair have their run-ins. A lot of them. It seemed to me that Pat would have prepared lines, he'd deliver a good one at Joe's expense, a funny one, but Joe would just whack him all over the place. He's the last man on this island who I would try to take on verbally, he's a barrister in Belfast so he's able for anyone.

Joe, and Dessie Dolan, had a right go at Pat over his comments on Diarmuid Connolly when he was involved in an incident with a linesman during Dublin's Leinster championship game against Carlow last year. Connolly eventually got a 12-week ban.

Pat had referenced the GAA rulebook to argue that Connolly should have been sent off for pushing the linesman. It was the only time I ever saw Pat learning a rule off by heart; he wouldn't know them normally.

Joe, who would have a big affection for the Dublin lads, said: "It was like watching counsel for the prosecution, Pat had everything on but his Kerry blazer and his Kerry tie," the implication being that because he's a Kerryman that was Pat's motivation for highlighting the incident to ensure Connolly was suspended.

Dublin manager Jim Gavin weighed in too, reckoning Pat was forcing the GAA to take action by highlighting the incident as he did and the rule that was broken, 'minor interference with a linesman'.

Pat had a go back in his *Sunday World* column, and a dig at me too, saying that while I tried to act as 'an honest broker', it wasn't one of my better performances.

Maybe he was right, but I felt I had defended him, or at least tried to. Especially when Joe said it sounded like Pat was reading off a script. I assured him that he wasn't, I wasn't sitting beside him, he had notes, as he always does, as many of our panellists do. And even though, personally, I thought Connolly's punishment was harsh, Pat simply described what happened and read out the relevant rule. I made that clear too.

Not that I've always got it right when it comes to standing up for people who have been attacked. Kevin Walsh springs to mind.

• • • • • • •

It would often be said to me, "ah, you're always defending people", but when one of the panellists is criticising a player, a manager, a referee, whoever, I just see it as part of my job to give a voice to that person when they're not there to defend themselves, it's only fair. It's important that the programme is done in a responsible way.

RTÉ doesn't influence the panellists at all, and I don't influence them, but if they're going to have a go at somebody I need to know, I need them to tell me in advance. Donal Óg was always very cagey about that. "Why do you need to know?" I'd tell him if he's going to have a go at, say, the Cork county board about their underage structures, which he did, I need to make a couple of calls in advance to find out about those structures and give their point of view. I want to be prepared.

But talk of agendas – Donal Óg had so many of them, especially with the Cork county board. And he regularly wouldn't tell me he was going to do it. We used to have this cat and mouse game. He'd know an ad break was coming up so he'd launch in to a tirade just before it knowing there wouldn't be enough time for me to balance it. He'd look across at me, the eyes, 'gotcha'.

And my eyes were telling him, 'you bastard'.

There'd be a tension between us. Donal Óg was heavily involved in the setting up of the Gaelic Players Association, which I wasn't sure about, I worried there'd be a push for pay-for-play which, for me, would be a major mistake. I think that created a distance between us. Which was no harm. But he's a good man, I've great time for him.

I think our panellists have a much tougher job than our soccer or rugby guys, and a greater responsibility too. It's the easiest thing in the world for Eamon Dunphy to say that Ronaldo is a clown or a show pony, to be sitting in Dublin slagging the multi-millionaire over in Madrid or Turin – Ronaldo doesn't give a sugar about Eamon Dunphy, or any of our soccer pundits. And the rugby players are paid professionals too, making a good living. I'm not saying they should be criticised more because of that, but we have to be conscious that our GAA players and managers are amateurs, most of them have college or jobs, regular day-to-day lives, they're not shielded from it all by professionalism. I just believe we have to bear that in mind. It doesn't mean we can't do honest analysis, but we should be mindful about the nature of it, we have to be responsible about it.

I was reminded of that back in 2013 when Eamonn O'Hara launched what was, to me, an astonishing attack on the Sligo manager, Kevin Walsh.

Eamonn had been an incredible servant to Sligo football, a fantastic player and a brilliant athlete. He was signed up for the programme so that we would have a Connacht voice on the panel and his first night on was after Sligo had been beaten by London in the Connacht Championship, a huge shock.

I started by asking him why he wasn't still playing for Sligo. He said that Kevin had asked the players to make themselves available for training from November 1, but Eamonn was unable to make that commitment until the start of January. Kevin said he would stick with the players who had trained since November, so that was that. Eamonn announced his retirement from inter-county football a couple of weeks before he appeared on the programme.

It wouldn't be surprising under those circumstances if there was some bad blood between the pair, but I was still completely taken aback by what Eamonn said, I just felt it was over the top.

"Kevin Walsh made big calls this year and last year but every one of them has backfired. For me I think he lost the players throughout the year. These players deserve an awful lot more, to be quite honest with you…Kevin Walsh has a lot to answer for."

"That's very strong coming from you, do you think he will go?" I asked.

"I think he will and I think he should do the county board a favour. There are a lot of problems within the county board from the top down. We have a lot of infighting…Kevin Walsh's results over the last two years have gone unnoticed because of this Infighting. He hasn't been held accountable for this. We got to a Connacht final last year, but we were papering over the cracks. There are players there who deserve better quality training, better quality management and I think going forward Kevin should make the right decision for the sake of Sligo football and not for anybody else."

Losing to London was a terrible result for Sligo so it was natural that Eamonn would be critical and would ask questions of the manager, but I felt it was too personal and that Kevin deserved better, particularly in light of what he had achieved with Sligo – he had, after all, taken them from division four to division two in the National League, winning two titles along the way, and had reached a Connacht final by beating both Mayo and Galway. That was some going for Sligo.

And this is what I should have been arguing with Eamonn in Kevin's absence. But I had upstairs shouting in my ear, "go, go, go, you need to move on, you need to move on." We had run out of time and I didn't have the chance. We had the highlights of three more matches to show and we only had 12 minutes left. So it was left there. And that was desperately unfair on Kevin.

Everyone there felt Eamonn had been far too hard on Kevin.

"Jesus, what was that about?" I asked.

"I was only giving my opinion," he said.

We want strong opinions, but they have to be fair too. And I didn't think Eamonn had been fair at all. I think he was trying to make an impact, to show he wasn't afraid to speak his mind, which is an admirable thing. Brolly gets people talking about him because of that, and I think that might have influenced Eamonn. When we had our meeting before the programme he didn't tell me he was going to do this, he sprung it on me.

There was a huge reaction to it, and while I don't know Eamonn particularly well, I'd say he was very rattled by it. The former Armagh footballer Oisin McConville had a go at him, saying his comments "sounded as if he had a personal axe to grind with Kevin Walsh." I think Eamonn's credibility was damaged by it, it just came across as personal. It's not in his nature to be nasty at all, but it was ill-judged.

Kevin accused *The Sunday Game* of being "very unfair, very unbalanced in its presentation" and that allegations made by Eamonn "were allowed to be made without challenge and debate". And he was absolutely right. The reasons for why it happened, that we were stuck for time, were irrelevant, they were no help to Kevin. He deserved better.

It rumbled on and on, more and more columnists were writing about it and it was all over social media, so eventually, three or four days later, I just thought I needed to ring Kevin.

His wife answered. She was very nice, but she did say "God, that was very harsh on Kevin the other night." And she told me their kids were of school-going age, "they're not babies." It drove it home, the repercussions on a personal and family level after a slating like that.

Kevin didn't make a fuss at all when we spoke, both he and his wife were very classy about it. Which, of course, only made you feel worse.

• • • • • • •

The Sunday Game analyst who has probably ruffled more feathers than most in 2018 has been Sean Cavanagh, the three-time All-Ireland winner with Tyrone and one of the great players of recent times. His impact on joining the programme was immediate, he's a straight-talking Nordie with a smiley persona, I think he's brilliant. He says unpopular things, and it's easier to be unpopular in GAA than most other sports because people are so tribal about their counties.

When he forecast that Mayo, All-Ireland finalists in four of the previous six years, wouldn't make the 2018 Super Eight, he got dog's abuse from some quarters, being accused of having an agenda against the county.

But I never believed he had. Sean strikes me as someone who is just honest and speaks his mind and knows no other way. He has a very strong personality, he doesn't set out to please or upset people, as others often do, he's not interested in making a punditry name for himself in that way. He's not interested in playing that game.

And because he was such a great player, that gives him credibility. The key point about his prediction on how Mayo's 2018 would go was that it was based on his own experience with Tyrone after their last All-Ireland victory in 2008 when the team, "with an awful lot of miles in the legs", began to tire and pick up injuries. He'd been there.

He sensed the same would happen with Mayo in 2018.

And it did.

He was right.

But while the Eamonn O'Hara/Kevin Walsh business had made me uneasy about the nature of the criticism sometimes dished out to managers and players, the reaction to Sean's critical comments about the impact of his former manager Mickey Harte's defensive tactics on the forwards in his team made me see it from the pundits' side too.

Sean argued that Harte had damaged, and was continuing to

do so, the careers of Tyrone forwards during his time in charge of the county by deploying such a defensive system, a criticism that was met with a major backlash from several Tyrone quarters, among them his Moy club-mate Philip Jordan.

"Sean is obviously thinking about his media career and he's learning from Joe Brolly and Pat Spillane about making the headlines," he wrote in his RTÉ website column.

That a club-mate would make such a comment showed how deep the loyalty to Harte went.

It was, to me, also unfair.

By all means criticise Sean for not speaking out during his playing days, which was one of the complaints, but I genuinely don't believe this is about promoting his 'media career', I stand by the view that he's just a man who calls it as he sees it, and doesn't worry about the consequences.

I texted him in the middle of it all to see if he was okay.

He was fine.

A while later Marc Ó Sé, the former Kerry All-Ireland winner, in his *Irish Mail on Sunday* column, had a go at Sean for his criticism of Harte, as well as calling him a 'snitch' for an incident in a January 2018 All-Ireland Intermediate Football Championship game between Moy and An Gaeltacht, and claiming that Sean's account of telling him at the end of the game that it was "an absolute honour to play against one of the best defenders the game has ever seen" had never happened.

I have no clue about the truth of all that, it's one word against another, but it just left me realising that when you become an outspoken analyst on national television, you need to have thick skin to take what comes your way.

Sean Cavanagh?

I think he can handle it.

34

Looking Up

*'Life, for all the darkness it can produce,
can still give us moments of wonder and
beauty, moments that revive us. And I choose
to look on the bright side of life because it
makes the journey a whole lot easier'*

I started this book by talking about what a lucky man I've been, but having taken a lengthy trip down memory lane to tell my story, I now realise just how much good fortune I've enjoyed.

Mountains of it.

It was a couple of months back, in the summer of 2018, that I heard Gay Byrne reflect on his life and career with RTÉ in a radio interview, and he talked about his regrets, how he wished he hadn't devoted himself to his job as much as he had, that he wished he had spent more time with his family, especially when his daughters were growing up.

That resonated with me because I would have similar regrets. I wish I had been around more too when Paul and Amy were young, not least for Caroline's sake. Because the nature of my career has made family life very tough for her. I wasn't there enough, I was away so much.

I've worked virtually every weekend through our marriage, starting at nine in the morning on Saturdays and getting home around 10 at night, and then working all day through to midnight on Sundays in the summers.

So I've rarely been around for weddings, christenings and just the simple things, like the neighbours having a barbeque. Caroline has had to go to all of these events on her own, and no matter how used to it she became, it can never have been easy.

I'm not complaining at all about that schedule, from my own point of view, if you're a sports journalist you work weekends, that's how the job is. I hear some of them now who want every second weekend off and I'm thinking 'how can you be a sports journalist and want weekends off?' Maybe I'm old school. It's changed since I started out, of course, sport is stretched through the week now, but back in the day it all happened on weekends, so you just accepted you would be working.

But I wonder about it all, even though you can't change any of it now. It's only when you hear someone like Gay reflecting on his own life, and you can relate to a lot of what he is saying, that you stop and think about it. In the middle of it all, of course, you're just getting on with life.

It was a shame to hear Gay having such regrets because his career was outstanding, his impact on Irish society as a broadcaster immense. He helped air issues that were just never talked about, issues that needed to be discussed. I genuinely feel he helped make this country a better place by shining a light on so many dark places.

But I understood why he might have felt that way, maybe he's spending time with his grandchildren now and is getting a sense of what he missed. Caroline and myself have a little fella who stays with us sometimes, we're just helping out in a difficult situation, we love having him with us, but it does drive it home for me just how much I missed out on during Paul and Amy's childhoods.

For 20 years the kids take over, there's so much going on, then it goes quiet again. It all goes so quickly. Although Paul and Amy have both turned in to fine young people, I'm so proud of them both, they seem reasonably well adjusted despite it all, and would I rather have been at a World Cup or a parent teacher meeting…? (No comment).

But I think, to balance it a little, my career has given us all a good lifestyle, with lots of wonderful experiences and so much fun along the way.

I think of a trip we had to America one time to mark our wedding anniversary, Paul and Amy coming with us. I still laugh about it because it summed up the personalities of the family.

It was Patrick's Day, we were driving down from Miami to Key West. We passed a little wooden church and in the car park there was a truck, a tractor and a golf buggy bedecked in green, white and gold ribbons.

Paul says: "That looks like a Patrick's Day thing, let's go back!"
I hit the brakes and try to turn.
Caroline says: "If you go back there I'm getting out of the car."
Amy says: "Me too – you are NOT going near this."
Soon after, Caroline and Amy were sitting on a truck near the head of the parade, surrounded by a group of Floridians dressed up as red-haired cailíns, complete with red curly wigs.

They were mortified.

Paul couldn't have been happier, though, he was loving it all, especially because he had been given a couple of cans of beer, having struggled to get any in Florida because he was around eighteen. They'd have sold him a gun alright, but no beer.

I'd had to drive five or six miles before I could turn back. When we'd got to the car park there were about 30, 35 people there.

I said: "Hiya, we're from Ireland."

"OH MYYYYYYYY GOD!!! We've never had anyone from Ireland at our Patty's Day parade!"

We were treated like celebrities. They couldn't get over that we were Irish, they actually wanted to touch us.

Their parade was only going a short way down a path, not even the road, to a bar where they were having a party. And to add to Caroline and Amy's mortification, I was asked to be Grand Marshal. I even had to get up and speak. "People of Florida!" I was a superstar, even though they wouldn't have known me from Adam.

Amy was like: "Jesus Christ, Dad."

Caroline didn't know where to look.

Mind you, she got up and sang in the end, so she got in to the spirit of Patty's Day. We had a brilliant day, and never, ever stopped laughing about it.

● ● ● ● ● ● ●

So, there's been no end of fun, no end to the laughter, although there have been challenges for Caroline, extremely testing ones.

Like when I got five stars on *The Restaurant* and as I'd be walking down the street with her there'd be women waving five fingers at me, thinking I was Shankill's Jamie Oliver.

"Oh he's fantastic! You're such a lucky woman!"

How blessed she was by the Lord to have me.

And she'd smile and nod, then whisper to me, "if only they knew you're feckin' useless." This is true. It's rare that I've whipped up culinary delights for the family, the odd ham sandwich maybe.

The star of my menu was a Malaysian curry that was based on one I'd eaten regularly in the Langkawi in Baggot Street, Alex, the chef there, bringing me in to the kitchen to show me how to make it. Tom Doorley loved it. And my rack of lamb went down well too, as did my Champagne Berries with Lemon Meringue Ice Cream.

I'd say Caroline was close to throwing the remote control at the telly. I've yet to serve her Champagne Berries with Lemon Meringue Ice Cream, but I will one day.

So I got my five stars and later was put in a cook-off against Dermot Bannon. Dermot insisted that he wasn't a good cook but his mother, if I remember correctly, was a home economics teacher and his brother a chef. And he came in armed with all these notes. I was like "you lyin' fecker."

He beat me. But only because I hadn't time to prepare (get over it, Des). Jesus, he's done well for himself since appearing with me on telly. The impact I have on people's careers.

• • • • • • •

Anyway, if there's been no end to the fun, there's been no end to the big decisions Caroline and myself have had to make along the way too.

I do sometimes think about what life would have been like if we had chosen to stay in Kerry where we were so happy and had a lovely relaxed lifestyle. And then there was 1986 when I was offered a job in Perth, Australia.

I had gone over to do a programme in advance of an Irish International Rules series and while in Perth I met Mel Moffatt, a Scotsman who had been the soccer correspondent in the *Irish Press* before moving to Perth where he became sports editor with *The West Australian*. I met him for lunch and he said: "There's a job for you here if you want one."

I remember him showing me his house and his garden, the apple and orange trees, and thinking what a perfect climate it was, what a great quality of life you could have there, what a great place to raise kids.

I was sure Caroline would say no because of the large family she had at home, how close she was to them all. But when I said it to her after I got back she said: "Yeah, absolutely, let's do it."

I agonised over it. In the end I opted to stick with RTÉ and in no time I was covering Roche and Kelly in the Tour de France, the Olympic Games, European Championships, World Cups, and so on. Career-wise, then, it all worked out, but I don't know how many times Caroline has said: "Imagine if we were in Perth?"

I don't regret it, but I do often wonder how it would all have worked out if I had made a different choice.

But sure, life is full of decisions, you make them, and hope you've chosen the right path. No regrets, you move on.

Anyway, I have so many nephews and nieces in Australia now, I probably wouldn't have had a minute's peace from them.

We'd be thinking about moving to Killarney.

• • • • • • •

I have also been incredibly lucky health-wise throughout my life. The only scare I had was on my return from Shanghai after the

Special Olympics World Games in 2007. I'd been blessed with good health before that and have been since.

It was never actually discovered what had caused it, but the assumption was that I had picked up a virus, possibly in my hotel in Shanghai or on the plane coming home. It went to my head, stomach and bowel, I was in bits.

The memories are miserable ones.

I was in an overcrowded ward in Loughlinstown hospital, the man in the bed next to me was dying. They pulled the curtains to give him and his family privacy, but one of the daughters was sitting on my bed. Suddenly I got a headache that was so bad I thought I was going to die. I know that sounds very melodramatic, but the virus was quite serious. I started kicking her backside to get help. I didn't want to cry out, they were literally saying goodbye to their father. I could hear it all. I was in agony. It felt like my head was going to burst open.

When I finally recovered and got out of hospital, myself and Caroline went down to Doonbeg in Clare for a few days.

It felt fantastic to be out of hospital. I had two pints in Tubridy's pub and felt great but then I woke up next morning feeling ill all over again. They wanted to admit me to Ennis hospital, but headed back to Loughlinstown where I stayed for another week.

I was out of work for around two months in the end. Thankfully, it wasn't the tumour they initially thought it was. They never really got to the bottom of it, but in the end they found the right treatment and I was fine again. It was a worrying time, the not knowing the worst part, but most people endure much worse during their lives, so I consider myself fortunate.

I'll be 60 in December 2019, but retirement is far from my thoughts. I see myself being very busy in the years ahead, I'm still youthful for my age…and weight.

I'm actually so enthusiastic, it might be quite alarming for Declan McBennett, the new boss. When I have ideas for programmes, on radio and television, I can sound like a little fella in the class in school – 'can I do this, can I do that?'

The bosses have to allow other people to do programmes, they have to cultivate new talent, develop new presenters, you're a part of a team, you can't do everything. My own podcast could allow me to do stuff without cutting across other people, so that's something I'm thinking about. And I see myself getting involved in that digital space, I have loads of ideas but the cost of transferring them to television can be expensive, that's why I think digital might become more of an outlet in the future.

I relish all those advances, rather than being intimidated by them. During the 2018 World Cup, Belgian TV did an interview with a hologram of Eden Hazard who was sitting in a dressing room back in Russia, but 'popped up' in that Belgian studio, so it was like any live interview. It was Star Trek stuff, amazing. It's all evolving and changing, the technology is extraordinary, and I'm intrigued by that.

I have a head full of ideas. I'd love to do programmes about some of our historic but often untold events, not necessarily just sport. There are some fantastic Irish stories, not all happy, that should be captured now while people are still alive and capable of giving first-hand accounts, rather than interviewing their children or grandchildren years later.

I'd love to do a documentary on some of our great election stories, for example, some of which I witnessed myself in Carlow and Kerry. There's endless material out there that has yet to be covered. I'd love to contribute to unearthing and broadcasting it.

• • • • • • •

Something else I'm grateful for is that I get the same joy from sport that I did 50 years ago. It's undiminished. After Cuala won a club match recently one of the young lads turned to me and said: "I bet you'll sleep well tonight." He knew how much it all means to me.

And I did sleep well that night.

Journalism is definitely a profession that can suck that joy out of you, it can, after time, leave the people in the business cynical and world weary, which, I think, is a shame.

Life has its bleak and dark sides, but if you dwelt solely on them you'd be blinded to the pleasure it can also bring.

Sport is just the same. Between drugs and cheating and commercialism and exploitation of the people within it, especially young people so ruthlessly cast aside.

Are you naive not focussing on that dark side?

I would often have been criticised for that down the years.

My view is that if you focus solely on that bleakness, life becomes a miserably tough journey, and while you can't ignore that dark side, there are some incredibly uplifting and positive things out there, including the most inspirational of people, and sport regularly reflects that. And choosing to be lifted by all that is, I think, no bad thing.

It's a personal decision, how you choose to look at life.

And life, for all the darkness it can produce, can still give us moments of wonder and beauty, moments that revive us.

I choose to look on the bright side of life because it makes the journey a whole lot easier and a whole lot more enjoyable.

It's a journey that, I hope, has many more adventures ahead, for me, Caroline, Paul and Amy.

I think it will too.

After all, I'm a lucky man.